NON-ADHESIVE BINDING

The Revised & Expanded Edition
1999

BOOK NUMBER 128

NON-ADHESIVE BINDING

KEITH A. SMITH

KE◉TH

First Edition March 1991
Second Printing July 1991
Second Edition, First Printing January 1992
Second Edition, Second Printing May 1992
Second Edition, Third Printing December 1992
Second Edition, Fourth Printing June 1993
Third Edition December 1993
Third Edition, Second Printing July 1994
Third Edition, Third Printing May 1995
Third Edition, Fourth Printing January 1996
Third Edition, Fifth Printing July 1997
The Revised & Expanded Edition January 1999
The Revised & Expanded Edition, Second Printing October 2001
The Revised & Expanded Edition, Third Printing October 2003
The Revised & Expanded Edition, Fourth Printing August 2005

Published by *keith smith BOOKS*

Distribution, wholesale & retail sales:
keith smith BOOKS
1115 East Main Street
Suite 219, Box 8
Rochester, New York 14609-6152
Voice Mail or FAX: 585 482 2496
email orders: keith@keithsmithbooks.com
www.keithsmithbooks.com

Library of Congress Catalogue Card Number: 98-91061
ISBN: 0-9637682-6-3

TABLE of CONTENTS

Part 3   COVERS and SUPPORTS

Part 4   REFERENCE

INTRODUCTION

Binding without adhesives requires no presses or other heavy equipment. Although paper folded down into sections ideally is placed under a weight overnight before sewing, a press is not necessary. All that is needed for these bindings is a needle and scissors and a few other minor tools. Non-adhesive binding is an exciting offshoot from the traditional approach to hand-bound sewn and pasted books.

Hard Cover

Separate side-covers of book board, wood or plexiglass can be attached. For Coptic Sewing, page 207, the sewing stabs through pre-drilled stations to attach the boards. The Blanket Stitch with Slit Strap, the Supported Concertina Sewing are types of Sewing onto Tapes. The tape supports, leather or book cloth, can be laced through the board. Or, the support can be stitched or glued to the board for attachment.

Wood or plexiglass eliminates the need to cover the board with decorative paper. Book board generally is covered. An adhesive is almost always used to attach papers to the boards, yet the binding, the sewn book block, remains non-adhesive. For the purist who wants no paste or glue whatsoever, decorative paper can be attached to the board by folding it around the board and tabbing it into position. See page 306.

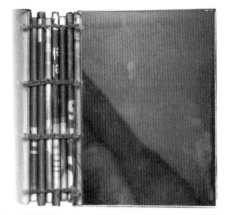

COPTIC SEWING by Scott McCarney. The boards, in this instance, plexiglass side-covers, are attached *as* the book block is sewn. See *Coptic Sewing,* page 207.

SEWN ONTO TAPES by Bert Weijermars. If the book block is sewn onto tapes, the supports can be used to attach the separate side-covers. Supports can be laced through, stitched or glued or nailed onto the boards.

Paper Cover

The majority of non-adhesive binding utilizes a paper cover. This eliminates the need for adhesives and speeds up the binding process.

These striking and substantial bindings bring new meaning to paper covers. The general connotation of hard cover and paperback is that the former represents quality and the latter is disposable, dowdy and cheap. Paper cover books are thought of as inferior because almost all commercial paperbacks have an adhesive binding referred to in the trade as perfect bound: Single sheets are stacked, held together only by adhesive across the backbone. As we all have experienced, they fall apart easily. Some paperbacks utilize sections and are Smythe-sewn. This text is an example.

Binding without paste or glue can yield fine bindings, some of which are hard cover. That is not to apologize for those bindings which have paper covers. The paper cover bindings described in this text are functionally well-made. They are archival, not only because they use good materials, but also because they lend themselves easily to repair, since no glue is involved. Aesthetically, they represent a love of materials and just as importantly, they facilitate access to their content.

Excellence in binding goes beyond skill of the craft. It is integration of the binding with the other elements of the book: pages, text and/or pictures, the revelation and display. When the binder works in collaboration with the author, artist and publisher, binding is able to reach its ultimate. It then is not only part of the statement, it helps determine the content.

This text will describe basic to very elaborately constructed bindings. With an investment of less than $50 for paper and tools, you can be involved seriously in the art and joy of fine binding.

Finally, I should say it is a joy to revise and expand this edition. Some of the bindings I devised for this book have been tried by various binders and book artists who have sent me slides. I have reproduced many in this edition. It is kind of like seeing my children come of age.

Bert Weijermars, Eys, The Netherlands, 1995. Reading the first edition of this book, Bert made samples of the various bindings described in Volume I, *Books without Paste or Glue*. Many of these bindings will be shown throughout this Revised and Expanded Edition of this manual.

PART 1

PREPARATION FOR BINDING

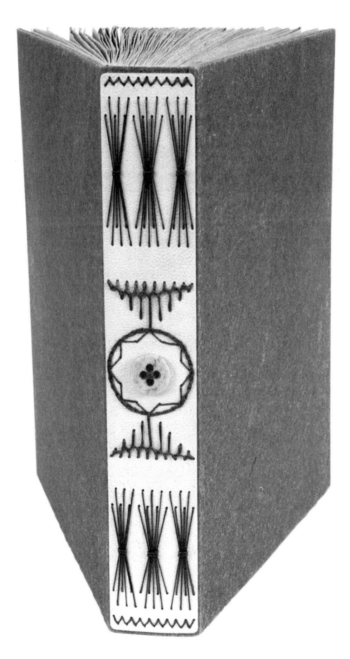

Gary Frost, untitled, Langstitch und Kettenstitch, 1990. This blank book has a leather spine over the paper covers.

ONE ONE-FOLD BOOK

Day one:

The first bindings are the most difficult. The beginner has a far greater challenge than the expert. The more simple the binding, the greater the challenge.

Fold a sheet of paper in half. The surface for display of text or picture has now been removed from the two-dimensional world of the single-sheet format. The resulting folio is now two connected planes, movable, able to arc in space because of the created hinge. The hinge-fold also delineates four surfaces as four pages.

The concept of using paper for text or pictures has been totally altered by the simple act of folding a piece of paper and understanding the consequences. Learning to see requires vigilance so that actions are not taken for granted.

I examine the paper I have folded in half. The term for this is a *folio.* Where the two planes meet, the fold creates a valley.

That is not true. It is equally a mountain peak. It is my point of view which creates the valley. If I turn the folio over, the fold then appears to be a mountain peak. I must be alert, not to assume a "truth" but to understand that *fact* is dependent upon context.

That *act* has created four pages and two implied sheets. Building comprehension requires paring down to bare necessities. Again, I look at the sheet I have folded. I concentrate on the crease-as-hinge: The valley is referred to as the *gutter.* The mountain peak is the *back,* or *backbone.*

Since the sheets are connected, this is a hand-bound book. I think about how these pages are seen. Their display is interdependent: there is no "front" side, as the surface in view is the front only while it is being viewed. It becomes the back when the page is turned. Context. I need no longer concern myself with single, unconnected sheets of paper imaged on one side, which have a front and a back. I must not think in terms of one-sided display. The fold has created a book—a totally different stage upon which to perform.

Recto means the right-hand page of an open book. *Verso* is the back of that page. An opened book presents, on the left, a verso of the previous recto. On the right is a recto. It is important to understand *both* pages in view are *front* sides until the page is turned, then each becomes a back side. *Verso* is not synonymous with *back*. A recto in view is always on the right of the gutter. A verso in view, on the left.

A single sheet imaged on one side has a fixed front and back. In the codex, fronts are pages in view, which become backs when the page is turned.

The *now* of a book is the opened folio.

Since the four pages cannot be seen simultaneously, they are experienced *in time,* like a play in four acts, a symphony with four movements. Time and movement are a necessary part of this format. Any art form revealed in time must be paced. Rate of turning pages is not standard or arbitrary. Each page is paced by the maker. The viewer can perceive the precise pacing of each page.

The fold *physically* holds together this blank book. Anything added to the surfaces in the form of text or pictures must conceptually tie the surfaces together. Otherwise, each surface is treated as an island where content is marooned, isolated, rather than acting as a multi-directional navigation. *Island* is a concept relevant only in the single-sheet format.

A book may be bound using single sheets rather than sections, but organization of the content has nothing in common with the single-sheet format. I must make concerted effort to remove myself from single-sheet mentality. This is a whole new world. A book is not the act of compiling information, but the process of timely construction of an organization.

Bookbinding at its ultimate realization is not a physical act of sewing or gluing, but a conceptual ordering of time and space. It is not sewing but structure of content that ties together pages of a book. Binding must begin with the concept of text and/or pictures.

The single sheet allows an overall view of everything; it has a narrow sense of time. Movement in the single sheet is limited to scanning. The viewer moves to the next single sheet, takes in a general view of everything and scans scant bits of information or carefully plows row by row this flat field.

This is not the manner in which a book should be experienced. It is not an easy transition from working in the single-sheet format to moving into the book format. To treat a book as no more than a stack of sheets would be a denial of inherent movement as fronts evolve into back sides. A codex is more than a *group.* The progression through a codex is more than a *series* in which the eye absorbs one page then moves in a straight line to the next, to the next. Such structure is linked, each successive idea dependent upon the previous.

With the content referring back and forth and the fronts evolving to backs, the structure of ideas *and the pages* are contingent upon events other than the adjacent. This is in addition to contiguous movement forward, page to page to page.

Single sheets can have common theme. But every page of a book is totally dependent upon every other, necessitating a complexity of movement. Content of pages moves back and forth by cause and effect—

in addition to the steady linkage forward.

This movement is within the boundaries of what is stated, and beyond by what is implied. The book artist structures the gap between the pictures just as an author speaks between the lines. But what is even better is for the artist and the writer to compose the space between the pages as thoughtfully as what is printed upon the surface. A book is *not* a running manuscript or compilation but a structuring of pages as an integral part of the content. This creates a *gestält*.

The multiple-page format has its own demands based on the inherent properties of the book. The multiple-page format also has options, totally new possibilities unavailable in single sheets. These new possibilities of movement stem from an understanding of how the multiple-page format differs from a collection of single sheets. The key is not to "add" in the sense of treating the book as an empty vessel into which things might be stuck. Rather, learn to see the blank book for its power and its potential.

Gary Frost, a blank book, sewn onto tapes which are laced through wooden boards.

The p o w e r of a blank book is that it is not *blank* in the sense of being empty, but is an entity complete in itself: It has a beginning and an end. Turning pages move through time and space. Even a blank book presents a group, series *and* a sequence. Every book is a format. The western codex utilizes two-sided display bringing new definitions to patterning, pacing. It is far removed from the single-sheet format. Since this format exists in space, it is nearer to sculpture than painting. Since it exists in time, it has more properties of cinema than the still-photography it might contain. A book of text or prints is *moving pictures.* Rather than a compilation of single sheets, each book is an organized totality, a union of states, each sheet subordinate to that union.

Folding a sheet of paper has created the most basic of book bindings. By understanding the power of *what* has been created, I can begin to appreciate and investigate the potential of the blank book.

The p o t e n t i a l is not to stick things in, but to allow ideas to emanate *from* the format as text and/or pictures. It is to revel in the book as action, to reveal the plane of activity, then help it relinquish center stage as it curls in the light and turns on its hinge into shadow, to disappear. In its place comes forward the next plane to entertain and inspire.

At any point in time, the reader is at the opened folio, at the fronts of pages. Indeed, it is impossible to ever realize the "back side" since on turning the page, the verso changes into an opened folio and, like magic, becomes a front.

This movement through pages is timed. The bookmaker builds in a rate of page turning. Yet, unlike cinema or dance, the reader can override the pacing of the author and linger at any point, retreat to some other page, or sneak a preview of what is yet to unfold.

Content is the process of coming to understand the essence of a blank book and to proceed from any inherent characteristic as a point of departure.

The power is *what;* the potential is *how.*

What is binding? One thing I feel strongly is that text can be so written that the words create the pages. The pages, as well as the writing relate back and forth, tying together all the elements into a unified flow. One would ask no less cooperation from all the instruments of an orchestra.

This inter-connection of all the *elements of a book— binding, the page, text and/or pictures, turning pages* and *display.*It is conceptual bookbinding, sewing on the ultimate level.

TWO TWO-FOLD BOOKS

SKETCH NUMBER 1: *two folds in opposite directions*

Day two:
Today I take another sheet of paper. This time I make two folds, reversing the direction of the second. The result is an Oriental fold book. How does this differ from the one-fold book which is a codex? That one-fold book merely suggests an Oriental fold book.

By making two alternating folds, I have the essence of a fold book. This book I have hand bound can also be seen as a compound codex. Back to back, it is what is termed a *dos-à-dos*.

There are *simple* bindings, meaning the elemental *types of books,* as opposed to easy to make. These are the fan, blind, codex, and the fold book.

There are *compound* bindings, which are a combination of two simple bindings. *Concertina Binding,* page 261, is a codex/fold book. The *dos-à-dos,* page 253, is two connected codices. Any dos-à-dos can also be thought of as a single Oriental fold book with side issues:

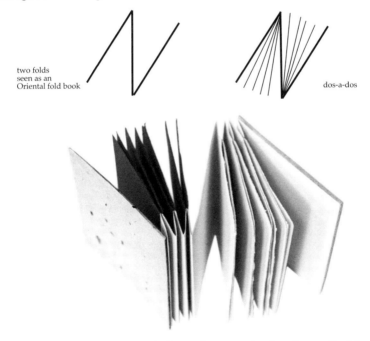

two folds
seen as an
Oriental fold book

dos-a-dos

Two books attached by a single back cover in common is referred to as a *Dos-à-Dos*. It is a traditional form, often used for two related books. See page 253.

SKETCH NUMBER 2: *two folds in the same direction*

I fold another sheet of paper twice, this time both folds in the same direction. What do I see? My question ought to be, "Where did I make the folds?" How did I *determine* where to make the folds? I must not act without thinking. I may spontaneously respond and then think, but I cannot take for granted. I made the folds equidistant. What are the permutations of folding a sheet twice, with both folds the same direction? They are the following:

1. creating three leaves of equal width, folds equidistant.

2. creating three leaves, two of which are equal in width, the third much wider than of the total of the other two.

3. creating three leaves, two of which are equal in width, the third far narrower than either of the other two.

4. creating three leaves, two of which are equal in width, the third the width of the total of the other two.

5. creating three leaves, each a different width.

Each of the five examples represents a compound binding, a codex/codex. What can you do with permutation 1, *equidistant folds* as a book? I might use this as units to be stacked and sewn. Each unit is a folio with a foredge throw-out:

Example 2 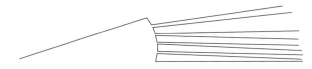 does not interest me, at least not as much as 1 and 4, because it does not completely hide the third leaf in the unit. There are more possibilities of content combination when the third page can be hidden by closing the other two. Opening and closing the pages allow some information to come forward while other imagery completely disappears. This permits the element of surprise.

I dismiss permutation number 5 because the action of the two hinges is limited. The movement is flawed because the longest leaf cannot be turned to rest within the opposing fold. The shortest leaf must always be positioned between the middle and the longest leaf.

Example 3 seems useless to me as well. It will not close flat, so I summarily dismiss it. However, some other bookmaker will take time to see, finding this to be the most ideal permutation of two folds as units for binding. The third shorter leaf would not be seen as a page, but become part of the backbone. Only the two longer sides would be pages. The accumulation of these units would swell the back deeper than the foredge accommodating folds-out or pops-up within the longer leaves.

Cross section of the book shown below.

Scott McCarney, untitled, 1982. One-of-a-kind, imaged by cutting into the page to form pops-up. Type of binding attributed to Joan Flasch uses strips of woven paper rather than thread. 12.5 x 12 cm.

In fact, example 3 has even more potential I have over-looked. Still another book artist would look at example 3 and see the shorter leaf as the foredge rather than the spine. Units would be compiled and bound at the opened ends of the longer leaves.

Rather than assuming the binding of the units should be a codex, Lisa LaLonde has bound the units as a fan book, allowing the units to telescope open to a tunnel formation and collapse shut.

Lisa LaLonde, *They Say,* self-published 1990.

In "turning" the pages, partially telescoped units overlap. At certain points in this movement a partial image on one unit is completed by the remainder of that picture on another. At these same points, incomplete text on one leaf is completed on the next. This creates precise points of pause positioning the leaves in the act of examining the structure.

Pages create their content.

Example 4 is a potentially strong format. Like example 1, this hybrid could also be stacked as units and sewn. However, in compiling and sewing, units lose their original character. Now, it becomes a book with every other leaf short, alternated by a longer leaf with a fold-out. The pages of such a book do not evoke or extend the essence of the unit.

I must take time to investigate example 4 for the quality of the single unit. Observation takes great effort. The artist is aware more than most that all of us are blind. We only truly see at brief points of inspiration. One way of seeing the unit is as two facing codices with a large back page in common. The two front pages are equal in width and tangent.

Tangent is the key, for it is the essence of this format, a feature unique to all the examples. What does it mean? Tangential pages offer two facing stages instead of one. But any codex opened to any point has two facing pages. This is the *opened folio.* However, example 4 has two hinges, ⎯⎯⎯⎯⎯ compounding the action.

The two shorter pages can be imaged separately. One image or text can cross from one to the other page. Opening, that is turning either the right or left page, reveals half of what is on the third (or back) page. This half must function compositionally with the remaining front page which has not yet been turned, as well as with the back side of the page which has been turned. Opening the second front page will further complicate the movement basic to this format.

I see the potential of example 4 not as units to be compiled and sewn, but as a *what* to exploit the inherent movement of this format, which is the interplay of tangential pages. This format is referred to as *French Doors*. It is described on page 257.

French Doors format

Adding additional tangent pages to each facing codex extends the interplay of permutations.

1. *Related Volumes* One facing book can be viewed while the other remains closed. It is a play in two acts. Or, instead of two related volumes, it might be a before and an after or an either/or concept.
    At every point in turning the pages of one volume while the other remains closed, each opened folio must incorporate or juxtapose with the closed cover of the unopened book.

2. *Implied Single Volume with Double Opened Folio* Both books can be viewed simultaneously like opening double French doors. Both covers are opened at once, both first pages are opened at the same time, et cetera. This sets up a series of compositions across the four panels of the two opened folios.

3. *Interacting Volumes* The two books can be seen alternately, intermittently randomly, turning one or more pages first of one book, then the other. Compositionally, this requires every possible permutation of combined imagery and/or text.

The artist and the craft person must always find the essence of an idea and extend it to its full potential. It's like telling a joke. You don't reveal the punch line at the beginning. You build on it for all it's worth.

Bookbinding is not a mindless task of rote repetition. Bookbinding as an art is severely limited if it is after the fact, rather than part of the statement.

I tell myself
> take another sheet of paper.
> think of what you are holding.
> think as you are folding
> think as you.
> think.

Gary Frost, two binding models, one in vellum, both with leather on the spine. Stitches on the spine have been tied or used as warp threads for the thicker woof weaving. The bindings are Long Stitch/Link Stitch, which is described on page 177.

The essence of refining a binding is getting it down to bare necessities.

TRIADS

When I think about bookbinding, I cannot determine *how to* without addressing, again and again, the question, *why?*
Why must be answered before *how to* can become meaningful.

What is needed will determine *how.*

It is one thing to learn mechanically how to sew a particular binding. It is much better to begin binding from a far more fundamental approach in order to see the process in its simplest terms, for only then can the imagination leap to invent the complex.

What is meant, what can be bent to be seen as the term *binding?* The most obvious answer is to dwell on the various means of constructing an order of pages.

Binding is the activity of folding down and/or attaching to. One sheet can be folded to construct a book. Various ways of folding and cutting will create different bindings which allow longer journeys and other itineraries through the format.

Sewing and adhesives are obvious ways of connecting. What about interlocking slits, weaving pages together, hinges, pockets, snaps, grommets and velcro?

What is the most obscure, seemingly irrelevant definition of basic terms for *sheet, cover, adhesive, sewn* and *bound?* Terms must be defined, but not confined; they must be expanded. The first tools to pick up are not a bone folder and needle, but time, thought, pencil and notebook.

Yet, for others, it is best to jump right in and make a binding so that the product encourages continuation. Later comes introspection on how to approach the concept of binding.

NUMBER GAME

Understanding ways of attachment in bookbinding may not come from making lists *or* hands-on labor. At times I take an indirect approach to a problem. One way is by equation. I think of the book in numerical divisions.

The number one concern is the totality of a realized book. Orchestration is not possible without each element relinquishing sovereignty to its union.

When I think of the number two, many pairs come to mind: recto/verso; text and pictures; space and movement; planned itineraries and random reading. Order and chaos are intertwined. The preconceived is balanced by the intuitive. There is the shelved book-as-receptacle, with its latent content in opposition to the book coming to life as it is read. There are practical as well as aesthetic concerns. If I had to choose the most basic two-of-a-book, it would be the content and how its order is maintained, displayed, revealed, protected and properly stored. This is its binding. Content plus binding equals book. That does not mean binding and content are of equal value. Binding serves content.

Three-of-a-book is an easy answer for me:
• Concept of the content and binding.
• Visual aspects of both.
• Physical needs of the object.

The   BOOK   is organized.

The order of the   CONTENT   is maintained by the   BINDING.   Each is revealed through

CONCEPTUAL   VISUAL   and   PHYSICAL

transitions.

There are many paths through this pyramidal hierarchy:

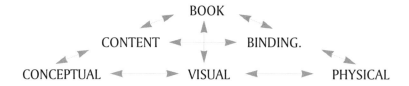

BOOK

CONTENT ◄——————► BINDING.

CONCEPTUAL ◄——————► VISUAL ◄——————► PHYSICAL

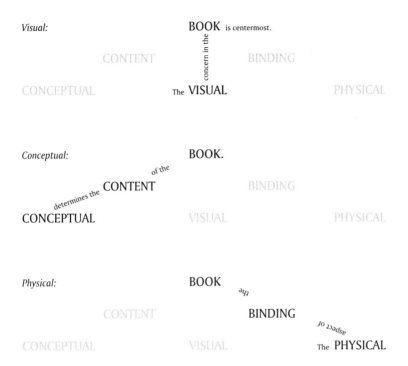

Visual: BOOK is centermost.

CONTENT   concern in the   BINDING

CONCEPTUAL   The VISUAL   PHYSICAL

Conceptual: BOOK.

             of the
     determines the CONTENT   BINDING

CONCEPTUAL   VISUAL   PHYSICAL

Physical: BOOK
                            the
CONTENT   BINDING
                              aspect of
CONCEPTUAL   VISUAL   The PHYSICAL

The book, constituted by everything in the pyramidal hierarchy, is always top and center, the totality and must dominate. Each decision on any element within is subordinate to the realized book. If the binding dominated, the book would be superficial. If conceptual, visual and physical organization were not considered, the content of text and/or pictures would be merely a compilation of islands, rather than an orchestrated totality.

It would appear that at one extreme, the content is quite separate from the process of binding. For me, nothing could be farther from ideal. I sometimes think about the *physical object*. There is concrete space between words and/or pictures. Movement is constructed through content, which determines the rate of turning pages.

At other times I think about *conceptual approaches*. There is the implied space within ideas of simple or complicated content. This requires creating a binding structure which can best facilitate revelation of the content. The itinerary may be straightforward, convoluted, cyclical or overlapping. At times, this requires an unique, non-traditional binding to best facilitate the itinerary through the book.

Still, other times I concentrate on *visual concerns*. Do I want to work with the book as spartan or elaborate, use a range of materials or processes, texture, pattern? To what extent do I want emphasis on graphic design, typography, the layout of the pages?

It quickly becomes clear that any visual concern is also a concern for conceptual ideas and the physical object. Modifications of the physical object affect the conceptual and visual aspects. Whatever I conceive determines the look of the end-product. Although one element may dominate, the physical, conceptual and visual decisions are interwoven. Each of the three areas speaks of both content and binding. That is why it is farce not to consider the binding until after the contents are completed. Each element of the hierarchal pyramid is essential and interdependent:

Binding: In the display of a BOOK

                 CONTENT   is facilitated by its   BINDING   which relies upon the

CONCEPTUAL   to materialize the   VISUAL   as form and upon the   PHYSICAL
to function as *ACTION*.

Content: The   BOOK   is ideal

          when CONTENT   is served by the proper   BINDING   to reveal

CONCEPTUAL   as well as   VISUAL,   and sometimes   PHYSICAL
transitions.

Movement

Some people could relate the pathway through content to ideas found in cinema or patterns in dance; but for me, I see so many parallel terms in musical composition.

Organization

Structure of the binding is similar to collage or a picture puzzle. The intended order of the content is maintained or can be reconstructed. A stack or portfolio dropped, like a raw egg, is irretrievable. Binding and content are movement and structure.

As Gary Frost[1] says, it is *the-book-as-action*.

This brings me back to thinking on the most simple basic level of what is meant by maintained: glued, sewn, folded, interlocked, bound and layered information: sheets, covers, text, images.

In collage, puzzles and binding, maintaining is a concern for attaching or interlocking. Unlike collage, the binding must allow access to the layered information—attached single sheets or the introduction of folded sheets. This is the concern for action.

One of my favorite artists is John Wood. He makes books and collages among other things. John sometimes gives workshops in collage and stresses ways of attaching. Gluing is an obvious solution. The activity of investigating attaching disparate elements demonstrates how function affects form. This is true in collage; it is equally true in physically inventive binding procedures.

The physical action in proficient binding of traditional formats influences the content. Unique means of attachment result in a binding which alters content: subject matter, mood and pacing. Non-traditional formats offer more radical opportunities of binding/imaging. Physical movement through the object may not take a straight path because of folds other than at 90° or because of compound hinging. Hybrid bindings require new ways of seeing and rethinking itineraries through a book. See the various *compound bindings* on pages 249-280.

Dwelling upon numerical divisions to define a book, I do not make it past the number three. Just as well. If I got much higher it would mean I was not allowing my imagination time to become engrossed in order to find that for which I am searching.

Keith Smith, *The Photographer in Search of His Image,* 1998. Half leather raised cord. Cover image is a postcard from a friend, his self-portrait, Torrence, CA, 1969.

AGGRESSIVE BOOKBINDING

The best bindings are more than craft which facilitates turning pages and providing a protective cover. Bindings should never be an after-thought; they are not independent of content.

If the binder is not the author, care must be taken that the binding is appropriate to style, mood and intentions of content. The binding should not be intrusive. It should not be too much nor too little. That is the advice of the renowned accompanist Gerald Moore. He says that in German lieder the piano is an equal with the singer. Sometimes he is accused of drowning the singer, but he replies that the piano must support the voice, creating a duet. Balance is the art of the accompanist. Not too much, not too little. And so it is with binding.

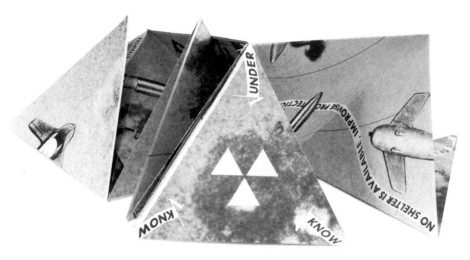

Scott McCarney, *In Case of Emergency:*, Nexus Press, 1985. Three-color offset edition of 400. Two intersecting fold books are pamphlet sewn together. Pages are folded on a 60° angle to further compound the itinerary through the book. The complication of reading reinforces the subject matter—evacuating a large city in case of nuclear attack. 15.2 x 15.2 x 15.2 cm.

If the binder *is* the author, or works in collaboration with the author, there is far more leeway. Binding becomes a broad horizon of potential. In producing a new book as opposed to re-binding an existing one, content and binding evolve simultaneously in a give-and-take situation.

Binding ideally is an integral part of the total experience, an element of the content, part of the statement. Mass-produced or one-of-a-kind, a binding should at least work in harmony from conception to finished piece.

Binding should be more than just appropriate. Sometimes, imaginative approaches to binding influence and reinforce content. In the ultimate collaboration, binding determines content.

Margaret Kaufman, *Aunt Sallie's Lament*, Janus Press, 1988. Book design by Claire Van Vliet based on a binding structure developed by Hedi Kyle and made with Linda Wray. Box is by Judi Conant. The spine strap can be removed. The codex transforms into a fold book, allowing all the pages to be seen at once.

Pamela Spitzmueller, Long Stitch/Link Stitch Models with vellum covers. The long stitches on the spine are elaborated with weaving and macramé. 1986.

THE DOVETAIL

A book is a combination of its content and its physical binding. Concerns for one flow back and forth into the other.

BINDING CAN BE CONTENT

Binding can be content to be limited to modest attachment of pages within a protective cover. Aggressive bookbinding is the rare interplay of all elements of the book.

Approach to binding can be aggressive or remain traditionally passive. Content does not have this option.

CONTENT MUST BE BINDING

Text and/or pictures must weave back and forth tying everything together, not merely connecting one page to the next. Sticking a running manuscript into a book treats the sheets as nothing more than surface to support the content. Resulting text is organized; pages are ordered only on the shallowest of levels—in a numerical sense. The pages do not relate back and forth. It does not show an awareness of the power and potential of the *format*.

Binding and content should be mutually dependent.

The *act*, rather than the result of folding is the essence of a codex book. The action should be with full knowledge of the ramifications of bringing into being the only art form with planar two-sided display. As I have tried to portray in the first demonstrated binding, the one-fold book, the time/space event is as much a part of the book experience as anything printed on the pages. Regulation of time through space alters anything printed on the page, as much as tempo alters melody.

To me, style in writing varies with a change in format, just as words in a conversation are different from an impromptu speech. Writing words to be delivered as a lecture is different from conceiving a running manuscript as a handout. Writing in the single-sheet format, such as a hand-out, is vastly different from text composed as a book experience.

Marbled and decorative papers from around the world. I am constantly buying papers. Once I asked Mrs. Aiko for a particular decorative paper. She said only two people in Japan made it. One retired; the other moved to a city for a better job. The paper was now extinct. After that, each time I am in a different city, I visit paper stores and buy every paper to which I am attracted, with no idea when they will be used. Now I have a vast store of papers from which to choose. For sources of paper check out the *Sources* on my web site.

COMING to TERMS

The book as physical object is an exploration. Each element presents opportunities as well as challenges in facilitating particular tasks through elaboration of design. The conceptual, visual and physical elements of content and binding unfold through time and space. In understanding the role that each element can perform best, I begin to orchestrate.

A book can be created through a play upon the action of turning a page. Indeed, a life time's work can have as one under-pinning the exploration of what physically transpires in turning the page.

Becoming involved and excited about any aspect of the physical book can reveal potential which, once understood, can easily be expanded as theme. Only then is subject matter, mood and point of view considered. A book grows out of an understanding of its inherent properties, rather than the inclusion of outside elements. Conception springs from the physical format, evolving into a realized book. It is the opposite of sticking things into a blank binding which disregards orchestration of all the elements—binding, the page, text and/or pictures, turning pages and display.

Compilation can never yield a book.

A sense of the format is glimpsed through introspection, but it is only achieved by making many, many books. Each resolved in a different way expands vocabulary. Work is the activity of play through discipline. Without discipline, there is no freedom. Without play, craft and skills are sterile. Play, but play for keeps—be willing to *say* something. Don't play it safe and make pretty, but meaningless objects. What you say reveals who you are. It's not easy to reveal oneself. I think that is what Matisse was saying in 1905, when he said, "Art is as a crime."

PARTS of a BOOK

Examine a book, stripped of content, so that all that is seen is its elemental characteristics. The blank book is richly laden, part by part.

Terms are often explained as they are introduced in this text. Also they are defined in the *Glossary of Terms,* page 335. Common words are preferred to jargon of the trade. But it is important to use words in a way which will not conflict with the established vocabulary of bookbinders.

This text has been edited to conform to *A Vocabulary of Terms for Book Conservation Practice* by Gary Frost.

SUPPLIES

Tools and materials for non-adhesive binding are few and inexpensive. There is no need for presses or other heavy and costly equipment. If you are a vegetarian, you need not use leathers, nor animal adhesives.

TOOLS

ITEM	QUANTITY
bone folder or plastic substitute	1 per student
2½" curved needles	1 per student
3" curved needles	1 per student
straight needles to fit #18 thread	1 per student
small (#11) X-Acto® knife and blades	1 per student
elf-sealing cutting base, about 18 x 24"*	1 per student
scissors	1 per student
steel rule	1 per 3 students
right triangle	1 per 3 students
bradawl, a straight shafted awl (or bodkin)	
See *Glossary*	1 per 2 students
twist paper drill or hand punch	1 per 4 students
gouge (curve-bladed chisel)*	1 per 4 students
dividers*	1 per 4 students
paper cutter*	
punches*	1 per 4 students

* Not a necessity, but eventually would be worthwhile.

MATERIALS

Stocking a working space with a few tools and materials can be done for under $50 for an individual, $200 for class of a dozen students:

QUANTITY	ITEM
straight needles to fit #12 thread	1 per student
1 roll unbleached #18 linen thread	
1 roll unbleached #12 linen thread	
1 ball of #6 or 8-cord linen twine	
beeswax	1 per 3 students

Book Board

cover boards (Davey Red Label binder's board
    is suggested)   1 per student
    .060" deep, x 26" x19" (thin board)
    .080" deep, x 26" x19" (medium board)
    .100" deep, x 26" x19" (thick board)

Papers

sheets of smooth white paper, 70 or 80 lb. text,
    approximately 17 x 23"   30 per student
smooth white paper, 70 or 80 lb. cover,
    approximately 17 x 23" (Mohawk Superfine
    is an inexpensive archival paper)   10 sheets per student
assorted colors, 70 or 80 lb. text, approximately
    17 x 23" (Classic Laid or Strathmore Charcoal)   10 sheets per student
assorted colors, 70 or 80 lb. cover, approximately
    17 x 23" (Strathmore Grandee or Canson)   10 sheets per student
Marbled and fine combed papers

As you become more involved in binding, you might start building an inventory of various 100% rag printing papers and a collection of marbled and handmade papers. In addition, you might purchase a used compositor or stamping machine with type for printing covers.

Try not to buy machine-made papers in individual sheets. They are far less expensive if purchased in increments of 100 sheets, with an even larger discount by the ream.

SOURCES

Membership in guilds gives access to their directories. Contact:

Guild of Book Workers
521 Fifth Avenue
New York, NY 10175
http://palimpsest.stanford.edu/byorg/gbw/g
bwnews.shtml

The Book Arts Guild
Sandra Kroupa, Membership Secretary
515 N. 49th
Seattle, WA 98103
http://bookartsguild.org

The Canadian Bookbinders and Book Artists
Guild (CBBAG)
176 John Street, Suite 309
Toronto, ONT M5T 1X5 Canada
T 416 581 1071   F 905 851 6029
http://www.cbbag.ca
Email: cbbag@web.net

UK Directory of Suppliers available for £5.50
from:
Designer Bookbinders
Publications Ltd to Lester Bath
DBPL, 8 Bryn Coetmor, Bethesda, Bangor
Gwynedd, LL57 3NL UK
email:
publications@designerbookbinders.org.uk

TYVEK

Some people are beginning to investigate the use of Tyvek as a paper substitute and even in place of book cloth. I investigated printing on it with my laser printer. DO NOT USE TYVEK IN YOUR PRINTER! It melted. But Tyvek has many non-printing possibilities.

Tyvek is spun boron, an inert material, flexible, tough, with tremendous strength. It cannot be ripped. Various shippers, United Parcel Service and the Postal System now make their envelopes of this material, rather than paper.

Tyvek is used as a house wrap. One side faces out. It allows moisture to go out, but not back through. A roll 9' x 50' costs $200. I could not find any without advertising printed over the entire surface.

However, Tyvek is available from commercial paper suppliers in three thicknesses. It is not expensive. Purchased in 100 sheets, 23" x 35", it is about $1.40 a sheet. Grain direction is not a problem. See *Paper grain,* page 45.

As Pages

Archival, flexible and strong, Tyvek seems perfect for pages in a book. It can be sewn.

As Book Cloth and Hinges

Since it is strong, it can be a substitute for book cloth. PVA must be used as the adhesive, not wheat paste. It can be a substitute for jaconette, which is often used as a hinge under a paper or leather hinge to reinforce the weaker material.

Counterpoint

Some binders are skeptical. They say in time Tyvek may lose its plasticizer. Like rabbit hide glue used in the 19th century, it may eventually dry out and shatter.

Keith Smith,
10 Dictionaries,
prototype, 1998.
Sewn onto tapes. Quarter binding, using tyvek with pigment rubbed into the surface.

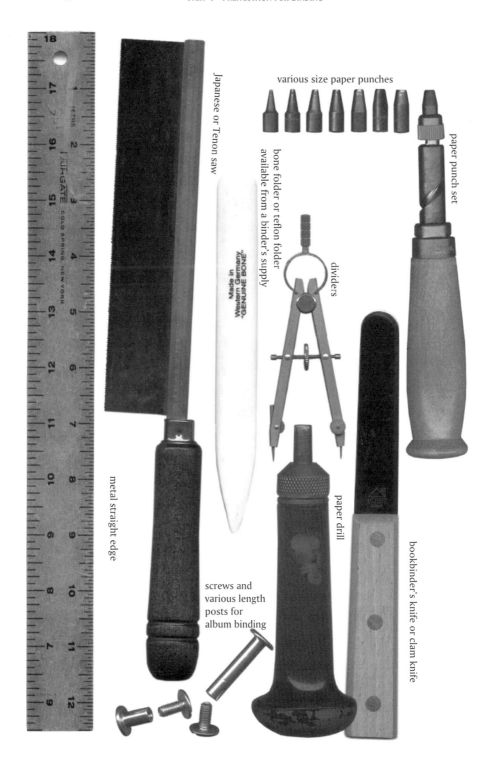

various size paper punches

paper punch set

Japanese or Tenon saw

bone folder or teflon folder
available from a binder's supply

dividers

metal straight edge

paper drill

screws and
various length
posts for
album binding

bookbinder's knife or clam knife

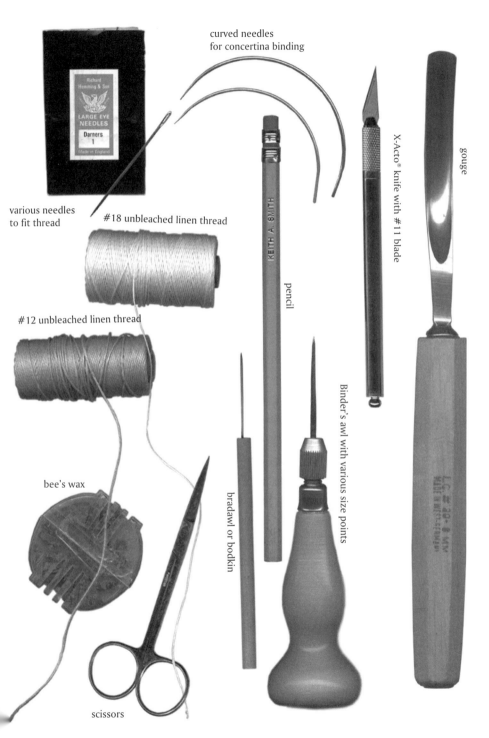

curved needles
for concertina binding

X-Acto® knife with #11 blade

gouge

various needles
to fit thread

LARGE EYE NEEDLES
Darners
1
Made in England

#18 unbleached linen thread

#12 unbleached linen thread

KEITH A. SMITH

pencil

Binder's awl with various size points

bee's wax

bradawl or bodkin

scissors

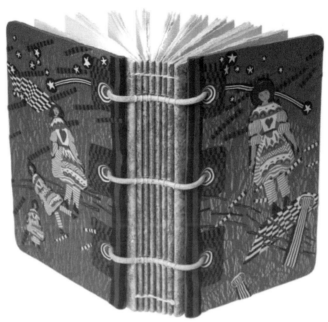

Kathleen Amt, *Alice,* 1990. Sewn onto leather cords with clay covers. For sewing onto tape supports see pages 187 and 191. For sewing raised cords see page 193.

This part of the book is preliminary reading before the descriptions of the bindings. Certain information and operating procedures about paper, thread, sewing procedures and covers common to all the bindings are discussed.

PAPER

In making paper by hand, the pulp is allowed to settle randomly, assuring that the fibers are multi-directional. The resulting paper folds as easily in one direction as the other. When paper is mass-produced, the water flows across the surface in one direction, causing more of the fibers to settle in the direction of the flow. Because of this, most commercial paper tends to fold easier in one direction than the other. This is referred to as the *grain* of the paper.

In planning how to fold down a sheet, the final fold, which is at the spine, must always be *with the grain* of the paper.

Grain of the paper, like the board for the side-covers, always runs parallel with the spine of the book. This is so that in turning pages the paper naturally curls from side to side, aiding turning the page rather than the page curling up from the head and tail.

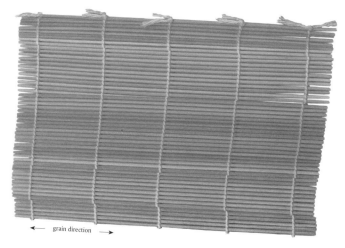

← grain direction →

DIRECTION OF GRAIN: In workshops, Scott McCarney demonstrates grain direction by showing a sushi mat. The direction of the wooden sticks represents the direction of the grain in paper or book board. Just as the mat rolls easily in only one direction, so does paper. Confusion comes when some say, "Paper bends *parallel with the grain,* while others term the same action as *against the grain."* Everyone will not agree on the term, but hopefully will understand the principle.

Grain Direction

Viewing a horizontal sheet, if it curls from side to side easier than from top to bottom, it is referred to as *grain short*. If the horizontal sheet bends easier from top to bottom, it is called *grain long*.

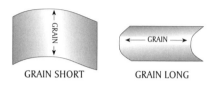

GRAIN SHORT   GRAIN LONG

Grain runs parallel with the direction of the paper in which there is less resistance to folding. Sometimes it is difficult to determine grain direction. Some papers are balanced and can be used in either direction. Other papers have a strong grain direction, but the small size of the paper can cause confusion. If bending the paper first one way and then the other does not show which direction has less resistance, there is another way to test for grain. Dampen a scrap of the paper and it will curl immediately. The axis of the curl is *parallel with the grain*. The curl shows the direction the paper should be folded. Grain runs up and down the sheets, parallel with the sewing.

Specifying the Direction of Grain

Paper is usually grain long. Paper companies generally list the direction of the grain as the second dimension: 23 x 35". Other companies will point out the direction of the grain by underlining that dimension: 17½ x 23". This smaller sheet might come from the mill 23 x 35", grain long, but they are selling it cut in half. Sold as a half sheet, the 23" figure would be misleading listed second since it is actually the shorter side of a sheet that has been cut down.

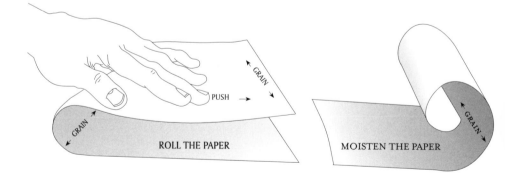

PUSH →   ROLL THE PAPER   MOISTEN THE PAPER

TESTS FOR GRAIN DIRECTION: Roll a sheet of paper without creasing it, first in one direction, then in the other. The direction in which the rolling is less resistant, the grain is parallel with the fold. If you cannot tell, moisten a scrap piece. It will curl with the grain.

Specifying Dimensions of a Finished Work

The dimensions of a book, section or a photograph are always listed with the height first, then the width. If the work has a third dimension, it is listed third. This book is 9 x 6 x $1^{5/32}$".

Marking the Measurement

Indicate the measurement to be folded on the sheet. Never use ink or ball-point. A light pencil dot can be erased, but is inaccurate because of its width—leaving to chance whether the fold is on the left, right or center of the mark. A pin prick is better. The ideal tool is the edge of your thumbnail. The indentation along the top edge of the sheet is the start of the fold. Use the top edge as a guide.

To Fold Paper

Start a loose fold with the measured mark on the outside of the fold. Crease the paper down an inch at the dot. Line up the two top edges of the sheet and firmly hold in place with one hand, while completing the crease lightly with the other. The single stroke should go downward and outward, away from the point where the two top edges are being held aligned. This insures the fold is at a right angle to the top edge. Give the fold a permanent crease with a bone folder. Do not use several strokes with the bone folder as this will cause the paper to shine.

To Score with a Bone Folder

Keeping the straightedge held firmly in position, score with a pointed bone folder. Hold the straightedge with one hand and fold paper back against the straightedge, along the indentation. This can help in the process of creasing to obtain a clean fold. A bone folder indents to score, whereas a knife incises to form a score on heavier stock paper or book board.

To Score Thick Paper or Board with a Knife

Cut $1/8$ the way down through the thickness of the paper or board with an X-Acto® knife. Heavy stock used for covers or a fold book should give a clean fold when it is parallel with the grain of the paper. If it tends to crack at the crease, the paper will first have to be scored, that is, slightly incised where it is to be folded.

Position a right angle lining up with the bottom edge of the cover paper. Cut along the edge of the right angle. If you cut too deeply, you will weaken the paper. Make the fold with the cut on the mountain peak.

Alternate the cuts with the other side of the sheet. Be consistent in lining up the right angle either with the top or the bottom edge.

If the paper has been cut slightly off from 90°, the top and bottom edges will not be parallel and neither will the resulting folds.

To Tear Paper

Torn paper edges are often attractive in a hand-bound book. They are impossible in a commercially-made production book, which makes them all the more desirable in hand-bound small edition and *one-of-a-kind* (single copy) books. Sometimes the deckled-edge is incorporated in the binding but the sheet is larger than the page. The other edges must be either machine cut or torn. Tearing paper can imitate the deckled-edge. Instead of placing all deckled-edges at the head and your torn edges at the tail, alternate the deckled-edge with the torn to offer less comparison between the two. Each method of tearing gives a different edge:

1. Lay a straightedge where the paper is to be torn. Firmly hold it in place with one hand, while you tear against the straightedge.
2. For a more exaggerated torn edge, use a wooden ruler which has a metal edge inserted. Since the metal is raised above where the paper is held down to the surface of the table, the tear will peel as it frays. The higher the metal edge is from the surface, the more exaggerated the tear. You can increase the height of the metal by placing masking or duct tape on the bottom of the ruler.
3. The most extreme and perhaps the best imitation of the deckled-edge by tearing is accomplished by a different approach. Fold and crease the paper where it is to be torn. Reverse the fold and crease. With a damp sponge, stroke the folded edge. Do not run the sponge on the surface of the paper, only across the edge of the fold. Reverse the fold and stroke it with the sponge. Open the paper and gently pull it in two at the weakened fold. The paper will fray more than tear, leaving an edge of hairy fibers.
4. Run a Rapidograph™ filled with water along a ruler for Eastern papers with long fibers. Hold ruler in place and gently pull. If an area resists, scrape the fiber with an X-Acto® blade, but do not cut.

To Cut Paper

Cutting and trimming paper by hand should be done with a sharp blade using a metal straightedge as a guide. Slits are made in the same manner. Whenever this text says *cut* or *slit,* this is the assumed procedure. An X-Acto® knife with a #11 blade is recommended as it has a narrow point which is easily positioned and is thin so it does not throw a burr on the paper.

Never cut directly on the table, not only to protect the furniture, but to avoid a ragged cut. Always use a self-sealing cutting mat under the sheet to be cut. Scrap book board is a poor substitute.

Your cut will be imperfect if it extends over an area where the book board is incised from a previous cut. Only use #11 blades with a self-sealing mat. Heavy-duty blades will shorten the life span of the mat. A cutting mat may seem expensive, but it is a valuable tool and a pleasure to use.

Paper Cutters: An ideal paper cutter has a clamp-bar close to the blade to hold the paper in position so it does not creep as the blade slices through the paper. The clamp-bar should come down parallel with the plate, so it must be hinged at both ends. A cutter with a clamp-bar having a single hinge located near the fulcrum of the blade is to be avoided.

The right angle bar may be located along the top or bottom edge. It should be adjustable and all paper cutters should be checked monthly with a large metal right angle to determine if the angle bar needs adjusting. Do not take it for granted that all paper cutters cut at a right angle. Few do. Only those capable of being adjusted and which are serviced regularly will give you an accurate cut. In folding, especially concertinas, it is impossible to achieve acceptable folds if you do not start with a sheet with 90° corners.

Never try to cut several sheets of paper at once. The bottom sheets will be ragged and probably not cut at 90°. The practice abuses the hinge of the blade.

Never cut book board or card on a paper cutter. If you do not have a board shear, cut by hand using a heavy-duty mat knife and straight edge. Place scrap book board underneath. Do not use mat knives on self-sealing cutting mats.

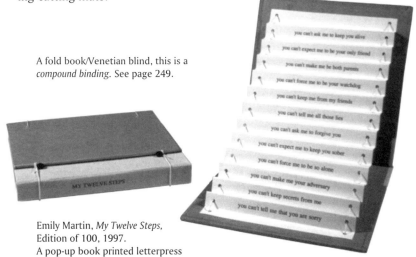

A fold book/Venetian blind, this is a *compound binding.* See page 249.

Emily Martin, *My Twelve Steps,*
Edition of 100, 1997.
A pop-up book printed letterpress
on cream colored Rives heavy weight paper. Case bound with flax and moriki paper over acid-free binders board. Bamboo and cotton pull cord and bead stops for closing.
15.2 x 15.2 x 2.5 cm.

SHEET

A *sheet* is one piece of unfolded paper with a front and a back side forming two pages.

Several unfolded sheets can be compiled and bound as a book, either as *fan, venetian blind* or a *codex*, as the *Album Binding* or a stab binding.[2]

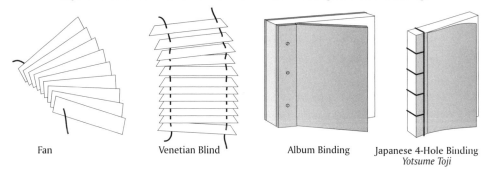

Fan   Venetian Blind   Album Binding   Japanese 4-Hole Binding
                                                                    Yotsume Toji

In compiling single sheets to form a codex the paper grain direction should be parallel with the backbone.

Three kinds of single sheet codex bindings are described in this text: *Album Binding*, page 133; *Single Sheet Pamphlet Stitch*, page 106; and *Stab Bindings*, beginning on page 107.

A single sheet can be altered to become several pages by alternately folding it back and forth upon itself to become an *Oriental fold book.*

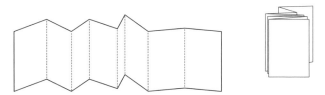

A sheet of paper can be folded down to become a book. The alternating folds are parallel with the grain of the paper. This is the *fold book.*

A sheet folded down into a section becomes a *codex.*

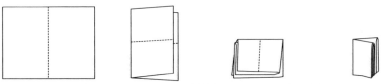

a SHEET folds in half to become a FOLIO which folds to a QUARTO which folds to an OCTAVO

FOLIO aka *fo*

Folding a sheet in half yields a folio. The fold is the back bone and parallel with the grain. A folio consists of 4 pages. With a folio, the terms *front* and *back* are irrelevant.

Each surface is a front during the act of viewing. Each is a back when that page is turned. To consider the right side of a two page spread as the "front" to be imaged and the left as a "back" to remain empty, is to negate 50% of display.

The Western codex is unique in all of art because it is *two-sided display*. It cannot be seen at once, but is revealed through time.

SECTION aka *signature*

Assembled Sections

SHEET

Two or more folios, one inside the other as a sewing unit, is a section, as shown on the right. The section is *compiled.* On the left, sections are shown *folded down.*

Folded Down Sections

FOLIO

In production work, compiling folios into sections is not an efficient procedure. It would require printing each individual folio at a time. Or, several folios would be printed on the same sheet, then each cut and assembled into units as sections. This would be cost-prohibitive.

QUARTO

In production printing signatures are machine-folded down. If it is not a blank book, it is first printed in imposition. A machine folds the sheet in half, two or more times. The folds alternate against and with the grain. The head, tail and foredge are trimmed leaving only the fold along the back-bone. Trimming is generally done after sewing, when all the sections, called the book block, can be trimmed at once. If there is a paper cover, this is attached to the book block prior to trimming. This saves time and insures uniformity, since all the units are held in position by the binding.

OCTAVO

FOLDED DOWN

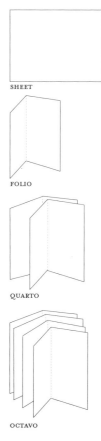

SHEET

FOLIO

QUARTO

OCTAVO

COMPILED SECTIONS

In hand binding, sections are hand-folded down. Folding down a sheet into a section requires two or more folds. Each fold after the first consists of folding layers of paper and folding against a fold. This tends to result in unsightly wrinkling at the second and third folds.

To avoid this, after each fold, slit the fold more than half way, but less than ⅔ the length of the fold. Use a dull knife, such as a clam knife. Make the next fold, then slit it in the same manner. The slits relieve the pressure, allowing the additional folds to crease neatly without wrinkles at the corners, referred to as *crow's feet*. The part of each fold that is not slit holds the section together until it is sewn and the slits are extended to the backbone with a knife or the edges are trimmed with a blade.

Cross Section of a folded down octavo.

The binder tends to fold down sections if making a blank book. The book artist tends to compile sections placing folios within folios. This is because the pages are imaged prior to binding. It is easier to image a folio than an octavo. Also, if a mistake is made in imaging one page, the entire octavo would be distorted. Only four pages of pictures are at risk in imaging a folio.

Cross Section of four folios sewn separately.

Both the folded down octavo and four compiled folios shown above will give 16 pages. There are other considerations of whether you should choose one over the other.

The compiled folios will require sewing four rows. Thread inside the folds will swell the backbone much thicker than the foredge. This is referred to as *swell*. It is a disadvantage because the covers will not be parallel. Storing on a bookshelf, the spine-edge will collapse. It is an advantage to sew individual folios if you are going to tip in pictures. This will tend to bring the foredge to the same thickness as the spine-edge.

Sewing the octavo has the advantage that it is quicker, since there is only one length of sewing instead of four with the compiled folios. Sewing the octavo has the disadvantage if you tipped in pictures into a folded down section because the foredge would bulge open. The covers would not be parallel and it would look stuffed.

You can sew a folded down section and tip in pictures. *Spacers* will leave space for a tipped in picture. See *Swelling the Back,* page 68.

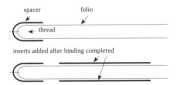

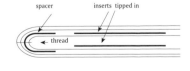

FOLIO with a spacer to tip in two pictures.   SECTIONS can have one or more spacers.

Quarto aka *4to*

A section consisting of 8 pages is made by folding the sheet in half, first against the grain. The result is then folded in half again, with the second fold perpendicular to the first.

In folding down a section, the final fold is always with the grain, since it will be at the back, aiding the hinging action.

Octavo aka *8vo*

Folding a sheet in half three times yields a 16 page section. The first fold is with the grain, the second against and the final fold is with the grain.

A very thin paper might be able to be folded in half four times, giving a 32 page section. However, the inside folds tend to wrinkle and pages within may slightly vary in size. In addition, when the book is sewn, it tends to gap open at the center folio. If 32 pages are needed, it is better to use four quartos or two octavos.

Sexto aka *6to*

A 12 page section is constructed by first folding the sheet in thirds, against the grain. This is referred to as a Z-fold. The result is then folded in half perpendicular to these folds, with the grain.

STEP 1: Fold in thirds against the grain. STEP 2: Fold in half with the grain.

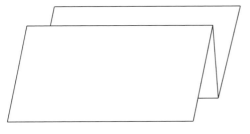

Folding down a twelve-page section referred to as a *sexto*. The final fold creates the spine-fold. The final fold must always be with the grain.

PROPORTION and SIZE of BOOKS

Proportion and size of the book depends upon the manner in which a sheet is folded into a section. For economy of paper, sheets are usually folded down utilizing the entire sheet. If the sheet is 18 x 24" and two inches is cut off the shorter side, to give a sheet 16 x 24", over 11% of the paper is wasted. Cost of production rises that amount.

If the book is to go into production, dimensions of the book are affected by three factors:

1. Standard sizes in which reams of paper are sold.
2. The direction of the grain of those papers.
3. The maximum size of sheet the printing press will accept.

One of the first considerations in creating a book must be where it will be printed. Different printers have different size presses. Next, the paper must be selected, as it may not come in a proportion that will cut down efficiently to fit that press. The desired paper may be grained the wrong direction and another paper must be chosen.

Whether the book is to be a production or a one-of-a-kind, size of paper is a limitation with which to contend. If the sheet is 18 x 24", the following are the options of proportion and size of the resulting book, when the full sheet is folded down.

If Grain Short

Sections created with an <u>18</u> x 24" sheet, halved with each fold are shown on the facing page. The sheet folded down creates the following:

18 x 12" Folio (1 fold, 4 pages)
18 x 6" Quarto (2 folds, 8 pages)
9 x 12" Quarto (2 folds, 8 pages)
9 x 6" Octavo (3 folds, 16 pages)
4½ x 12" Octavo (3 folds, 16 pages)
6 x12" Sexto (12 pages) A section created with a <u>18</u> x 24" sheet with a Z-fold yields a sexto, also referred to as 6to.

If Grain Long

Sections created with an <u>24</u> x 18" sheet, halved with each fold are illustrated on page 42.

24 x 9" Folio (1 fold, 4 pages)
24 x 4½" Quarto (2 folds, 8 pages)
12 x 9" Quarto, (2 folds, 8 pages)
12 x 4½" Octavo (3 folds, 16 pages)
6 x 9" Octavo (3 folds, 16 pages)
8 x 9" Sexto (12 pages) A section created with a 18 x <u>24</u>" sheet, with Z-fold is also called a 6to.

GRAIN SHORT

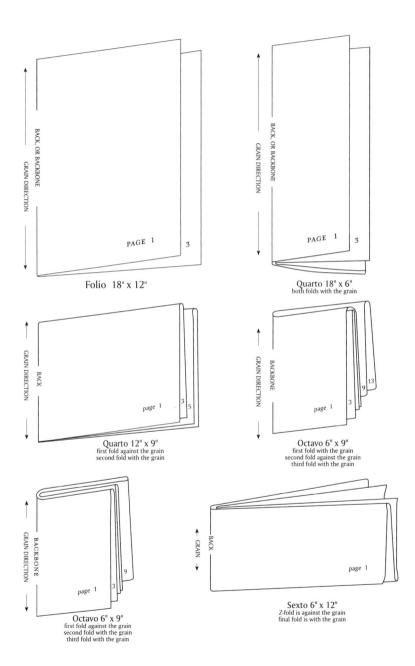

Folio 18" x 12"

Quarto 18" x 6"
both folds with the grain

Quarto 12" x 9"
first fold against the grain
second fold with the grain

Octavo 6" x 9"
first fold with the grain
second fold against the grain
third fold with the grain

Octavo 6" x 9"
first fold against the grain
second fold with the grain
third fold with the grain

Sexto 6" x 12"
Z-fold is against the grain
final fold is with the grain

GRAIN LONG

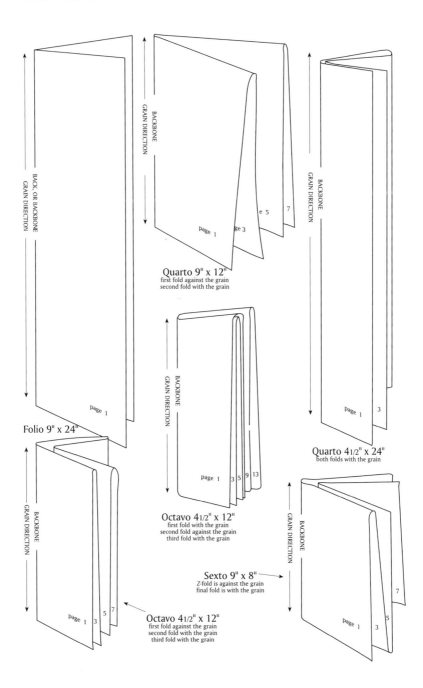

Quarto 9" x 12"
first fold against the grain
second fold with the grain

Folio 9" x 24"

Quarto 4½" x 24"
both folds with the grain

Octavo 4½" x 12"
first fold with the grain
second fold against the grain
third fold with the grain

Sexto 9" x 8"
Z-fold is against the grain
final fold is with the grain

Octavo 4½" x 12"
first fold against the grain
second fold with the grain
third fold with the grain

IMPOSITION

The *imposition* of a sheet is the laying out of page numbers on a sheet, so that they will be in numerical order when the sheet is folded down into a *section*.

In commercial printing, the sheet of paper is printed, upon which are many pages, unless it is a broadside (poster). This sheet is then turned over and the corresponding pages are printed on the back. The first side is called *Side A*. The other side of the same sheet is referred to as *Side B*. Number of pages are determined by how it is folded down, into a folio, quarto, octavo, sexto, duodecimo, et cetera.

Looking at the flat sheet, the layout of pages is not in numerical order and some pages might be upside down. See *Chart of Impositions,* page 60. The layout of the sheet is in a constructed order. It is *imposed,* so that the pages eventually will be upright and in consecutive order, after the printed sheet is folded down into a section referred to specifically as a *signature*. See *Glossary*. The layout of this constructed order on the flat sheet is referred to as *imposition*.

One or more sheets may be printed, resulting in that number of signatures in the finished book. This text book was printed on twenty-two sheets, creating that number of 16 page signatures, making a 352 page book. Put another way, this book is a 22 sheet octavo. Since the page size is 9 x 6", it was printed on an 18 x 24" sheet.

FOLIO

Imposing a folio is simple. The right hand side of Side *A* is page 1, while the left is page 4. Side *B* is page 2 on the left, 3 on the right.

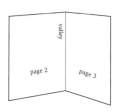

Front and back or Side *A* and Side *B* of the same sheet folded to a *folio.*

QUARTO, *folded down*

Imposing the numbers on a sheet to be folded down into 8 pages or more is difficult on a flat sheet. The easiest method is to take a scrap sheet. Fold it down to whatever number of pages desired. In this instance, 8 pages. Start at the front of the section/signature and number the pages in numerical order, 1 through 8.

GUIDE TEST: A scrap sheet is folded to a *quarto* and numbered while still folded. It is opened flat and examined.

Open the section to a flat sheet. Examine it.

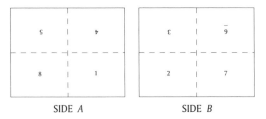

SIDE *A*   SIDE *B*

GUIDE TEST: The folded quarto at the bottom of the previous page is opened flat. On the left is one side of the sheet with the pages that appear on it. Two pages are upside down when opened. On the right is the other side of the same sheet.

One side, Side *A*, is page 1, as well as the final page, 8. Notice that pages 4 and 5 on this side of the sheet are upside down.

Side *B* is not a separate sheet, but the back side of the same sheet. Notice that page 2 backs up with page 1. Page 2 is across the gutter from page 7. They are not in numerical order, but they are definitely in an order: The numbers are in their *imposed* order.

If you were designing a flat sheet that later would be folded down, you would lay out the pages in their imposition, as in the illustration, above.

QUARTO, *compiled*

Rather than folding down a sheet to 8 pages, you might compile 2 separate folios as a quarto.

Folio 1 would not be numbered as a folio, diagrammed at the top of the previous page. It would be numbered as part of a quarto.

Instead, on Side *A* of Folio 1 would be page 1 on the left, but page 8 on the right.

Side *B* would be pages 2 and 7, as shown to the right on the folio which will be on the outside of two compiled folios.

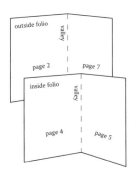

Two folios compiled as a QUARTO. SIDE *B* of both sheets is shown above.

Folio 2 would be slipped inside the first to form a quarto.

Side *A* of the inside folio would be pages 6 and 3. The other side of the second folio is Side *B*, the valley. It will contain pages 4 and 5, as shown above.

IMPOSING A COMPILED QUARTO

Looking at both sides of the compiled quarto shown at the bottom of the facing page, you can see how the page numbers are imposed.

Side A is the Peak

It is important to remember in compiling folios to form a section, that Side A always represents the *mountain peak* of the fold. Side B is the *valley* of that same fold—it is the other side of the same sheet.

FOLIO 1

First Sheet, Side A   First Sheet, Side B

FOLIO 2

Second Sheet, Side A   Second Sheet, Side B

FOLIOS 1 & 2
COMPILED AS
A QUARTO

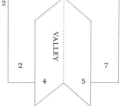

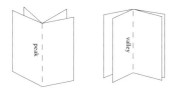

"Front" and "back" are irrelevant terms. Each page of the section is a front when opened to it. The same page becomes a back as that page is turned. Thus, the sheet is referred to as Side A and Side B.

Illustration on page 60: CHART OF IMPOSITIONS
One sheet, 4 pages and 2 sides are shown imposed, at the top, as a folio. Next, the same size sheet is imposed as a quarto. Thirdly, if the sheet is folded down into an octavo, the page numbers would be imposed as shown. At the bottom, a sheet would be folded against the grain with a Z-fold, then in half to form a sexto. The sheet is imposed as a sexto.

CHART OF IMPOSITIONS

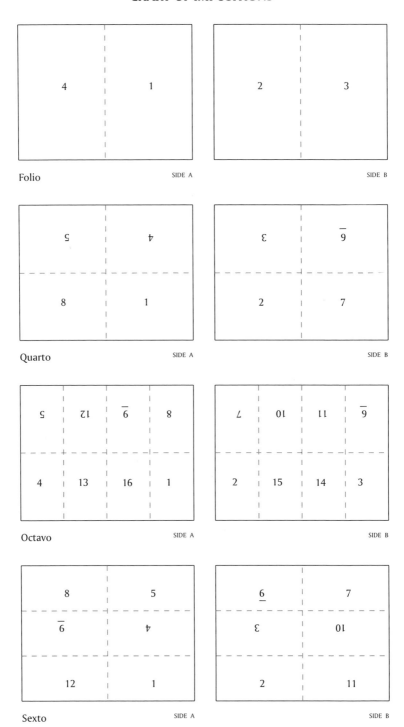

ENDSHEETS

Often the first and last sections of a multi-section binding are a different paper than the remainder of the book block. These are endsheets at the front and back of the book. If you wish, they might be a folio or quarto, even though the remainder of the book block is octavo or larger.

Endsheets are often a fine laid paper. The text weight paper is the same or lighter weight than the book block. Often they are a color different from the book block. They may be the same color as the cover. I see endsheets, cover, jacket, liners, supports and thread as the opportunity to introduce additional colors to the binding.

The function of endpapers is much like a mat on a framed picture. It isolates the content, serving as a pause to clear the mind, before entering the text/image. Turning several blank endsheets slows the viewer in anticipation. Just as when the curtain rises on the stage or the cinema, it says, "hush, we are about to begin."

The term *end papers* refers to adhesive binding. It is a folio, half of which is pasted down on the inside of the board cover. The remainder extends across the gutter as the first page of the book block.

William Drendel, *Jaula de la Serpiente,* 1993. Sewn onto Tapes. Goat skin with snake skin onlays. Box has a glass window. 15.7 x 13 x 11.4 cm.

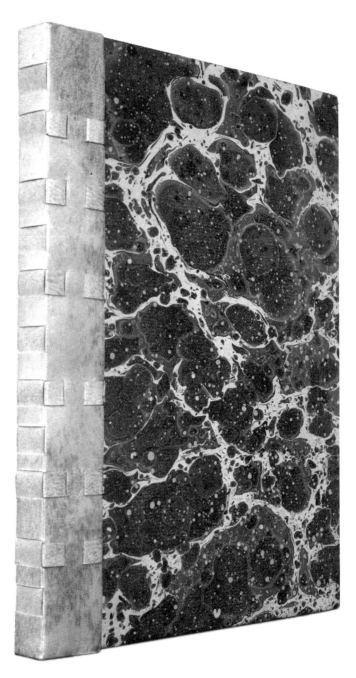

Gary Frost, untitled, sewn onto vellum tapes which are laced into the side-covers. A vertical tab is laced onto the spine, covering the sewing.

SEWING

Although the type and pattern of sewing varies with different bindings, all codex bindings have certain preparations and procedures in common.

SEWING STATIONS

The holes through which you sew are called *sewing stations*. All binding starts with pre-piercing the sewing stations. Piercing is done with an *bradawl, bodkin* or a *pointed needle* as a substitute.

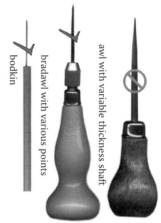

Do not use an awl designed for piercing leather. The shaft of an awl increases in diameter farther up from the point whereas a bradawl or bodkin has a shaft constant in diameter. The resulting hole should be smaller in diameter than the needle with which you will sew. To keep the sewing tight, the needle should have to slightly enlarge the sewing station as you sew.

Sewing is with a binder's needle which is also called a ball-point needle, as it has no sharp point. It cannot be used for piercing the paper. Pre-piercing the stations and then sewing with a ball point needle will permit speedy sewing, without the risk of accidentally scarring the paper, piercing an unwanted hole or stabbing your finger.

PIERCING FROM THE OUTSIDE TO THE INSIDE

The sewing stations may be pierced from the peak to the valley (outside to the inside) or from the valley to the peak. The latter is described on page 67.

Marking a Single Section Book

A single section binding has sewing stations on the mountain peak of the cover, as well as the section, but the stations are marked only on the cover. Cover and section can be pierced at once. The disadvantage is that the marking my show on the outside of the cover. If the booklet were marked and pierced from the valley to the peak, the cover would be free of any marking.

Always use a pencil, not ball point. Use a sharpened pencil to keep the dots small. Piercing should eliminate any sight of the pencil mark. Mark lightly, so you can erase if the dot is too big.

Marking a Multi-Section Book

Sewing stations in a multi-section book are generally marked and pierced from the mountain peak to the valley. It is quicker to mark all the sections and faster to pierce, it a saw is used.

Only one section of the book block needs to be measured and marked. It is then used as a guide to mark the remaining sections. You can use a scrap piece of paper as your guide, as explained on the following page.

With the marked section on top, the book block is assembled. It is jogged on the head, then on the backbone. It is then carefully laid on the table, so that the stack will not go askew. Jogging at the head, instead of the tail keeps the text in alignment.

A small right angle is stood on the table against the backbone. It is positioned at one station and a pencil is drawn down across the folds of the remaining sections. The sewing station at that location on the backbone is marked on all the sections at once, across the edge of the folds.

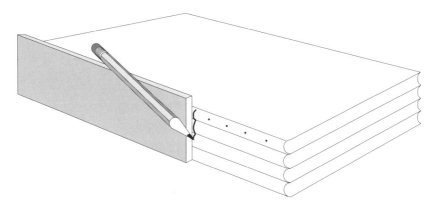

MARKING THE STATIONS USING A RIGHT ANGLE: Measure and mark the top section, only. Jog the book block. Place a right angle against the backbone at each dot. Use a sharp pencil to make a precise line down across each section. Never use ink; it can bleed. Never place a station closer than 3/8" in from the head or tail. It could rip. Stations are usually not more than 1½" apart in order to securely sew the book block.

Stations should be lightly marked with a sharp pencil to achieve the precise location to be pierced.

If the stations were marked on the inside of each section, each would have to be measured and individually marked. Since it is faster to mark the outside of the sections, the piercing must be on the outside.

Do not disassemble a section and mark all the folded sheets. Mark only the outermost fold on each section. Pierce through the remaining folds of that section with a bradawl or bodkin. Mark the sections only on the fold, not onto the surface of the page, as it would be seen in the book. Do not use ink or ball point pen, as they might bleed or smear.

Scrap Paper as a Guide in Marking the Book Block

I do not mark one of the sections as a guide. The number and locations of the stations can be measured and marked on a scrap sheet of paper the exact height of your sections. If you do not like the position of the stations, as in example 2 below, simply adjust the position of the stations keeping the same space in between the sewing stations. In example 3, the scrap guide is slid towards the head to allow more space between the tail and the sewing station.

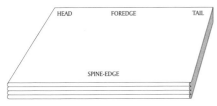

1. Assembled book block

2. Scrap guide marked and laid on top. Too little space between final section and the tail.

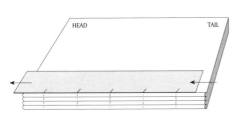

3. Guide adjusted for more space at tail. Sections are marked with a pencil using a right angle.

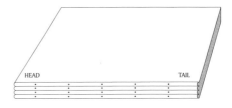

4. Guide is removed. Stations are pierced.

A scrap piece of paper is used as a guide to determine not only the space between the sewing stations, but also a pleasing position on the backbone.

With a scrap piece of paper as a guide you can play with the space between stations and adjust all the stations at once, up or down, towards the head or tail. Keep in mind the distance from the tail to the station closest to the tail is generally larger than from the head to the station closest to the head.

• Visually, this gives a base to the look of the spine. Otherwise, the station closest to the tail will look too low.

• Practically, it is especially helpful when neither the front and back cover have text or pictures. Simply by looking at the spine, the larger space at the base clues the reader to which is the front and which is the back cover.

Some bindings will have rows of sewing stations on the cover, such as the *Long Stitch/Link Stitch,* page 177. Other bindings have slits on the cover to correspond with the heights of the sewing stations on the sections. An example is *Long Stitch through Slotted Wrapper Cover,* page 141.

After the stations are marked on the backbone, each section must be opened and individually pierced from the outside in. If it is not a blank book, take care to keep the sections in their proper order. Hold the bradawl erect, to pierce perpendicular to the fold. This will insure the point will pass through each successive fold and not veer onto the pages. Use a bradawl which will leave a hole slightly smaller than the needle which will be used for the sewing. This will allow the sewing procedure to leave as small a hole as necessary, wounding the paper as little as possible.

Try using the crack in the middle of an expandable dining room table. Or, construct a board with a slot in the middle, a foot long and a quarter inch wide. The section is laid flat on the surface with the fold aligned with the slot. One hand firmly holds the section in position, while the sewing stations are easily pierced with no fear of kinking the paper causing a dimple.[3]

Piercing the Sewing Stations Using a Knife

With practice, some prefer to extend the book block off the edge of the table. Use a thin bladed sharp knife, such as an X-Acto® or a knife with break-off blades. The stations are not "pierced" but are slit. The stations do not have to be marked onto the sections. Align the scrap piece of paper on top as a guide to where are the sewing stations. Slice the stations, similar to sawing.[4]

PIERCING FROM THE INSIDE TO THE OUTSIDE

Since the sewings described in this book are not multi-sectional, the one to eight section bindings do not require piercing from the outside to the in. You may choose to pierce from the valley to the peak. Even when there are many sections, binders often prefer piercing in this direction using a *cradle.*

Piercing the Stations Using a Cradle

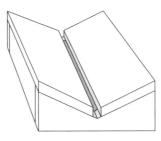

Piercing several sections is easier by setting up some sort of a jig. The best is a cradle, into which opened sections are individually laid. Stations are pierced from the inside to the outside, making sure the angle is bifurcated. This will insure that the bradawl pierces all the layers of the section precisely on the fold.

WOODEN CRADLE with slot

A sheet of stiff paper can be marked as a guide for the locations of the sewing stations. This is laid inside the section after it is placed in the cradle, eliminating the need to mark the stations on any of the sections.

The cradle might be constructed out of book board and can be used time and again. The bradawl will pierce the seam of the scored and folded diagonal boards.

A permanent cradle can be constructed out of wood. In this instance, a small slot is left between the two diagonal boards to allow the needle to pass through the gap between the boards.

Piercing with a cradle does not require marking any sections. A scrap piece of paper can be used as a guide.

BOARD WITH SLOT

You could construct a board with a slot in the middle, a foot long and a quarter inch wide. Screw a ruler as guard at the bottom to center the section.

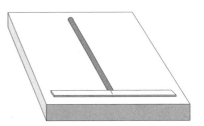

The section is laid flat on the surface with the fold aligned with the slot and ruler. One hand firmly holds the section in position, while the sewing stations are easily pierced with no fear of kinking the paper causing a dimple.

BOARD with SLOT is not as accurate as a cradle, which centers the section.

Ball Point Needle

Sewing is with a binder's needle which is also called a ball-point needle, as it has no sharp point. A substitute is to use sand paper on a sharp
needle to dull it.

A ball point needle cannot be used for piercing the paper. Pre-piercing the sewing stations, then sewing with a ball point needle permits
speedy sewing, without the risk of accidentally scarring the paper, piercing an unwanted hole or stabbing your finger. That said, I do not sew
with a ball-point needle; I use a pointed darners needle.

THREAD

Archival materials should be used. Linen thread is generally considered to have more strength and longevity than cotton.

Non-traditional sewings might use copper wire or some other linear
substance. Plastic fishing line is strong and will last, but risks ripping the
paper. After knots are tied, they would have to be fused with a match.
Although these substitutes have a nice unusual appearance, they do not
function as well as cotton and linen thread.

Swelling the Back

Size of thread which should be used depends on several factors. If the
binding contains many sections, generally a thinner #18 thread would
be used, rather than a thicker #12. This is because the thread increases
the thickness of the fold. The spine-edge of the book block swells.

This is not desirable unless a number of prints will be tipped-in bringing the foredge up to the level of the spine-edge.

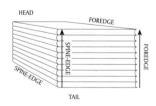 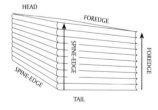 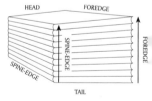

1. Sewn with covers parallel
is desirable unless prints
are to be tipped-in.

2. Thick thread swells the spine.
This is not desirable unless prints
are to be tipped-in.

3. Foredge bulge from not
providing swell on spine
to accomdate tipped-in prin

SWELL must be considered in sewing. When completed, the book should look like
figure 1, so that the covers will close parallel. The spine will not collapse on the shelf.
Figure 2 is sewn with thread that is too thick, unless prints will be tipped-in after the
sewing is completed. The tipped-in prints will bring the foredge up to approximately
the same height as the spine-edge.
Figure 3 represents a book sewn as in figure 1, but then tipped-in prints were added.
The foredge has bulged.

It is difficult to gauge how thick a thread is needed in order to expand (swell) the backbone in sewing to accommodate the prints that will be tipped in. A safe solution is to sew the sections onto a concertina pleat or guard. See *Concertina Binding* page 261. The pleat expands or contracts, keeping the sections level.

Another method to swell the backbone is to add *spacers,* a strip of paper about an inch wide by the height of the book, on the back of each section, building up the depth of the backbone.

Spacing strips are pierced along with the sewing, which holds them in place. Width of the backbone can be increased further by adding a strip of paper not only on the back of each section, but also within.

Photographic albums require spacers (stubs) between every page to compensate for the thickness of the added prints. The following illustration suggested by Betsy Palmer Eldridge uses single sheets for the sewing, sewn as a unit, suggesting a quarto. The sheets are all the same dimensions, flush at the foredge.

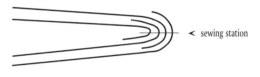

< sewing station

Start with the center page and add to the outside. Alternating the direction of the folded stubs results in their length being gradually decreased with each additional sheet added to the unit. Since the tapered stubs do not end at the same point, pages are less likely to be dented.

However it is sewn, the completed book should not be wedge-shaped. Visually, the book looks better if the closed covers are parallel. Functionally, a wedged-shaped book will be smashed on the book shelf. The spine-edge or foredge, whichever is larger will be distorted, collapsing on itself.

Waxing the Thread

Thread should be waxed prior to sewing. Waxed thread is stiffer and will become less tangled as you sew. Stitches will tend to cling in position, remaining tighter during sewing. After sewing, turning pages will have less friction and the book will wear better.

To wax the thread, run a length of thread across the edge of a cake of beeswax. Speed is important, as it will create friction, causing the wax to melt upon the thread. Run the length of cut thread two or three times across the wax until the thread seems a little stiff.

Binding suppliers sell unbleached (an unwaxed) linen thread. Craft stores often handle spools of pre-waxed linen thread in various colors.

Threading the Needle

Use as small a needle as you are able to thread. Too large a needle will create larger holes in the paper than the thread can fill.

Sewing is usually a single thread stitch. If the binding needs a short length of thread, cut off the approximate amount and pull about four inches through the needle. Sew with the single length. If the binding requires a large amount of sewing, cut the amount needed or up to a limit of an arm's length. It would be awkward and time consuming pulling this entire length through the sewing stations. Thread the needle, pulling a little more than ⅓ of the thread through the needle. This will cut the distance the thread must be pulled through the sewing stations almost in half, without giving a double thread stitch. As more and more thread is used up in the sewing, adjust the needle closer to the loose end of the thread, so that the stitches are not of double thread.

Guiding the Needle

Sewing usually attaches the section and paper cover at the same time. It is often difficult to guide the needle through the section and find the proper sewing station in the cover in a single push of the needle. If you are using a pointed needle, you risk missing the pre-punched holes and coming through the paper at a point other than the sewing station.

If you are on the inside of the section, it is often faster to sew if you place the needle through the section only far enough to see the point of the needle. Then, direct the point into the proper sewing station of the cover.

Only at that time do you take the remainder of the needle through the section and cover and pull the sewing taut.

When the needle is slightly showing through the mountain peak, direct the needle into the cover by examining on the side of the section in the direction that you are proceeding in the sewing. Never backtrack.

If you are on the outside of the cover, taking the point of the needle through the cover and position the needle into the section. Examine the side of the section which is on top.

Whenever the directions say to take the needle through to the outside or inside, it is taken for granted that you will pull all the thread through the sewing station to the other side. Pull gently until the sewing is taut.

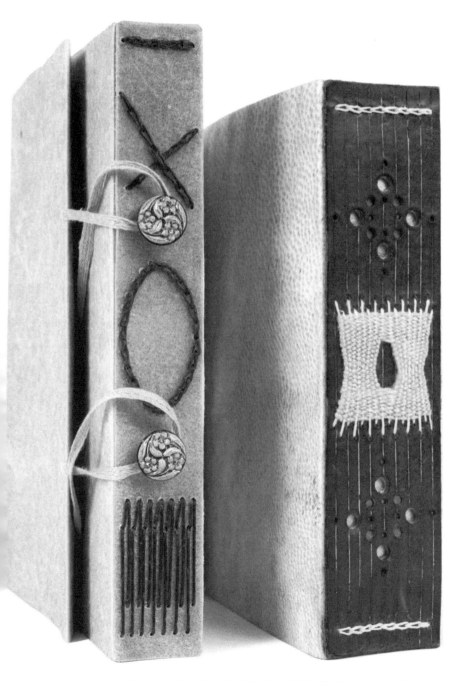

Pamela Spitzmueller, Long Stitch/Link Stitch Binding Models. On the right is a vellum cover with leather spine. 1989.

KNOTS

The bindings demonstrated will require knowledge of only a few knots: the *Square Knot, Half Hitch* and the *Weaver's Knot*. The Square Knot requires two loose ends of thread and is used at the beginning of most sewings. The Half Hitch is used to tie-off when there is only one loose thread. The Weaver's Knot is required whenever you run out of thread in the middle of the sewing and need to add more thread.

Start with an Overhand *K*. The second knot is in reverse direction.

Both knots above are a loosely tied Square Knot.

Square Knot

Every sewing which has two loose threads should be tied off with the use of a square knot, also known as the *reef and* as the *flat K*.

After the knot is tied, clip the loose ends to about ¾ inch. Do not clip close to the knot to get rid of the loose ends, thinking they are unsightly. The knot might work itself loose and the sewing will come untied. Do not be ashamed of hand-tied knots. They are evidence of the individual and should not be down-played. They are part of the craft of hand-binding.

Tightening the Square Knot.

Tightened Square Knot.

REEF, SQUARE KNOT or FLAT K
This knot is commonly called a *square knot* in the States. In Australia, it is known as the *Reef Knot*.

Procedure for Tying a Square Knot

Grasp one loose end of the thread with your left hand with 1" of thread extended from your grip. This will be referred to as the left thread. Grasp the other thread with your right hand in the same manner. Lay the left thread over the top of the right. Hold this into position with your left thupmb and forefinger. Take your right thumb and push the left thread under and around the right, through the loop. Both loose ends are now pointing upwards. This configuration is known as the *overhand knot.*

Go through this procedure for a second time. Grasp the left thread with your left hand and the right thread with your right hand. Lay the left thread over the top of the right.

Hold this into position with your left thumb and forefinger. Take your right thumb and push the left thread under and around the right, but not under and around the overhand knot. Grasp the loose ends and pull. Both of the overhand knots will tighten. When it is tied, this is a single *square knot*.

Half Hitch

Often at the end of a sewing there is only a single thread with which to make the final tie-off. This loose thread is tied around on of the stitches on the inside of the final section. A square knot is impossible since there are not two loose threads. The knot required is the *half hitch*.

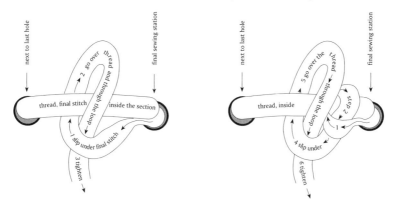

Step 1 TYING THE HALF HITCH   Step 2 TYING THE HALF HITCH

HALF HITCH: The half hitch forms a knot with the use of a single loose thread, whereas the Square Knot requires two ends of thread in order to form.

Weaver's Knot

The Weaver's Knot is needed when you run out of thread before the sewing is completed. It is tied on the inside of the section, so it is not seen on the backbone or spine-cover.

When you run out of thread, only an inch need protrude on the inside of the section. A slip knot will be placed over this dangling end of thread. Pulling on the longer and shorter end of the *new thread* will tighten into what is called the Weaver's Knot. Do not pull on the old dangling end of thread, as this will open the noose of the knot, rather than tightening it.

To make the Weaver's Knot, you must first form a slip knot. Wax a new length of thread and thread one end with your needle. Take the other end and form a slip knot, also known as the *running K*.

Forming the Weaver's Knot

To form the Weaver's Knot, first a *slip knot* is made:

1. Grasp the end of the new length of thread and form a loop, maintaining it with the fingers of one hand.
2. Grasp the longer end of the thread with your thumb and forefinger and bend the longer thread as shown in Step 2 on the facing page.
3. Push this newly formed are of thread over the original loop.
4. Pull the longer thread slightly through the loop maintaining the arc.
5. Hold onto the arc of the longer thread while you tighten the the original loop, which is now a knot. Do not tighten it totally, but simply enough to reduce it in size.
6. The arc of thread is now the new loop. Adjust it until this new loop is smaller, about the diameter of a pencil. Be careful not to tighten the knot completely. That will happen when the Weaver's Knot is completed.

This is a *slip knot*. Now you are ready to make a Weaver's Knot. Bring the new length of thread containing the Slip Knot to the opened section of the sewing-in-progress. The old thread is very short with the needle attached. If possible, you should have run out of thread at a sewing station near the middle of a section, so that when you tie the Weaver's Knot, the clipped ends will not dangle out of the head or tail of the closed book.

Remove the needle from the old thread. Place the *new loop* of the Slip Knot over the dangling end of old thread protruding from the section. *Do not place the knot* of the Slip Knot over the old thread. Push the loop all the way down to the surface of the section before tightening. Otherwise in continuing the sewing, you might have to pull the Weaver's Knot through the next sewing station.

To make the Weaver's Knot, grasp both the short and long end of the thread of the Slip Knot and pull to tighten around the old thread. *Do not hold onto the* old *thread*—that would open the Slip Knot. Grasp only the new thread, the long and short end of the Slip Knot.

As you tighten make sure the new thread does not slide up on the old thread protruding from the sewing. It must be tied close to the sewing station, so that the Weaver's Knot will not have to pass through the next station when the sewing is resumed.

When you tighten, holding onto the shorter and longer ends of the new thread, you will hear or at least feel the knot tighten with a clunk. Now grasp only the longer part of the new length of thread and tug to check if the Weaver's Knot is secure. If the new length of thread slips off the old, start again. This process is illustrated on pages 76 through 78.

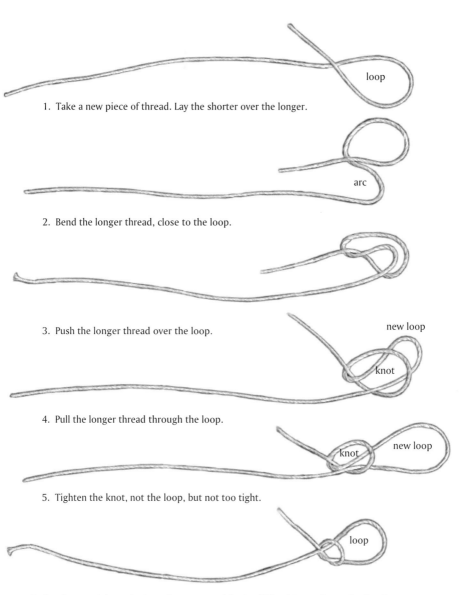

1. Take a new piece of thread. Lay the shorter over the longer.

2. Bend the longer thread, close to the loop.

3. Push the longer thread over the loop.

4. Pull the longer thread through the loop.

5. Tighten the knot, not the loop, but not too tight.

6. Continue to tighten the knot, but not too tight. It will be tightened completely when forming the Weaver's Knot. Adjust the size of the loop to about the diameter of a pencil.

FORMING A SLIP KNOT
The Slip Knot is used in forming the Weaver's Knot which is described on page 76-78.

The Weaver's Knot is used to attach a new thread to the old, when you run out of thread while sewing. The reasons it is used rather than a Square Knot are these:

It makes less of a bulge than a Square Knot.

The Weaver's Knot is easier to tie precisely where you want to attach the new thread.

STEP 1

Place the needle with a new length of thread. Form a Slip Knot on the other end of the thread, following the directions on pages 74 and 75.

STEP 2

The Weaver's Knot is the choice of knot because you do not have to pull on the old thread, which might distort the sewing. It is tied on the inside of the section, so it is not seen on the spine or spine-cover.

In tying the Weaver's Knot, it is important to slip the *loop* of the new thread over the old thread. Do not slip the old thread though the knot of the Slip Knot.

Form the loop and the knot a little smaller than shown in Steps 1 and 2. They are illustrated a little large for clarity.

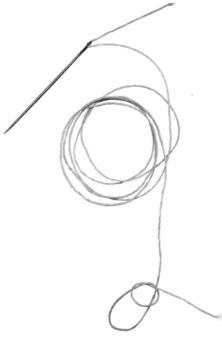

Step 1: To form the *Weaver's Knot,* thread the needle. On the other end, form a *Slip Knot,* shown above and described on page 74 and 75.

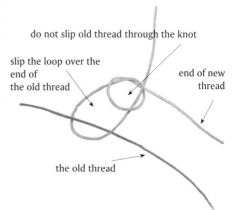

do not slip old thread through the knot

slip the loop over the end of the old thread

end of new thread

the old thread

Step 2: To form the *Weaver's Knot,* slip the loop of the Slip Knot over the end on the old thread.

STEP 3

Pull the new thread until the knot is very small, but not tight. Adjust the loop until it, too, is small.

Move the Slip Knot onto the old thread, illustrated as darker for clarity, to the precise position you wish to tie the Weaver's Knot.

STEP 4

Tighten the knot by pulling on both ends of the *new* thread. Pull in opposite directions to tighten. When you have tightened sufficiently, you will feel a slight click when it locks.

Do not pull on the old thread. This will loosen the loop and the new thread will slip off.

Pull on the old thread only to untie the Weaver's Knot.

To test if the knot is secure, tug on the new thread. If it slips off, you did not tighten enough in Step 4.

Step 3: Make the knot smaller, but not tight. Make the loop smaller, but not tight.

Step 4: Place the loop precisely where you wish the Weaver's Knot to be tied. Pull on both ends of the new thread to tighten. Do not touch the old thread. Tug on the longer new thread to check to see if it is secure.

The WEAVER'S KNOT *tightened*
Front and back views at 500%. The new thread is the lighter color. The darker color is the old thread.

NOTE: The two views of the Weaver's Knot shown on this page have not yet been tightened, so that you can see the formation. If you left the knot like this, without tightening it, the new thread would slip off.

Weaver's Knot, shown here, not tightened, as the front and back views, magnified 500%. The tightened view is at the bottom of the previous page.
A darker thread was used as the old thread, in the illustrations on this and the previous pages, to differentiate it from the new thread.

The old thread through the loop of a Slip Knot, plus the Slip Knot, once tightened, forms the *WEAVER'S KNOT*.

SEWING ON THE BENCH

Placing the book on a table and sewing back and forth is referred to as *on the bench.* This may be done with a sewing frame, but it is not necessary for the bindings described in this book.

All the instructions and illustrations herein are described for sewing back and forth across the sections on the bench. The wording does not preclude sewing up and down the vertical sections of a hand-held sewing.

All the bindings are described sewing face up, head to the left. This is the German method. With the book on the bench, this requires sewing from the back of the book to the front. Therefore, sewing the "first" section means the section adjacent to the back cover.

If you wish to sew from the front to the back of the book, sew face down, head to the right. This is in the manner of the English.

Coptic Sewing

When I learned the Coptic Sewing, it was by standing the book on its tail. Sewing in and out of the sections required a curved needle.

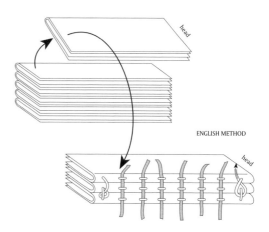

ENGLISH METHOD

SEWING FACE DOWN: This is the English method of sewing. Be careful to sew each section in proper order, with none upside down. The foredge of the unsewn sections face you. Flip each to be sewn 180° as you sew the next section. It does not matter if you start the sewing from the front or back of the book block.

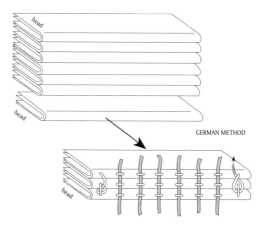

GERMAN METHOD

SEWING FACE UP: This is the German method of sewing. Be careful to sew each section in proper order, with none upside down. The spine-edge of the unsewn sections face you. Grasp the next section to be sewn from the bottom of the stack. It does not matter if you start the sewing from the front or back of the book block.

Betsy Palmer Eldridge showed me how to sew on the bench. Coptic sewing is by far easier if sewn on the bench. It eliminates the need for a curved needle, which is difficult to manage. Uniform shape of the links is easier to manage on the bench. The description begins on page 207.

When I say I learned "the Coptic Sewing," I should qualify that by saying the particular Coptic which is described in this manual. There are many Coptic sewings. Betsy taught me nine others, which, thanks to her, I have described in Volume III of *Non-Adhesive Binding,* titled *Exposed Spine Sewings.*[5]

HAND-HELD SEWING PROCEDURE

It is almost always easier to sew on the bench as both hands are left free for sewing. There are exceptions:

Pamphlet Sewing

Some sewings, such as *Pamphlet Sewing,* pages 89-106, are so rapid they can be hand-held. I prefer to sew all the link stitch bindings hand-held, except for the Coptics, which would be extremely difficult to sew if hand-held.

For sewing which is not done on the bench, it can be stood on its tail and sewn with the right or left hand. The other hand is used to grasp the section and cover at the head or tail with the thumb and forefinger. Left-handed sewing starts at the back cover, with the final section and sew towards the first section and front cover. In this direction, you are not sewing across your right hand, which would be awkward and difficult to see the stations and pressure of the stitches.

Right-handed sewing would start with the front section and sew towards the back cover.

Concertina Binding

Pamphlet sewing the sections onto a pleat for the *Unsupported Concertina Sewing,* page 261, is easier hand-held than sewing on the bench. I stand the pleat on the table and hold it and the section I am sewing.

If you are making a *Supported Concertina Sewing,* page 271, that also is easier hand-held. Stand the *Unsupported Concertina Sewing* on the table. This leaves your hands free to hold the tape or leather strap support, as you begin wrapping the thread around it. This is referred to as *packing.*

Long Stitch / Link Stitch

I prefer to hand hold this sewing to place the tip of the needle through the section in order to insert it in the proper hole of the cover as I exit to the outside. I have to watch carefully to find the proper sewing station.

GENERAL REFERENCE on COVERS

Standard procedures in measuring, folding and constructing covers which are basic to all covers will be stated only in this section. They should be read prior to constructing a cover for one of the bindings.

PAPER

Paper covers must use stock which is heavy and rigid in order to protect the text block. Unlike most text blocks which require text weight paper, covers must use 80 or 100 pound cover weight paper. Strathmore Grandee is a good paper with a range of colors. Canson is thinner, but appropriate for smaller books.

Grain of the cover paper must be parallel with the hinge-folds. This allows the cover to bend as it is turned and insures a clean fold. If it tends to crack or crease, the paper will first have to be scored, before it is folded.

COVER MEASURING PROCEDURE

Most non-adhesive bindings have a one piece paper cover which must be measured and cut before sewing begins. This is because the text block and cover are sewn simultaneously with a single thread.

In describing how to measure and cut a cover, the sheet of cover stock is always on the table, with the inside of the potential cover facing up. Dimensions are listed as a progression across the sheet. Widths are listed from the front cover foredge turn-in, if any, to front cover, spine, back cover and then back cover foredge turn-in, if any. This means measuring proceeds from the right to left on the sheet, since the inside of the cover is marked.

Dimensions for a cover, as well as procedure of folding, will be given simultaneously. Each use of the word *plus* in the stated measurements also denotes the position of a fold on the cover. Mark these positions with your thumbnail, a prick with a pin or if you must, a faint pencil dot along the head or tail of the cover.

REINFORCING PAPER COVERS
Turns-In

A paperback tends to become dog-eared at the corners. To help prevent this, the foredge can be reinforced. The foredge can be turned-in to the inside of the side-cover. They are usually not glued down. The two layers at the foredge make it twice as strong. The foredge is 2-ply. Certain paper covers have turns-in at the head and tail, as well as the foredge, for rigidity. See *Flat Back with Borders,* page 287.

Optional Liners

A *Flat Back with Borders,* page 287 or *Bordered Paper Side-Covers,* page 289, can have a sheet of paper underneath the bordered turns-in to make a stiffer cover. This *liner* is also cover weight paper of the same or a different color than the cover. It is cut ¼" less in height and width than the book block. It is seen on the inside of the side-covers adding a different color and texture to the inside of the cover.

The liner is held in place by the turns-in, but should be tipped-in, tabbed or sewn into position to give structural rigidity, making the side-cover 2-ply. A tab might be laced through the bordered turn-in and liner. A design of tabbing with slits might be anywhere on the side-covers, lacing the liner and side-cover. See *Interlocking Tabs,* page 306.

Slots

A *slot* is an opening, constructed by two slits, parallel and no more than about ⅛" apart. A cut is made at right angles at the ends of the parallel slits to remove the paper or board within the slot.

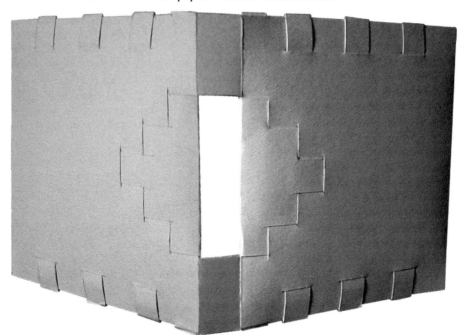

SLOTTED 2–PLY COVER: Outside view of a cover with turn-ins making the cover 2–ply.The turn-ins are tabbed along the head, foredges and tail. Tabs are folded around to the outside of the cover for insertion, decorating the cover. Since this cover is for a Buttonhole Stitch, page 171, the center of the spine has been removed. Diagram of this cover is shown on page 297.

Slots, rather than slits, are needed to accommodate heavy paper in weaving a strap or support into a cover. They are also used to insert photographs into album pages. Slots help prevent the backing sheet or page from buckling.

Cutting the thickness of a slot creates a very narrow rectangle. If you are not careful and over-cut the corners, the paper is weakened at that point and could rip when photo is inserted or when a strap is woven. The cuts extending beyond the corners looks unprofessional. Slots are more attractive if the extremes are started with a punch. The two resulting holes are connected with an X-Acto® knife and straight edge. The opening can be an oblong or shaped like bar bells.

SLOTS have two holes punched with cuts to connect for a clean shaped opening.

Punches

Punches come in different diameters. The best punches have a handle which has a twisting shaft as you lightly press down. The handle comes with a set of various diameter bits. See page 42.

Other punches are individual metal cylinders with one end hollow and sharpened for cutting. The other end is solid metal, to be struck with a hammer. Book board should be placed under the sheet to be pierced. This will protect the sharpened edge of the tool. Do not punch onto a self-sealing cutting mat.

Reinforced Spine

Often in sewing a paper cover, the spine is reinforced so that the stitches do not rip the paper spine. A strip of cover stock the width and height of the spine can be glued down on the inside of the spine.

If you wish to avoid pastes and glues, you can maintain a totally non-adhesive structure. One means is turns-in at head and tail, to give a 2-ply spine. See *Flat Back with Borders,* page 287. For a 3-ply spine, see *Flat Back with Fixed Foredge Turns-In,* page 285.

The spine can be reinforced by a cover with a support. Another means is a double or layered cover.

Cover over a Continuous Support

A book block can be sewn onto a single continuous support of paper, book cloth or leather. The paper cover is added separately. Sewing a book block onto a support that is the same height as the book block is similar to sewing onto tapes, but instead of several, there is only one *continuous support.*

For purposes of design, the support offers possibilities. The turns-in might extend to meet it. The vertical edge of the support and turn-in would be tangent. The turn-in and support would open like swinging doors to reveal text or picture on the inside of the side-cover. Or, they could be stitched together to form a 2-ply cover. The support would structurally not only reinforce the spine, but the side-cover as well.

Another variation is to cut an endsheet slightly smaller in height and width than the side-cover *plus* the spine *plus* the other side-cover. This would be sandwiched between the cover and support. The three would be sewn as a unit.

Layered Covers

Two covers can be sewn as a unit to a book block. The inner cover is $1\frac{1}{2}$" to 3" less wide than the outer. The outer cover has foredge turns-in which extend in to the spine-edge, covering the inner cover. The structural purpose of the support is to reinforce the spine for sewing. The spine is 2-ply and the side-covers are 3-ply making a sturdy cover. See *Flat Back Cover*, page 283 and *Flat Back with Foredge Turns-In,* page 284.

Measure the inside flat back cover to fit the book block. Cut and fold the inside cover. The outer cover will have side-covers and spine approximately $\frac{1}{16}$" greater in width. The height of both covers are the same. Measure and cut the outer cover, but do not fold.

Fold one hinge-fold of the outer cover. Place outer cover in position, snug on the back of the inner cover. Mark the position of the second hinge-fold of the outer cover on the inside. Remove and fold.

Place the outer cover snug against the back of the inner cover. Mark the positions of the foredge folds on the inside of the outer cover. Remove and fold the turns-in. This procedure for the outer cover of measuring as you go will allow enough extra width in folding, so the inner side-covers are not cramped and buckled.

Hold the two covers together as a unit and proceed sewing as if with one cover. If the turns-in are almost as wide as the side-covers, you will, in effect, have a 3-ply or layered cover.

Layered covers can have a turn-in at the head and tail of either the inner or outer cover. Foredge turns-in should only be on the outer. I would not recommend making a layered cover by using three flat backs, as this makes a 3-ply spine, which could give trouble in the sewing.

Layered covers can be attached other than sewing both flat backs as a unit. See *Jacket A,* page 153 and *Jacket B,* page 162.

All layered covers offer the possibility of cutting away parts of each layer to reveal composite designs. See example on page 174.

OVERHANG COVERS

Hard cover books almost always have the cover boards extended slightly beyond the head, tail and foredge of the text block for protection. The oversize cover is referred to as an overhang cover. The amount of protrusion is called the *square or square of the book*. With hard covers, the amount the board extends is usually 1½ times the thickness of the book board.

An overhang paper cover cannot be a single-ply. The square of the book would quickly become crimped with use. Overhang paper covers must have turns-in on the head, tail and foredge as reinforcement to protect the square. One such cover is described on page 287 as *Flat Back with Borders*.

Before marking the sewing stations using an overhang cover, center the section inside the cover, for an equal amount of overhang at the head and tail. Mark the stations on the spine, making sure the extreme sewing stations on the cover will catch the section. These stations must be slightly farther in from the head and tail than a cover which is the same height as the section.

Adéle Outteridge,
Envelope Book II,
used envelopes, Coptic binding, one-of-a-kind,
1995. 12 x 12 x 9 cm.

PART 2

DESCRIPTIONS OF BINDINGS

Part 2 describes and diagrams sewing procedures for non-adhesive bindings.

The simplest method of binding a single section codex is by means of a pamphlet sewing. Cover, endsheets and the section are sewn at once. This elemental sewing elevates a single section book from a stapled magazine to a hand-bound book. Magazines are technically not stapled, but saddle stitched. This is described in the glossary.

The following three demonstrations show how to pamphlet sew with either three, four or five sewing stations.

Keith Smith
Book 150, 1989.
Sections are pamphlet sewn
onto a pleat which is not as tall as the
sections. The two separate side-covers are
notched at the spine-edge to conform to the shape of the book block with pleat. Another
one-of-a-kind Concertina Binding with a shaped cover is on page 279. 45 x 33 x 4 cm.

3-HOLE PAMPHLET SEWING

PREPARATION

Book Block and Cover

Fold down a sheet to a section or compile several loose folios as a section. If endsheets are desired, add them on the peak of the section.

Place a folded cover over the mountain peak of the section. Cover should be the same size as the section, unless there are foredge turns-in. In which case, the cover will be cut wider.

WIDTH of the total cover equals:

width of the front cover foredge turn-in, if any,

plus width of the book block (front cover),

plus width of the book block (back cover),

plus width of the back cover foredge turn-in, if any.

HEIGHT of the cover is the height of the section.

Position of Sewing Stations

Three sewing stations are to be pierced along the fold. Position of the holes is important. The two end stations should be close enough to the head and tail for the sewing to provide support. But they should not be positioned any closer to the edge than $\frac{3}{8}$" or the sewing will weaken the paper between the hole and the edge. It could rip.

The middle station should be centered on the fold. Station 1 is at the tail. Pierce the three stations with a bradawl or bodkin. The cover and section are pierced at the same time.

Thread

The pamphlet sewing requires a thread which is $2\frac{1}{2}$ times the height of the back.

The pamphlet sewing makes a loop, beginning and ending on the same side, at the center sewing station. Determine if you want the knot tied on the spine or inside the section in the gutter. This is where you will start and end the sewing.

ELABORATED SEWING PROCEDURE

This description starts on the mountain peak or outside.

1. Start at sewing station 2. Take the needle through the cover and the section to the inside, leaving about 4" of loose thread hanging on the outside of the spine at the center sewing station.

2. Proceed on the inside of the section to sewing station 3. Take the needle through the section and the cover. Now that the thread is through two holes, you can pull the stitch taut without the thread slipping out of the first hole. If you had tried to leave only the desired shorter amount of loose thread in the initial station, it might have accidentally slipped through the hole. However, once the needle and thread have gone through two of the sewing stations, the thread is less apt to accidentally fall out of the station.

   Do not pull so hard that the thread is pulled out of the middle station, but hard enough to reduce the length of loose thread dangling on the spine at station 2 until it is 1½". This will be enough to tie a knot when the sewing is completed.

3. Proceed along the spine, to sewing station 1. Insert the point of the needle through the cover, to position the needle into the mountain peak of the section. Pull needle and thread through to the inside of the section. Carefully pull the stitches taut, without reducing the 1½" length of loose thread at the center sewing station. You are now on the inside of the section.

4. Proceed on the inside to the center station. Take the needle through station 2 to the outside, back to where you started.

   Examine the sewing before you tie a Square Knot. On the side you started, there is one long stitch, extending from station 1 to station 3. Flipping the book over, the other side has two stitches, each half the size of the one long stitch.

Look at the long stitch. At the center station is the two inch loose thread, as well as the opposite end of the thread where the needle is threaded. Are both of these ends of the thread on one side of the long stitch or do they straddle it? If they are on the same side, place the needle under the long stitch and pull that thread to the other side, so that the two ends of the thread straddle the long stitch. Now, when you tie the knot, the long stitch will be tied down at its center point.

In the future, when you take the needle through the final station of the pamphlet sewing, make sure the needle comes through the hole on the opposite side of the loose two inch thread, to straddle the long stitch. It will then be ready to tie a Square Knot and clip the loose ends.

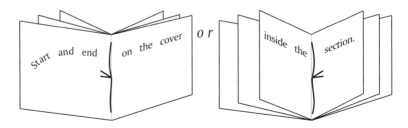

REVIEW or CONDENSED PROCEDURE

This description starts and ends on the mountain peak.

1. Go through station 2 to the inside. Leave 4" of loose thread hang on the outside of the spine.
2. Proceed on the inside to station 3. Go through to outside. Pull, reducing loose end of thread to 1½".
3. Proceed along the spine, to station 1. Go through to inside.
4. Proceed on the inside to station 2. Go through to outside of the spine. Tie a Square Knot around the stitch on the spine.

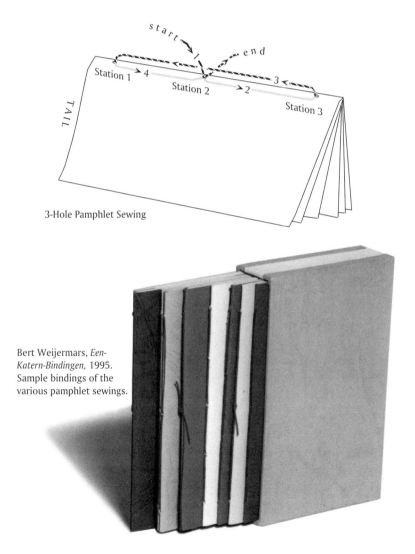

3-Hole Pamphlet Sewing

Bert Weijermars, *Een-Katern-Bindingen,* 1995. Sample bindings of the various pamphlet sewings.

4-HOLE PAMPHLET SEWING

PREPARATION

Sewing Stations

Prepare the section and cover. First, mark the first and fourth sewing stations on the spine. They should be no closer to the edge than $3/8$", no farther from the edge than 1".

Measure the distance between these two extreme sewing stations and divide it by three. This will be the distance between each of the four sewing stations, so that they are spaced equidistantly across the spine. Mark the remaining two sewing stations and pierce the four stations.

Thread

Length of the thread is $2\frac{1}{2}$ times the height of the spine. Start at station 2, either on the outside of the cover or inside the section.

ELABORATED SEWING PROCEDURE

This time, the illustration will start on the inside of the section. Take the needle through the section and cover at the second sewing station to the outside.

1. Pull all but 4" of the thread through the hole.
2. Proceed on the outside, up the spine to sewing station 3. Take the needle through the cover and the section, pulling the stitch taut. Do not pull so hard that the thread is pulled out of the station 2, but hard enough to reduce the length of loose thread dangling inside the section to $1\frac{1}{2}$".
3. Proceed on the inside to sewing station 4. Take the needle through the section and the cover at station 4, to the outside. Since you have reached the other extreme of the spine, you will proceed back in the other direction.
4. Proceed on the outside of the section to sewing station 3. Take the needle through to the inside.
5. Proceed on the inside of the section to station 1. Take the needle through to the outside.
6. Proceed on the outside to station 2 and take the needle through to the inside. You are now back to where you started. Make sure the two ends of the thread straddle the long stitch which crosses over the initial sewing station, then, tie a Square Knot.

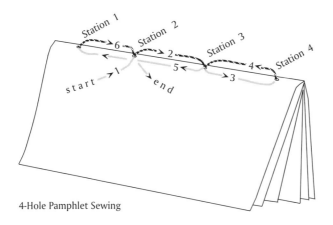

4-Hole Pamphlet Sewing

CONDENSED SEWING PROCEDURE

Description starts on the inside of the section.
1. Go out station 2. Pull all but 4" of the thread to outside.
2. Proceed to station 3. Go through to inside. Pull, reducing loose end of thread to 1½".
3. Proceed to station 4. Go through to outside.
4. Proceed to station 3. Go through to the inside.
5. Proceed to station 1. Go through to the outside.
6. Proceed to station 2. Go through to the inside. Tie a Square Knot around the long stitch which crosses over station 2.

Pamela Spitzmueller, *Triple Concertina*, 1987. Three fold books with differing size pages are pamphlet sewn at each valley. The pleated paper with the smallest width pages goes on the bottom, the largest pages on the top. The compound book can open to the full extent of the smallest. This determines the angle of the openings of the other two. 9.5 x 8.3 cm. closed. Fully extends to 48 cm.

5-HOLE PAMPHLET SEWING

PREPARATION

Sewing Stations

Prepare the section and cover. Mark the two end positions first, stations 1 and 5. They should be no closer to the edge than ⅜" and no farther from the edge than 1". Mark station 3, which is in the center of the spine.

Mark station 2 which is centered between stations 1 and 3. Mark station 4, which is centered between 3 and 5. Pierce the five stations.

Thread

Length of the thread is 2½ times the height of the spine. Thread the needle with waxed thread. Start at the center sewing station, either on the out or inside.

ELABORATED SEWING PROCEDURE

The illustration will start on the inside of the section.
1. Take the needle through the section and cover at sewing station number 3. Pull all but 4" of the thread through the hole.
2. Proceed on the outside to station 4. Take the needle through the cover and the section, pulling the stitch taut reducing the length of loose thread dangling inside the section to 1½".
3. Proceed on inside to sewing station 5. Take the needle through the section and cover to the outside.
4. Proceed on the outside back to sewing station 4. Take the needle through the station to the inside.
5. Proceed on the inside to station 2, by-passing sewing station 3. Take the needle through the section and the cover.
6. Proceed on the outside to station 1. Take the needle through to the inside. Since you have reached the other extreme of the spine, you will proceed back in the other direction.
7. Proceed on the inside to station 2. Take the needle through the section and cover to the outside.
8. Proceed on the outside to station 3. Take the needle through cover and section to the inside. Make sure the two ends of the thread straddle the long stitch which crosses over the initial sewing station. Tie a Square Knot.

CONDENSED PROCEDURE

The illustration starts on the inside at station 3.
1. Go out station 3. Pull all but 4" of the thread to outside.

2. Proceed to station 4. Go through to inside. Pull, reducing loose end of thread to 1½".
3. Proceed to station 5. Go to the outside.
4. Proceed to station 4. Go through to the inside.
5. Proceed to station 2, by-passing 3. Go through to outside.
6. Proceed to station 1. Go through to the inside.
7. Proceed to station 2. Go through to the outside.
8. Proceed to station 3. Go through to the inside. Tie a Square Knot around the long stitch which crosses over station 3.

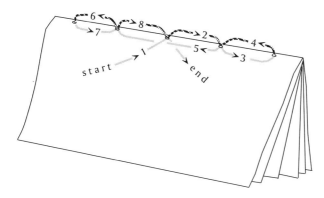

5-Hole Pamphlet Sewing

Introspection

When I examine a binding, I look for what is unique about it. What can I explore as variation on sewing? I read the blank book page by page and consider how I could image this book so that it would relate to its binding. The reverse is more difficult, to see how the binding can determine the content.

The *5-Hole Pamphlet Sewing* permits exploration of different size pages. Each folio of the section needs to be sewn at a minimum of three stations for stability. The *3-Hole Pamphlet Sewing* demands that every folio be precisely the same height. If I wanted a book with variable page size, I am limited to exploration of the foredge.

The *4-Hole Pamphlet Sewing* allows folios to vary only an inch or so in height and each still maintain at least three stations to secure it to the spine. With five holes, I can make a folio almost half the height of the others and still maintain three sewing stations. I can have a shorter folio resting at the tail. The smaller folio could be centered on the spine, attached at the three middle stations. Or, I could float it at the head, sewing the the smaller folio at the top three stations.

5-HOLE VARIATION

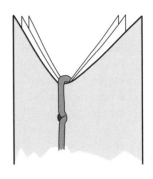

This is a lovely variation of the five hole pamphlet sewing. Only three stations are pierced along the spine. The remaining two stations are passive, the head and the tail. Looking down at the head, the wrapping comes over the spine to the inside of the section. It is not only lovely, but also holds the section to the extremes of the cover.

The sewing wraps around the head (and tail) in the middle of the section.

PREPARATION
Sewing Stations

Prepare the section and cover. Mark three sewing positions on the spine. One should be at the center. It is station 3. The remaining two pierced stations can each be half way between the center and head and the center and the tail. They need not be within an inch of the edge, since the edge in this instance is a sewing station.

Rather than a pierced station, the head and tail are wrapped stations. The tail is station 1. The first pierced station up from the tail is station 2. The center station is 3, the next pierced station is 4 and the head is the fifth station.

Pierce the three stations marked on the spine.

Thread

Length of the thread is 3 times the height of the spine. Thread the needle with waxed thread. Start at the center sewing station, either on the out or inside.

ELABORATED SEWING PROCEDURE

This illustration will start on the outside of the section.

1. Take the needle through the cover and section at sewing station 3. Pull all but 4" of the thread through the hole.
2. Proceed on the inside of the spine to station 2. Take the needle through the section and the cover to the outside, pulling the stitch taut, reducing the length of loose thread to 1½".
3. Proceed on the outside to the head, which is sewing station 5. Hold the thread taut from the previous station. Proceed along the spine, wrap the thread around the edge to the inside of the section.
4. Proceed to station 4. Take the needle through this station to the outside.

5. Proceed to station number 2. Do not go into sewing station 3. Take the needle through the cover and the section at station 2. Pull the stitch taut. You are now on the inside of the section.
6. Proceed to the first station, the tail of the book. Pull the thread taut along the gutter. Wrap it around the tail to the outside.
7. Proceed along the spine to station 2. Take the needle through the cover and the section to the inside.
8. Proceed on the inside, to station 3. Take the needle through the section and cover to the outside. Make sure the two ends of the thread straddle the long stitch which crosses over the initial sewing station, then, tie a Square Knot.

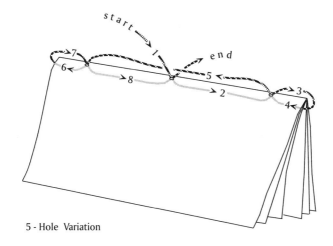

5 - Hole Variation

REVIEW, or CONDENSED PROCEDURE

Illustration starts on inside of the section.

1. Go out station 3. Pull all but 4" of the thread to the inside.
2. Proceed to station 4. Go through to the outside. Pull, reducing loose end of thread to 1½".
3. Proceed to the head (station 5). Wrap around head to the inside.
4. Proceed to station 4. Go through to the outside.
5. Proceed to station 2, by-passing station 3. Go through station 2.
6. Proceed to tail (station 1). Wrap around tail to the outside.
7. Proceed to station 2. Go through to the inside.
8. Proceed to station 3. Go through to the outside. Tie a Square Knot around the long stitch which crosses over station 3.

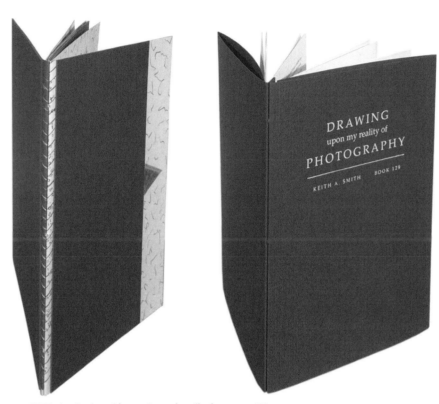

LEFT: *One Sewing without a Cover,* described on page 100.
Ruth Laxson, *(Ho + Go)² = It,* Nexus Press, Atlanta, GA. 1986. Artist book printed off-set in an edition of 500. This 2-section book uses a single pamphlet sewing. Both sections are opened to the center and the single sewing goes through the folds of each section, but without a cover. After it is sewn, both sections are closed. The front board side-cover is glued to the first page, slightly in from the spine-edge. A separate back side-cover is attached in the same manner. No board covers the spine. 26.5 x 21.5 cm.

RIGHT: *One Sewing with a Cover,* described on page 101.
Keith Smith, *Drawing Upon My Reality of Photography,* Book 129, 1989. Self-published in an edition of 300 copies. 21 x 14 cm.

When pamphlet sewing a single section booklet, two folds at the spine give a slight depth to the cover which allows the paper side-covers to close parallel instead of bulging open.

2-SECTION PAMPHLET SEWING

Pamphlet Sewing is almost always used to sew a single section binding with a paper cover. The cover is attached *as* the section is sewn. Three approaches to a 2-Section Pamphlet Sewing will be described. This doubles the number of pages and makes this sewing a most useful format for book artists and calligraphers.

WITH TWO SEWINGS

The most obvious solution for a two-section booklet would be to construct a cover with two valleys in which a section could be pamphlet sewn. I do not recall if I devised this or learned it from someone. The cover is first formed prior to the sewing by

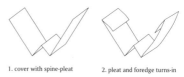

1. cover with spine-pleat   2. pleat and foredge turns-in

adding a pleat to a paper cover. This sets up two gutters inside the cover instead of one. When viewed on its edge, the pleated cover forms a *W*.

The pleat should not be larger than ¾" on each side. This means it adds an additional 1½" to the total width of the cover. The width of the paper for the cover must be even wider if you were to add foredge turnsin to the cover as in illustration 2 on the right.

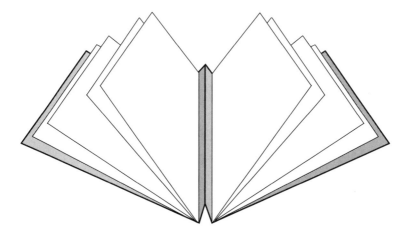

2-SECTION PAMPHLET created by two separate sewings. The cover has a pleat at the spine-edge to create two valleys on the inside of the cover. A section is pamphlet sewn into each valley.

Pamphlet sew one section in one of the gutters, then make a separate sewing of the other section in the remaining gutter. The procedure for each sewing would be the same as for *3-, 4- or 5-Hole Pamphlet Sewing* previously described.

ONE SEWING WITHOUT A COVER

Two sections can be sewn at once, with a single pamphlet sewing without a cover. The solution for a cover by Ruth Laxson, page 98, was to glue the board to the first page. Practically, this is not a good hinging solution as the paper is the only hinge and can wear out, losing the cover. My copy of that book has had only minor viewing, but viewing over a thirteen year period. The book is in excellent condition.

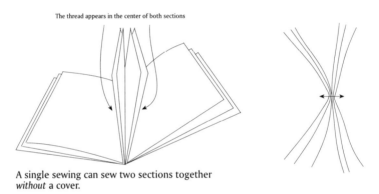

The thread appears in the center of both sections

A single sewing can sew two sections together *without* a cover.

Sewing Procedure

1. Pre-pierce the sections in identical locations. Set the two sections together and lay the book block on the table. Turn the first section 180° to the left so it is laid on the table tangent to the first. The end of the first section is visible on the left. The beginning of the second is seen on the right.
2. Lift the second half of the first section vertically. Lift the first half of the second section vertically.

Step 2

3. Hand-hold the book block as shown on the upper right illustration on this page.Proceed to pamphlet sew a *3-, 4- or 5-Hole Pamphlet Sewing* as previously described. Start the needle through the valley of the first section. After the point of the needle is seen peaking through the mountain peak, set the needle into the corresponding sewing station on the second section. Take the needle through. This insures you will not accidentally pierce the second section at other than the sewing station. Complete the pamphlet sewing and tie-off.

ONE SEWING WITH A COVER

My favorite method of sewing a 2-section booklet with the pamphlet sewing has a single sewing that sews *both* sections *and* a cover at the same time with a single pamphlet sewing. It is an economy of steps which makes it a little more difficult to juggle as you sew.

Cover

HEIGHT of the cover is the height of section.
WIDTH of the total cover equals:
   width of the front cover foredge turn-in, if any,
plus width of the book block (front cover),
plus width of the cover pleat ($\frac{3}{4}$"),
plus again, the width of the cover pleat ($\frac{3}{4}$"),
plus width of the book block (back cover),
plus width of the back cover foredge turn-in, if any.

Cut the cover to size. Fold in half to create the spine. Open flat with the mountain peak facing up and the head at the top. Measure $\frac{3}{4}$" from the fold along the head to the right and mark. At this point the cover will be scored and folded to the left. The new fold is parallel with the center fold. When making the fold, bring the right foredge across, aligning the top edge along the head.

Open the cover flat again. Measure $\frac{3}{4}$" to the left from the center fold onto the head of the remaining cover. At this point fold the cover to the right, aligning the top edges. This creates the cover pleat, in the form of a *W*. See page 99. Fold the foredge turns-in. Prepare the two sections.

Thread

Before assembly of sections and cover, thread the needle with thread which is $2\frac{1}{2}$ times the height of the spine.

ASSEMBLY and PIERCING of STATIONS

There will be three sewing stations. The cover and both sections will be pierced at once as you sew.

Assembly of sections and cover and maintaining their alignment while piercing the three sewing stations is somewhat difficult. It will be much easier the second or third time you do this binding. The sewing is the easy part.

1. Lay the cover on the table with the mountain peak of the pleat facing up and vertical. The valleys on each side of this mountain peak are the gutters, as well as the hinge-folds.
    Turn the cover 90° to the right, with the head at your right. Sit the first section, opened, in the top gutter.

The second half of the section is erect. Sit the second section in the lower. The section is opened to the middle.

The first half of the section is erect, tangent to the second half of the first section. Allow the front and back cover to lay on the table. Grasp the two sections with your left hand at the tail, your right at the head. Hold the sections in position, near the gutters, so that you are clasping the pleat as well as the sections.

The first quarter and the final quarter of the text block are resting against their respective covers. The center half of the text block is standing erect with the gutters of both sections showing and clasped firmly against the pleat.

2. Maintaining your grasp at the head and tail with thumbs and forefingers, lift the book into the air. With your middle fingers, push on the first half of the front section, so that it and the front cover point down. The book is somewhat in one vertical plane. The covers, along with the first and final quarter of the  text block are hanging down below your grasp. The pleat is sandwiched by the last half of the first section and the first half of the second. They point upwards from your grasp.

3. If you are right handed, reposition the grasp of your left hand inward almost to the center. Remove your right hand to pick up the bradawl. Remember to keep a firm grasp with your left hand to insure both sections rest snugly in the respective gutters on each side of the pleat. If a section slips out of position, lay the cover on the table, place the sections in position and start again.

4. Pierce the center sewing station in a single action, taking the bradawl through the center of the fold of the section nearer to you, through the center of both gutters of the pleat, out through the center of the fold of the remaining section. Remove the bradawl and place your pre-threaded needle half way through the sewing station to help maintain alignment.

5. Maintain your left hand hold on the book and grasp the head of the book with your right thumb and forefinger. Only clasp the pleat and the parts of the section which stand erect above the horizon of the spine. Reposition your left hand to the tail, grasping the pleat and pages which sandwich it. Pick up the bradawl with your right hand.

6. Pierce the far left sewing station within a half inch of the tail.

Again, the single action pierces the section nearer you, then the pleat and out through the other sewing station. Pick up an unthreaded needle and center it through the sewing station.

This will temporarily maintain alignment of all the pierced holes within this station.

7. Grasp the foredges of the erect part of the text block with your right hand. Rotate the book 180° so the head, which was at three o'clock, will be at nine.

Grasp the head of the book, which is now on your left, with your left hand. Clasp your left thumb and forefinger at the folds, so you are gripping the pleat as well as the pages.

8. Pick up the bradawl and pierce the final sewing station the same distance in from the head as you pierced in from the tail.

9. Continue to hold the book with your left hand. Lay down the bradawl, grasp the threaded needle at the center sewing station and make a *3-Hole Pamphlet Sewing* through these three pierced stations. Remove the unthreaded needle as you approach to sew that station.

Upon completing the sewing, lay the book down and tie a Square Knot. It will be tied at the middle opening of the second section. The protrusion of the pleat will be between the the two sections.

This binding is quick for a book which has a few more pages than can be folded into a single section. It also lends itself to a book in two parts or two short stories.

COMPARISON of TWO SEWINGS with ONE

Sewing two separate pamphlet sewings, one in each gutter, does not require the gymnastics of assembly of the singular sewn two-section pamphlet sewing. One sewing is more complicated to pierce, but sews twice as fast.

The main difference is how they are attached to the cover. One sewing stitches the pleat shut, while two sewings allows the pleat to open. There is limited use for the pleat to open. Unless you incorporate a purpose for it to expand, it will seem to be a mistake.

The action of the pleat opening, expands the space between the two sections. This action is rich with possibilities when you examine it. If the structure is compounded, there are even more possibilities: Make the cover with several folds in the pleat. Attach the sections on the mountain peaks, instead of in the valley gutters. This is a *Concertina Binding*. Many approaches to the binding are also described under *Spine-Pleats*.

Claudia Lee, various one-of-a-kind single sheet stab bindings, 1998. The thread stabs the book block and separate paper side-covers. The book at the bottom has an end-sheet around the book block which covers the spine. In some, the thread is tied around a chop stick as support. In others, the thread goes through elongated stoneware beads. Each book is approximately 22 x 16 cm.

There are very few bindings which utilize single sheets as units. Among these are the *Single Sheet Pamphlet Stitch;* the *4-Hole Japanese Binding* and its variations of stab bindings; and the *Album Binding.* Since often there is no choice but to bind a book with single sheets, the binder is always looking for some method other than spiral binding. It is the least attractive way to bind. Perhaps I am prejudiced. The spiral bound book opens totally flat. Plastic spirals allow for titles on the spine. They are just so aesthetically displeasing. The spiral is always wider than the thickness of the book and so they don't fit in a book shelf and can damage books on either side.

PROPERTIES of SINGLE SHEET BINDINGS

The hinge-fold of a section is neutral ground between leaves, ideally suited for sewing stations. In binding single sheets, there is no option except to place the sewing stations upon the page. This restricts movement of turning pages. Single sheet bindings have to be pried opened and held open to view.

In section sewing, the pages not only open flat, the total surface of the paper can be imaged. Single sheet bindings relinquish at least an inch margin along the backbone to the sewing stations.

Single sheet resistance to turning pages can be overcome. Single sheets can be altered into folios by pasting a thin strip of paper connecting successive pairs of sheets. However, instead of reducing single sheets to an imitation of folios, it is better to utilize the characteristics of the single sheets.

Very thin paper is one solution. In turning the page, the sheet slinks over to the other side and lies there. If stiff paper is used, a turned page will lie flat if it first has been scored parallel to and about $\frac{1}{2}$" in from the spine-edge. This creates a hinge fold, beyond the sewing, but at the expense of the total area of the sheet which can be imaged. For thick albums there may have to be a second hinge-fold, $\frac{1}{4}$" farther in from the spine-edge.

There are advantages to single sheet bindings. By eliminating folds, any number of sheets can be bound. The scrap book, described as *Album Binding,* exploits this advantage with posts and nut attachment. Additional single sheets can be added at any time, one at a time or several, after the book is bound.

The flip book makes use of stiff, stubby sheets to create sound with rapid movement through the pages.

Think of books which you can make, which are only possible because of single sheet bindings. For instance, if you wanted a different surface, color or weight of paper on each successive page, a single sheet binding is the only means. Constructing parameters, rather than accepting variables, fosters the imagination.

SINGLE SHEET PAMPHLET STITCH

Compile the single sheets to form the book block. Make a *W* cover, as described on page 99. Jog the book block on its tail and then on the back to align. Open the cover. Lay the book block into either or both of the two valleys on each side of the pleat.

Mark 3, 4 or 5 sewing stations on the top sheet, close enough to the spine-edge that the pierced holes will strike the pleat half way between the valley and the mountain peak. Pierce the sewing stations through the sheets and pleat at once.

Proceed with the Pamphlet Stitch.[6] It is not a "sewing", but stitching—it takes place in from the spine-edge of the book block, which is compiled single sheets, hence there are no folds. The stitching goes through both sides of the pleat. No sewing goes through any folds on the cover or on the side-covers. When the book is closed, the stitches are slightly visible within the cleavage of the two folds which constitute the spine.

STAB BINDINGS

INTRODUCTION

Covers

Traditionally, the front and back side-covers for a stab binding are separate sheets, allowing for an exposed spine. The side-covers might have a foredge turn-in. The approach to the covers is generally limited. To augment this, I will describe eight non-adhesive covers specifically devised for stab bindings. See page 127.

The Book Block

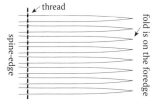

2-ply stab binding

The book block generally is a stack of single sheets. Often stab bindings utilize folios as the book block, bound along the *open edge,* stacked one on top of each other. The folds become the foredge of the book block. Fairly thin paper is used to allow the pages to slink when turned, since each "sheet" is now 2-ply.

Advantages of this approach are that pictures and/or text need be printed on only one side of the sheet. It is then folded to form a recto/verso. This cuts down cost in printing, while utilizing more paper. In constructing one-of-a-kind photographic books, this binding procedure allows freedom of design. Special photo paper, such as some photo mural, *A or N* Surface can be folded without cracking the emulsion. The recto/verso printing is side by side on the sheet, then folded back to back during binding. This allows for bleeds or printing around the foredge to the verso.

Text and picture can be printed, eliminating the need to paste either on the page. Mounting photographs onto blank sheets creates a cumbersome page. Compositionally the layout is imprisoned within borders. The photograph becomes an island, far more difficult to incorporate into the *composition of the book,* as opposed to the picture/page.[7]

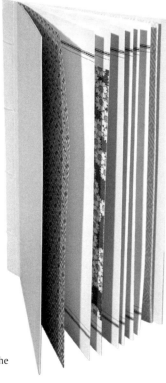

Philip Zimmermann, 1991. Japanese 4-Hole stab binding folios with the fold at the foredge. Lines on the sheet dot the foredge of the closed book giving a decorative border.

Printing on stiff double weight photo paper and then dry-mounting to a sturdy blank stock is a far inferior approach insisting upon borders. The blank stock is only for support. The page is not imaged, only the photograph. It is reluctance to compose the book and parts thereof and insistence upon working in the single sheet format, then compiling, rather than imaging the multiple page format.

Another advantage of folds at the foredge is that whatever is imaged across the fold is seen dotted on the folds when the book is closed, decorating the foredge of the closed book.

Rather than seeing stab bindings as just another binding, think of books which you can make which are only possible because of single sheet bindings. For instance, if you wanted each leaf a different color, that would be impossible with folios or sections. Make a list of the unique characteristics inherent to single sheet codices.

The cyclical pattern of sewing and wrapping the spine is common to all the stab bindings. I suggest you try the 4-Hole stab binding first, as it is the easiest. The other bindings will then be easier to follow.

The four Japanese stab bindings: Noble Binding, *Koki Toji;* Tortoise-Shell Binding, *Kikko Toji;* Hemp-Leaf Binding, *Asa-No-Ha Toji;* Japanese 4-Hole Binding, *Yotsume Toji.*

PREPARATION for STAB BINDINGS

Preparation for the following traditional stab bindings is the same in each instance.

Thread

No knots are visible on the outside of the bindings. If you run out of thread during the binding, it is difficult to tie a Weaver's Knot inside. Therefore it is best to start with an excess of thread to insure enough to complete the binding.

The *Japanese 4-Hole Binding* will need a length of thread approximately three times the height of the book block. The others require considerably more thread. For instance, the *Tortoise-Shell Binding* with a 6" tall book block needs 36" of thread to sew.

Covers

Construct the two covers and assemble the single sheets or folios-as-sheets. Various covers, other than the traditional, which might be utilized with stab bindings will be described in the following section. Place the covers on each end. Jog the unbound book on its tail, then on the backbone to align. You will be ready to pre-pierce the stations. Position and number of stations vary with each of the stab bindings.

How to Pierce Stab Bindings

Piercing through a book block is more a challenge than piercing individual sections. A motorized paper drill is ideal, but most binders do not have access.

To pierce with a bradawl, place blotters on each side of the covers and a piece of ¾" plywood on each side. Plywood and blotters should be near, but not extend over the sewing stations. Clamp with C-clamps. Lay another sheet of plywood under the exposed part of the side-cover for support. Leave ¼" crack between for path of needle along the line of the stations.

JAPANESE 4-HOLE BINDING

Yotsume Toji

SEWING STATIONS

The four sewing stations are ⅜" in from the spine-edge. Station 1 is ½" up from the tail. Station 4 is ½" down from the head. Stations 2 and 3 are equally spaced between. Pierce the stations.

Each station will eventually be sewn three times. Each time a station is sewn for the first time, the thread will be wrapped around the spine to form the small horizontal stitches from cover to cover.

The reason the stab sewings are never started at the end stations is to insure the knot does not hang out of the head or tail.

ELABORATED SEWING PROCEDURE

1. Pick up front cover and about half of the book block. Start the needle on the inside of book block at station 2, proceeding up through, coming out the front cover. Pull all but 4" of thread to outside. Lay this half back in position on top of the remainder of the book block. Make sure the loose thread inside the book extends towards the foredge. If it is near the backbone, it will become entangled in the sewing. It will need to be free in order to tie-off at the end of the sewing cycle.

2. Proceed around the spine, take the needle through station 2 of the back cover, coming out through the front cover.

3. Proceed on the front cover to station 3. Go through to back cover. Wrap around the spine to front cover. Go through station 3 to back cover. Tighten stitches as you go. Form the spine wrap, so it is at right angle to the spine-edge.

4. Proceed on the back cover to station 4. Go through station 4 on the back cover, through to the front cover. Wrap around the spine to back cover. Go through sewing station 4 on the back cover to the front cover.

5. Keep proceeding in the same direction. Since there are no more stations, the manner in which the sewing direction is changed is to wrap around the head to the back cover. Then proceed towards the tail to the next station, which is number 4.

   Take the needle through station 4 to front cover. Since the spine has already been wrapped, proceed on the cover to station 3.

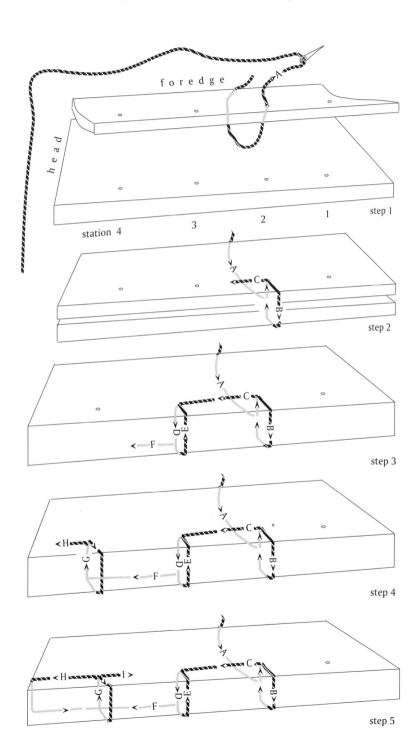

foredge

head

station 4   3   2   1   step 1

step 2

step 3

step 4

step 5

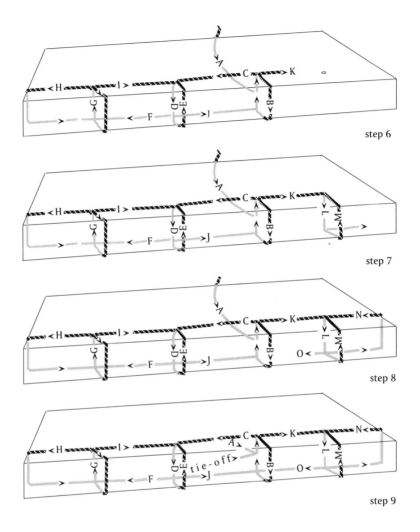

step 6

step 7

step 8

step 9

6. Go through station 3 to back cover. Since the spine has already been wrapped, proceed on the back cover to station 2. Take the needle through 2 to front cover. Since the spine has already been wrapped, proceed on the front cover to station 1.

7. Take the needle though station 1 to back cover. Wrap around the spine to front cover. Take the needle through station 1 on the front cover coming out on the back.

8. Proceed on the back cover to the tail. Wrap around the tail to front cover. Proceed to station 1 on front cover. Go through station 1 to back. Proceed on back cover to station 2.

9. Open the book to the middle page to the loose thread. Take the needle into station 2 on back cover and proceed to the middle page, bringing the needle out beside the loose thread. Tie a Square Knot, pulling the knot into the gutter. Trim loose ends so they do not hang out of the book block.

REVIEW or CONDENSED SEWING PROCEDURE

1. Pick up front cover with half of book block. Start inside at station 2, proceeding up through that part of the book block, coming out the front cover. Pull all but 4" of thread to outside. Lay this half in position on top of the remainder of book block, with loose thread extending towards the foredge.
2. Wrap around spine. Proceed to station 2. Go through to front.
3. Proceed to station 3. Go through to back. Wrap around the spine to front. Go through station 3 to back cover.
4. Proceed to station 4. Go through to the front. Wrap around spine to back cover. Go through station 4 to the front cover.
5. Wrap around the head to back cover. Proceed to station 4. Go through 4 to front cover. Proceed to station 3.
6. Go through station 3 to back cover. Proceed to station 2. Go through to front cover. Proceed to station 1.
7. Go through to back cover. Wrap around spine to front. Go through station 1 to the back.
8. Proceed to the tail. Wrap around the tail to front cover. Proceed to station 1. Go through 1 to back. Proceed to station 2.
9. Open book to the middle page to the loose thread. Go through station 2 on back cover and proceed to the middle page, coming out beside the loose thread. Tie a Square Knot.

Japanese 4-Hole Binding with two separate Z-fold side-covers with foredge turns-in. See pages 130, 131.

TORTOISE-SHELL

Kikko Toji

Sewing Stations

Each of the traditional four sewing stations has been compounded to triple units. These are denoted as stations *A, B and C*. Station 1B is ½" up from the tail. Station 4 *C* is ½" down from the head.

All the *A* stations are ½" in from the spine-edge. All the *B* and *C* stations are ¼" in from the spine. Measure and draw the stations on a scrap of paper which is the height of the cover. Place the paper as a guide on the front cover. Pierce the covers and book block stations.

ELABORATED SEWING PROCEDURE

The stations will be sewn in the following order: Station 2, 3, 4, 1 and back to 2.

Starting at an Even Numbered Unit

1. Pick up front cover and about half of the book block. Start the needle on the inside at station 2*A*, proceeding up through that part of the book block, coming out the front cover. Pull all but 4" of thread to outside. Lay this half back in position on top of the remainder of the book block. Make sure the loose thread inside the book extends towards the foredge. If it is near the backbone, it will become entangled in the sewing. It will need to be free in order to tie-off at the end of the sewing cycle.

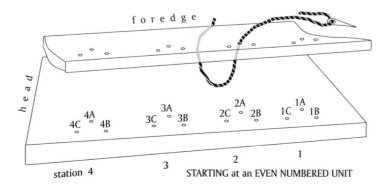

Steps 2 through 5 describe the remainder of the sewing for stations 2*A*, 2*B* and 2*C*.

Sewing an Even Numbered Unit

2. Proceed around the spine to the back cover. Take the needle through station *A*, coming out through the front cover.
3. Proceed on the front cover to station *B*. Go through to back cover. Wrap around the spine to front cover. Go through station *B* to back cover. Tighten stitches as you go to form the spine wrap.
4. Proceed on the back cover to station *A*. Go through station *A* to the front cover. Proceed to station *C*.
5. Take the needle through *C* on the front to back cover. Wrap around the spine to front cover. Go through *C* to the back cover. Proceed to station *A* on the back cover. Go through to front cover.

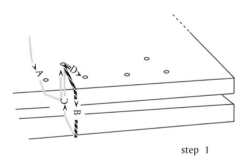

step 1

SEWING an EVEN NUMBERED UNIT

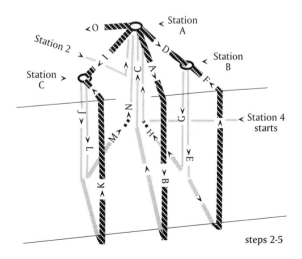

steps 2-5

Sewing an Odd Numbered Unit

6. Proceed on the front cover to station *A* of next odd numbered unit to be sewn. Take the needle through to the back cover. Proceed around the spine to the front cover. Take the needle through station *A* of the front, coming out through the back cover.

7. Proceed on the back cover to station *B*. Go through to front cover. Wrap around the spine to back cover. Go through station *B* to front cover.

8. Proceed on the front cover to station *A*. Go through station *A* on the front, to the back cover. Proceed to station *C*.

9. Take the needle through *C* on the back to front cover. Wrap around the spine to back cover. Go through *C* on the back to the front.

10. Proceed to station *A* on the front cover. Go through to back cover.

SEWING an ODD NUMBERED UNIT

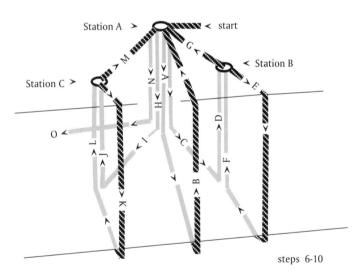

steps 6-10

Sewing Remainder of Units

Proceed on the back cover to station 4*A*. Go through station to front cover. Sew station 4*A, B and C* following the even numbered sewing procedure.

After completing unit 4, proceed around the head to the back cover. Take the needle through the *A* station to the front cover. Proceed to station 3*A*. Go through to the back cover. Proceed to 2*A*. Go through to the front cover. Proceed to station 1*A*. Follow steps 6 through 10 to sew the first unit.

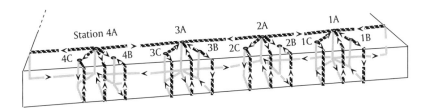

After completing unit 1, proceed across the back cover to tail. Wrap around tail to the front. Proceed to station 1A. Go through to back cover. Proceed across back cover to station 2A.

Open the book to the middle page to the loose thread. Take the needle through back cover at 2A, up through half the book block, coming out the middle page at the loose thread. Tie a Square Knot and clip the thread to ¾".

CONDENSED SEWING PROCEDURE

Starting at an Even Numbered Unit

1. Pick up front cover with half of book block. Start inside at station 2A, proceeding up through that part of the book block, coming out the front cover. Pull all but 4" of thread to outside. Lay this half in position on top of the remainder of book block, with loose thread extending towards the foredge.

Sewing an Even Numbered Unit

2. Proceed around spine to the back cover. Go through station A, to front cover.
3. Proceed to station B. Go through to back. Wrap around spine to front. Go through B to back cover.
4. Proceed to station A. Go through A to front. Proceed to C.
5. Go through C to back cover. Wrap around spine to front. Go through C to the back. Proceed to A. Go through to front cover.

Sewing an Odd Numbered Unit

6. Proceed on the front to station A of next odd numbered unit. Go through to the back. Wrap around spine to front. Go through A to the back cover.
7. Proceed to B. Go through to front. Wrap around spine to back cover. Go through B to front.
8. Proceed to station A. Go through to the back cover. Proceed to C.
9. Go through C to front. Wrap around spine to back. Go through C on the back to the front.
10. Proceed to A. Go through to back cover.

Sewing Remainder of Units

Proceed on back to 4*A*. Go through to front. Sew station 4*A, B and C* following steps 2–5.

After completing unit 4, wrap around the head to the back. Go through *A* to the front. Proceed to station 3*A*. Go through to back cover. Proceed to 2*A*. Go through to front. Proceed to 1*A*. Follow steps 6–10 to sew the first unit.

After completing unit 1, proceed across the back cover to tail. Wrap around tail to the front. Proceed to 1*A*. Go through to back. Proceed to 2*A*.

Open book to the middle page to the loose thread. Go through back cover at 2*A*, up through to the middle page at the loose thread. Tie a Square Knot and clip the thread to ¾".

Linda Grabill, variation on the Tortoise-Shell Binding, 1990. The spine-edge of the book block at the head and tail can be capped with paper pasted extending onto the head and tail to where the thread crosses. The book block without the covers is temporarily stabbed sewn at two stations near the head and at the tail. The thread does not go around the spine, so only the final sewing will be seen. The first sewing stabilizes the book block so the paper caps an be pasted into position.

HEMP-LEAF BINDING

Asa-No-Ha Toji

Sewing Stations

The traditional 4 stations have intervening stations, for a total of 7 sewing stations. There are two rows of stations. The *A* stations are ½" in from the spine-edge. Station 1*A* is ½" from the tail. Station 4*A* is ½" from the head. Stations 2*A* and 3*A* are evenly spaced between.

The *B* stations is ¼" from the spine-edge. These are evenly spaced between the *A* stations.

Measure and draw the stations on a scrap of paper which is the height of the cover. Place the paper as a guide on the front cover. Pierce the covers and book block stations.

ELABORATED SEWING PROCEDURE

1. Pick up front cover and about half of the book block. Start the needle on the inside at station 2*A*, proceeding up through that part of the book block, coming out the front cover. Pull all but 4" of thread to outside. Lay this half back in position on top of the remainder of the book block. Make sure the loose thread inside the book extends towards the foredge. If it is near the spine, it will become entangled in the sewing. It will need to be free in order to tie-off at the end of the sewing cycle.

2. Wrap around the spine to the back cover. Take the needle through station 2*A*, coming up through front cover. Proceed to station 2*B*.

3. Take the needle through station 2*B* on the front to the back cover. Wrap around the spine to the front cover. Proceed back through station 2*B* to back cover. Proceed to station 2*A*.

4. Go through station 2*A* on the back to the front. Proceed to station 3*A* and go through to the back. Proceed to station 2*B*.

5. Go through 2*B* to the front and proceed to station 3*A*. Go through 3*A* to back, wrap around the spine-edge and proceed to 3*A* on the front.

6. Go through station 3*A* to the back. Proceed on the back to station 3*B* and go through to front cover.

7. Wrap around spine-edge to back cover and proceed to station 3*B*. Go through to front. Proceed to station 3*A*.

8. Go through 3*A* on the front to back cover. Proceed to station 4*A*.

Go through to the front cover. Proceed to station 3B.

9. Go through 3B on the front cover to the back. Proceed to 4A and go through to front cover.

10. Wrap around spine, proceed on the back cover to station 4A . Go through station 4A to front cover.

11. Now you are at the head. Wrap around the head to the back cover. Proceed to station 4A. Go through to front cover. You will proceed back towards the tail.

12. Proceed to station 3A on the front cover. Go through to the back. Proceed on the back to sewing station 2A and go through to the front cover.

13. Proceed on front cover to 1B. Go through, wrap around spine. Come up on front cover, down through 1B. Proceed on back to 2A.

14. Go through 2A to front. Proceed to sewing station 1A. Go through 1A to the back.

15. Wrap around spine to front. Proceed to 1A and go through to back. Proceed to station 1B and go through to the front.

16. Proceed to station 1A and go through to the back. Wrap around the tail to front cover. Proceed to station 1A and go through to back.

17. Proceed to station 2A on back. Open the book to the middle page to the loose thread. Take the needle through back cover at 2A, up through half the book block, coming out the middle page at the loose thread. Tie a Square Knot and clip the thread to ¾".

CONDENSED SEWING PROCEDURE

1. Pick up front cover with half of book block. Start inside at station 2A, proceeding up through that part of the book block, coming out the front cover. Pull all but 4" of thread to outside. Lay this half in position on top of the remainder of book block, with loose thread extending towards the foredge.

2. Wrap around the spine to the back cover. Go through 2A, to front cover. Proceed to 2B.

3. Go through 2B to the back cover. Wrap around the spine to the front. Proceed through 2B to back. Proceed to 2A.

4. Go through 2A to the front. Proceed to 3A. Go through to the back. Proceed to 2B.

5. Go through 2B to the front. Proceed to 3A. Go through to back. Wrap around spine. Proceed to 3A on the front.

6. Go through 3A to the back. Proceed to 3B. Go through to front.

7. Wrap around spine to back. Proceed to 3B. Go through to front. Proceed to 3A.

8. Go through 3A to back cover. Proceed to 4A. Go through to the front. Proceed to 3B.

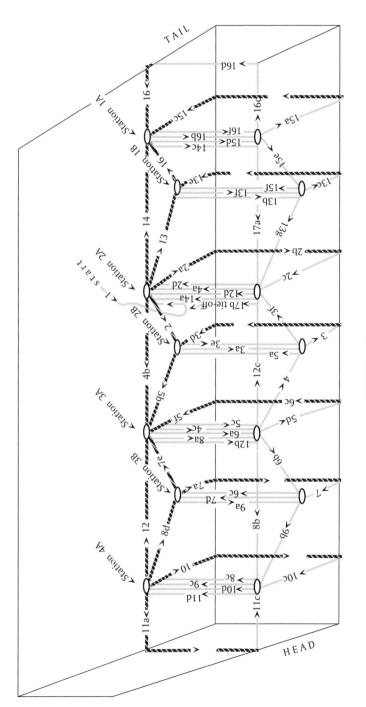

ASA-NO-HA TOJI
Hemp-Leaf Binding

9. Go through 3*B* to the back. Proceed to 4*A*. Go through to front.
10. Wrap around spine, proceed on the back to 4*A*. Go through to front.
11. Wrap around the head to the back. Proceed to 4*A*. Go through to front.
12. Proceed to 3*A*. Go through to the back. Proceed to 2*A*. Go through to the front.
13. Proceed to 1*B*. Go through, wrap around spine. Come up on front cover, down through 1*B*. Proceed on back to 2*A*.
14. Go through 2*A* to front. Proceed to 1*A*. Go through to back.
15. Wrap around spine to front. Proceed to 1*A* and go through to back. Proceed to 1*B*. Go through to the front.
16. Proceed to 1*A*. Go through to the back. Wrap around the tail to front cover. Proceed to 1*A*. Go through to back.
17. Proceed to 2*A*. Open book to the middle page to the loose thread. Go through back cover at 2*A*, up through to the middle page at the loose thread. Tie a Square Knot and clip the thread to ¾".

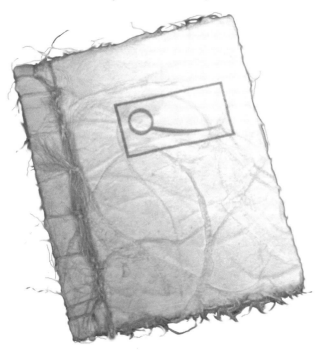

Rosemary S. Bell, *Querulous Q*. Noble Binding with folded foredge. Digital text and images on handmade paper. Edition of 14.5 x 15.3 cm.
Excerpt from text:
    symbol for the deep throaty sound of quoph ~
    a word meaning 'back of the head'
    a reference to insight and intuition.

NOBLE BINDING

Koki Toji

This binding is also called the *Kangxi Binding,* named after its reputed originator.[8]

Sewing Stations

The traditional 4-Hole Binding has two additional sewing stations, one at the top and bottom corners at the spine-edge. Station 1*B* is ¼" from the spine-edge and the same from the tail. Station 4*B* is ¼" from the spine-edge and the same from the head. Stations 1*A*, 2, 3 and 4*A* are ½" from the spine-edge. Station 1*A* is ½" from the tail. Station 4*A* is ½" from the head. Stations 2 and 3 are evenly spaced between 1*A* and 4*A*.

Measure and draw the stations on a scrap of paper which is the height of the cover. Place the paper as a guide on the front cover. Pierce the covers and book block stations.

ELABORATED SEWING PROCEDURE

1. Pick up front cover and about half of the book block. Start the needle on the inside at station 2, proceeding up through that part of the book block, coming out the front cover. Pull all but 4" of thread to outside. Lay this half back in position on top of the remainder of the book block. Make sure the loose thread inside the book extends towards the foredge. If it is near the spine, it will become entangled in the sewing. It will need to be free in order to tie-off at the end of the sewing cycle.

2. Wrap around the spine to the back cover. Take the needle through station 2, coming up through front cover. Proceed to station 3.

3. Take the needle through station 3 on the front to the back cover. Wrap around the spine to the front cover. Proceed back through station 3 to back cover. Proceed to station 4*A*.

4. Go through station 4*A* on the back cover to the front. Wrap around spine-edge to back cover and proceed to station 4*A*. Go through to front cover.

5. Proceed across front cover to head. Wrap around head to back cover. Proceed to station 4*A*.

6. Go through station 4*A* on the back cover to the front. Proceed diagonally to station 4*B*.

7. Go through station 4B on the front to the back cover. Wrap around the spine-edge to front cover. Proceed to station 4B.

8. Go through station 4B to back cover. Proceed across back cover to head. Wrap around head to front cover. Proceed to station 4B.

9. Go through station 4B to back cover. Proceed to station 4A. Go through 4A to front cover.

10. Proceed to station 3. Go through 3 to back cover. Proceed to station 2 on the back cover and go through station 2 to front cover.

11. Proceed to station 1A. Go through to back cover. Wrap around spine-edge to front cover. Proceed to station 1A.

12. Go through station 1A to back cover. Proceed to station 1B and go through to front cover.

13. Wrap around spine-edge to back cover. Proceed to station 1B. Go through station 1B to front cover.

14. Wrap around tail to back cover. Proceed to station 1B and go through to front. Proceed to station 1A.

15. Go through station 1A to back cover. Wrap around tail to front cover. Proceed to station 1A.

16. Go through station 1A to back cover. Proceed to station 2.

17. Open the book to the middle page to the loose thread. Take the needle through back cover at station 2, up through half the book block, coming out the middle page at the loose thread. Tie a Square Knot and clip the thread to ¾".

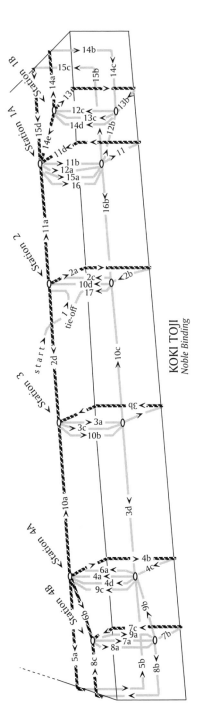

KOKI TOJI
Noble Binding

CONDENSED SEWING PROCEDURE

1. Pick up front cover with half of book block. Start inside at station 2, proceeding up through that part of the book block, coming out the front cover. Pull all but 4" of thread to outside. Lay this half in position on top of the remainder of book block, with loose thread extending towards the foredge.

2. Wrap around spine to the back cover. Proceed to station 2. Go through to front. Proceed to station 3.

3. Go through 3 to the back. Wrap around spine to the front. Proceed through station 3 to back cover. Proceed to station 4A.

4. Go through 4A to the front. Wrap around spine to back. Proceed to 4A. Go through to front.

5. Wrap around head to back cover. Proceed to 4A.

6. Go through 4A to the front. Proceed diagonally to 4B.

7. Go through 4B to the back. Wrap around spine to front cover. Proceed to 4B.

8. Go through 4B to back. Proceed to head. Wrap around head to front cover. Proceed to 4B.

9. Go through 4B to back. Proceed to 4A. Go through 4A to front.

10. Proceed to 3. Go through 3 to back. Proceed to station 2. Go through 2 to front cover.

11. Proceed to 1A. Go through to back. Wrap around spine to front. Proceed to 1A.

12. Go through 1A to back. Proceed to 1B. Go through to front.

13. Wrap around spine to back. Proceed to 1B. Go through 1B to front.

14. Wrap around tail to back. Proceed to 1B. Go through to front. Proceed to 1A.

15. Go through 1A to back. Wrap around tail to front. Go to 1A.

16. Go through 1A to back cover. Proceed to station 2.

17. Open book to the middle page to the loose thread. Go through back cover at 2, up through to the middle page at the loose thread. Tie a Square Knot and clip the thread to ¾".

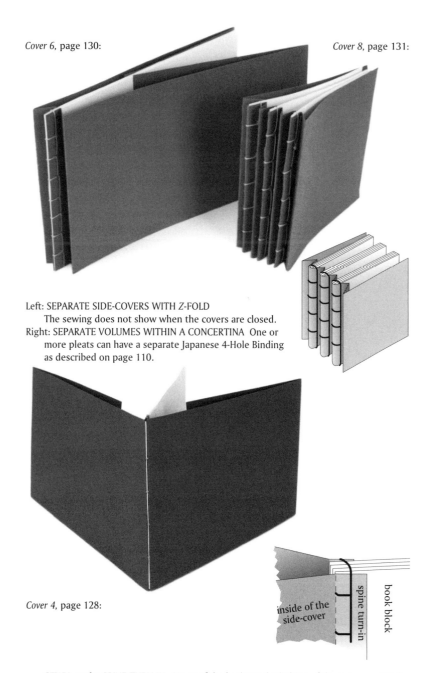

Cover 6, page 130:

Cover 8, page 131:

Left: SEPARATE SIDE-COVERS WITH Z-FOLD
   The sewing does not show when the covers are closed.
Right: SEPARATE VOLUMES WITHIN A CONCERTINA One or
   more pleats can have a separate Japanese 4-Hole Binding
   as described on page 110.

Cover 4, page 128:

inside of the
side-cover

spine turn-in

book block

SEWN on the SPINE TURN-IN: None of the horizontal stitching of the Japanese 4-Hole
Binding is seen on the outside of the covers. The binding is done with both covers fully open, piercing the covers through the hinge-fold.

STAB COVERS

Eight non-adhesive flush and overhang covers will be described, which are specifically designed for stab bindings. The four bindings are *Japanese 4-Hole Binding, Tortoise-Shell Binding, Hemp-Leaf Binding and Noble Binding*.

Three of these stab covers have the hinge-fold upon the side-cover, which is traditional. The other covers have the hinge-fold at the spine-edge.

SEPARATE SHEET SIDE-COVERS

The traditional approach for a cover for the stab binding is simply to have the first and last sheet of heavier stock. These are the covers. The stack of sheets between is the book block.

Each separate side-cover has the hinge-fold *in from the spine-edge,* beyond the stations. The hinge is made by scoring and folding the cover to facilitate opening. This is done after piercing the stations, prior to sewing.

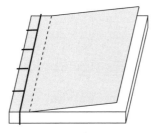

1. Separate Sheet Side-Covers

SEPARATE SHEETS with TURNS-IN

The separate side-covers may have foredge turns-in. The turns-in not only reinforce the foredge, but repeat the motif of folds at the foredge, if folios are sewn with their open edges at the spine-edge.

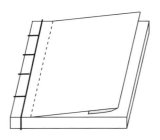

2. Separate Sheet Side-Covers with Turns-In

SINGLE PIECE COVER

A single sheet of cover-weight paper could wrap around from the front cover, over the backbone, continuing as the back cover. Sewing stations for the cover would be on the side-covers, pierced with the book block in place.

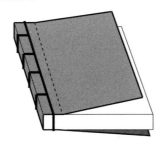

3. Single Piece Cover

Hinge-fold at the Spine

The stab cover can be hinged at the spine, rather than in on the cover. The following explorations place the hinge on the spine. Functionally, only the covers open better; the book block does not. These covers only offer play in design, a refreshing break away from the rigors of tradition. In each instance, re-positioning the hinge-fold hides or partially hides, the sewing when looking at the object with the covers closed.

SEWN on the SPINE TURN-IN

Each separate side-cover is given a spine turn-in. This results in a hinge for the side-cover at the spine. The turn-in offers a location for the sewing stations of the stab binding, rather than upon the side-covers. See illustrations at the bottom of page 126.

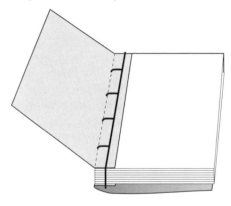

Wrapping around the spine at each of the traditional sewing stations will necessitate going through the cover at the hinge-fold. Additional sewing stations for the covers must be pierced on the hinge-fold, parallel with the sewing stations which go through the book block and the spine-edge turns-in.

4. Sewn on the Spine Turn-In

Sewing Stations

Stations for the book block remain the same. Measure and pierce the stations on the book block.

One set of stations on the cover is positioned on the spine turn-in. Use a pierced sheet from the book block as a guide to mark the stations on the turn-in. The second row of sewing stations for the cover are on the hinge-fold. Place a right angle at each station on the turn-in to find the position of the corresponding station on the fold.

The sewing procedure remains the same, except the book must be sewn with the covers fully opened.

HINGE-FOLD at SPINE with BORDERED TURNS-IN

This is the same as *Sewn on the Spine Turn-In* with the addition of turns-in on all sides allowing for an overhang. Each separate side-cover has turns-in at head and tail and at the foredge which will be tabbed down. The turn-in at the spine-edge functions as the hinge-fold.

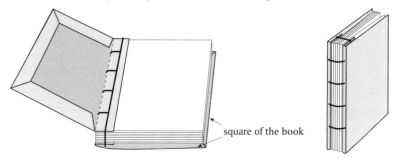

square of the book

5. Hinge-Fold at Spine with Bordered Turns-In. The turns-in along the head, tail and foredge of the cover reinforces the cover and offers the possibility of an overhang cover. This extension of the cover around three sides of the book block is the *square of the book.*

Preparing the Covers

The front and back side-covers are measured and constructed the same. Overhang on the head and tail each will be ¼". Overhang on the foredge will be ⅜". Turns-in are 1½" on the head, foredge and tail. The spine turn-in is ¾". If you wish a smaller turn-in, adjust the following measurements.

HEIGHT of one side-cover equals:

1½" turn-in at the head and an additional 1¼" for the overhang on the turn-in,

plus ¼" for the overhang at the head and the height of the book block and ¼" for the overhang at the tail,

plus ¼" for the overhang on the turn-in and 1½" turn-in at the tail.

WIDTH of one side-cover equals:

1½" foredge turn-in and ⅜" for the overhang of the turn-in,

plus ⅜" for overhang of the side-cover and width of the book block,

plus ¾" for spine-edge turn-in where the sewing stations will be positioned.

Measure and mark the cover sheets. Trim excess height and width. Lay the straight edge in position at each new fold and score with a bone folder, not a knife.

Folding the Covers

Order of folding the turns-in is important. First fold in from the head and tail, followed by the foredge and spine. After each fold, use the bone folder once across the fold to sharpen the crease and flatten the fold.

The turns-in are either sewn down or held down by tabs, described under *Interlocking Tabs,* page 306.

You may wish to add another sheet between the inside side-cover and its turns-in. This will add support if cover-weight and decoration if text-weight paper. See *Optional Liner,* page 82. The sewing stations and procedures are the same as the cover *Sewn on the Spine Turn-In,* described on page 128.

SEPARATE SIDE-COVERS WITH Z-FOLD

If you do not desire a foredge turn-in each side-covers is the width of the book block *plus* enough to make the Z-fold. The first fold is at the spine-edge turning in approximately 1½". This amount is then folded in half back on itself to form the Z. The edge of the cover paper is at the spine-edge. This gives ¾" width where the stabbing will occur.

The book is sewn with the covers extended forward. After sewing, the Z-fold is re-positioned which hides the thread except on the spine. The hinge-fold is at the spine-edge.

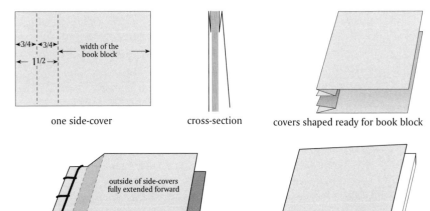

one side-cover   cross-section   covers shaped ready for book block

sew with covers fully extended forward   Separate Side Covers with Z-Fold

6. Separate Side-Covers with Z-Fold. Addition of foredge turns-in is recommended.

A foredge turn-in extending close to the Z-fold keeps the side-covers parallel and from creasing.

SINGLE PIECE COVER WITH Z-FOLDS

This is the same as the Single Piece Cover, page 127, with the addition of Z-folds at the spine-edge.

thin book block

For a book block of 4 or fewer sheets this cover is folded with double Z-folds. The center valley houses the book block.

For a thicker book block the cover requires an additional fold to give depth to the spine. See photo illustration below.

thick book block

7. Detail of Z-fold cover
with foredge turns-in

7. Single Piece Cover
with Z-Folds

SEPARATE VOLUMES within a CONCERTINA

Each pleat in this binding has a separate sewing. Each could be used to house separate chapters of the same book or several separate volumes. In the photo illustration at the top right on page 126 a three volume stab binding was sewn. Seven pleats were used. The two end pleats 1 and 7 are the hinge-folds. Pleats 3 and 5 do not house volumes; they are left empty as a motif, echoing the hinge-folds.

The three book blocks were sewn separately into pleats 2, 4 and 6.

Utilizing only every other pleat as a spine places space between the separate volumes. When the front cover is opened and extended, the volumes are pulled to the left. Benefits of an expanding spine are described under *Cover Pleat,* page 320.

8. Separate Volumes within
a Concertina

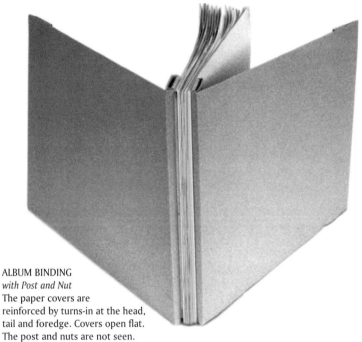

ALBUM BINDING
with Post and Nut
The paper covers are
reinforced by turns-in at the head,
tail and foredge. Covers open flat.
The post and nuts are not seen.
Below, an Optional Spine-Cover was added to cover the exposed edges of the book block.
See page 139.

ALBUM BINDING with Post and Nut

The album binding has always had board covers and the hinging required glue or metal hinges and screws. This album has paper overhang covers which are light weight but sturdy. Holes are drilled through the spine turns-in on the separate side-covers. Threaded posts are inserted into the back cover turn-in through the book block and bolted to the other cover turn-in. Covers open freely. Posts and nuts are not seen when the covers are closed, nor when they are opened.

Album posts and nuts are available in large office supply stores. The posts come in increments of $\frac{1}{4}$ to 3" lengths and are $\frac{1}{4}$" in diameter.

BOOK BLOCK

Single sheets of heavy stock. Rives BFK is a good weight and comes in black, gray, tan and white. Paper can be cut to size. Tear to size, if you wish to utilize the deckled-edge.

As with any single sheet binding, the entire sheet cannot be utilized for display. In this instance, a width of $1\frac{1}{2}$" at the spine must be reserved for the binding.

Drilling with Holes

Use one sheet as a pattern. Mark in $\frac{3}{8}$" from the spine at the head and tail on the template. Connect the marks with a pencil and ruler. Measure $\frac{3}{4}$" down from the head and mark across the vertical pencil line at that point. Measure up $\frac{3}{4}$" from the tail and mark the vertical line at that point. These two intersections are where you will center a $\frac{1}{4}$" drill.

Machine Drilling

Place blotters on each side of the book block and a piece of $\frac{3}{4}$" plywood on each side. Plywood and blotters should be near, but not extend over the drilling po sitions. Clamp with C-clamps. Drill.

A paper drill is ideal. Any electric drill can be used. If holes are slightly ragged, it is not that critical, since they are not seen. If very ragged, the book block will lose its shape. A hand punch would be preferable.

Hand Punching

If you are hand-punching, do not attempt to drill the entire book block at once, as it is easy to go off course. Punch through 5 to 10 sheets at a time, with the pattern on top to position the punch and a scrap sheet of book board underneath to protect the punch blade from being dulled.

Scoring the Sheets

Each sheet must be double-scored and folded, creating a compound hinge. This allows each turned page to lie flat in this single sheet binding. Use one sheet as a pattern to mark every sheet of the book block.

The first fold-as-hinge will be 1⅛" in from the spine-edge of the book block. When the covers are attached, this fold will be seen ⅜" in from the cover turn-in. The second hinge-fold will be ⅜" in from the first fold or, 1½" in from the spine.

Cut a piece of card the height of the book block, by 1⅛" wide. Cut another piece of card the same height, by 1½" wide. These will be used as a jig or template so that each individual sheet does not have to be measured. Lay one of the jigs on a sheet, flush at the spine-edge. Place a straight edge tangent to the jig. Hold straight edge in place and remove jig. Score the sheet. Lay the other jig on the same sheet, flush with the spine to position the straight edge. Score. Now fold both to make the hinge. Folds can be in either direction. Flatten the sheet and lay aside.

Follow this procedure to score and fold each sheet of the book block, without ever measuring or marking the sheets. Set the sheets aside and construct the covers.

COVERS

The cover for this binding is a variation on separate side-covers with borders.

Measuring the Covers

Each side-cover will be identically measured and constructed. The spine itself usually is not covered, but an optional spine-cover will be described on page 139.

Overhang on the head and tail will be ¼". Overhang on the foredge will be ⅜". Each cover has turns-in on all four sides. Turns-in will be 1½" on the head, foredge and tail.

The spine will have three turns-in requiring five folds. The extra folds are on each side of the area where the strip of book board is laid to accommodate its thickness.

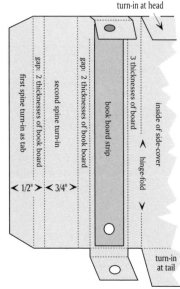

The three turns-in on the spine

Each sheet to be folded down as the cover should be laid down separately with the spine to the left and the foredge to the right.

One will be flipped over later when assembling covers and book block.

HEIGHT of one side-cover, measured from the head to the tail, equals:
  1½" turn-in at the head
plus ¼" for the overhang at the head and the height of the book
  block and ¼" for the overhang at the tail,
plus 1½" turn-in at the tail.
WIDTH of one side-cover, starting from the spine-edge to the
  foredge, equals:
  ½" for the first spine-edge turn-in which will serve as tab to fit under
  the board strip. See diagram on the facing page.
plus two thicknesses of book board, Trace edge of board twice.
plus ¾" for the second turn-in,
plus two thicknesses of book board, Trace edge of board twice.
plus ¾" This is where the book board will be positioned and holes
  will be drilled.
plus three thicknesses of the book board, Stand the strip of book
  board on edge and trace its depth three times. This last fold
  will be the hinge-fold.
plus width of the book block and ⅜" for overhang of the side-
  cover at the foredge,
plus 1½" foredge turn-in.

Measure and mark the cover sheets. Trim excess height and width. Lay the straight edge in position at each new fold and score with a bone folder, not a knife. Proceed to each measurement, score and fold all horizontal and vertical folds.

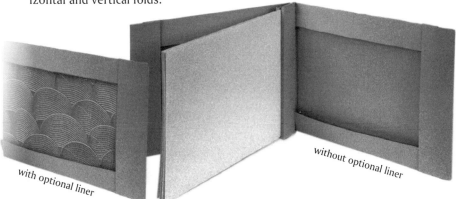

ALBUM BINDING with Post and Nut The turns-in at the spine are reinforced with a ¼" wide strip of book board, .060" thick. Height of the board is the same as the book block. An *optional liner,* page 137, can be on the inside of the side-covers.

Folding the Covers

Fold in from the head and tail, followed by the foredge. After each fold, use the bone folder once across the fold to sharpen the crease and flatten the fold.

The spine folds-in are begun from the outside and each additional fold to the right is folded and creased with the bone. Once the spine turns-in are made, unroll them and unfold all turns-in to a flat sheet.

Preparing the Tabs

The tabbing procedure at head and tail of the foredge is described on page 306, *Interlocking Tabs,* tabbing bordered turns-in. The tab at the spine-edge will be described. Cut, but do not assemble the tabs as follows: With the cover flat, locate the sections demarcated by folds at the head and tail of the foredge. Each will be 1½" high by 1½" wide.

1. Make vertical slits through the middle of these sections. This will create tabs at the head and tail of the foredge each which will be 1½" high by ¾" wide. See number 1 in the illustration.

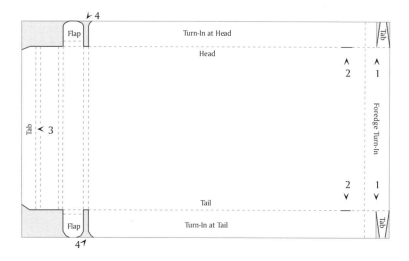

2. Temporarily fold in the head and tail turns-in. Then fold in the foredge turn-in, bringing the tabs around the head and tail to the outside of the cover. Place a pencil mark on the edge of the fold at the head, on each side of the tab. This will indicate where to cut the slit to insert the tab. Mark on the fold of the tail on each side of the tab. See *Edge-Tab,* page 307.

Unfold all turns-in and cut the two horizontal slits at the head and tail of the foredge. See number 2 in illustration above.

3. Cut away the areas denoted as light gray in the above illustration at head and tail of the spine-edge. This will taper the leading edge of spine tab, number 3 in the above illustration, to be fitted under the board strip after the holes are drilled.

4. Remove that area of the head and tail turns-in which is between the flap and the side cover. It is marked in gray above and the width of the area removed is 3 thicknesses of board. This will facilitate the wrapping of the board strip. Crease the flaps to allow for the thickness of the board when closing the flap over the board.

You might modify this binding with some other variation of tabbing procedure. See *Interlocking Tabs,* page 306. Or, instead of tabbing the corners, the turns-in can be held down by sewing.

Optional Liner

The cover is sturdy. To make it even stronger, if it is larger than 9 x 12" the cover can be reinforced with a optional liner, described on page 82. Place liner in position on the inside of the cover prior to tabbing.

Tabbing the Turns-In

Fold in the turns-in at head and tail, except for the foredge tabs. Turns-in go over the liner, if any. Fold in foredge turn-in. Insert tabs into slits to secure the head, tail and foredge turns-in. Weave the turns-in, drill holes and insert posts before tabbing the spine-edge.

Weaving the Turns-In

The head, tail and foredge turns-in tend to bow open unless they are attached to the cover. A few stitches with a colored waxed linen thread can secure the turns-in, increase the rigidity, as well as decorate the cover. I prefer weaving tabs of the same or another color paper as a fastener. It is important to have the head and tail turns-in fastened close to the spine-edge. Tab the center of the turns-in if they are long. If the cover is large, woven tabs can be designed in the center of the side-cover, holding the liner against the middle of the cover.

The turns-in can be secured by a long tab woven the length of the turn-in. Cut a strip of cover stock ½" wide. Lightly mark where the slots are to be cut on the turns-in. Cut the slots and weave the tabs. See *Woven and Tucked Tab,* page 310.

Short tabs can be woven in and out of two slots. Secure the tabs, by interlocking the ends. See *Weaving a Slit-Locked Tab,* page 309. Either tabbing procedure will not only hold down the turns-in, but will attach the liner to the side-cover making it more rigid.

Drilling the Covers

The head, tail and foredge turns-in should be secured by tabbing or sewing before the holes are drilled through the board strip, after flaps are closed so they will also be drilled as shown in illustration on page 134. There will be one hole drilled at each end of board strip, ³⁄₄" from the head and tail, so they are centered vertically on the turn-in. They are centered horizontally, ³⁄₈" in from the edge of the board strip. Place the marks on the flaps. Center the ¼" drill at the intersection of your marks, drilling through the flap, board strip and third spine turn-in. Unless you have access to a paper drill, a hand punch or paper drill is better than a carpenter's electric drill. Paper drills give a clean hole. They are illustrated on page 42.

Assembly of Book Block and Covers

Album posts come in varying lengths. Measure the depth of the book block, add the thickness of the two board strips. The total will be the length of album posts required.

Pick up one cover, with the turns-in facing you, with the spine on the left. This is the inside of the back cover. Unroll the spine turns-in. Place an album post into the drilled hole at the head, first through the flap, then board strip, then through third spine turn-in. Insert post at the tail.

Fold the second spine turn-in over the flaps, board strip and posts. Tuck the spine tab under board strip. Fold the wrapped board against the inside of the back cover. The shafts of the album posts are now protruding upright.

Hold the spine turn-in in this position or it might unfold. Add the bottom of the spine-cover, if any. Place the book block, a few sheets at a time, onto the album posts. After a few are added, the spine turn-in will cease wanting to unfold. When all the sheets have been positioned onto the posts, fit the other end of the spine-cover in position, if one is used.

Tab the foredge of the front cover, but do not insert tab on spine-edge. Pick up front cover with the turns-in facing up, with the spine to the right. With the spine turns-in unrolled, lower the spine turn-in until the drilled holes line up with the album posts protruding from the text block. Place the cover on the posts. Add the board strip and flaps over the posts. Screw a nut onto each post. Tighten with a screw driver.

Fold the second spine turn-in over the board strip and nuts. Insert spine-tab under the board strip. Close front cover. With use, the wrapped spine-cover turn-in will lie flat, covering the nuts. The first few viewings, the turn-in may have to be positioned over the board strip before the cover is closed.

Optional Spine-Cover

When the book is closed, if you do not wish to see the spine-edge of the book block, you can add a spine-cover. As additional pages are added to the album, a new, wider spine-cover can be installed.

The paper spine-cover will be the height of the book block. The width will be the width of the board strip *plus* depth of the book block *plus* width of a board strip.

The spine-cover fits over the spine-edge of the book block. The fold-overs must be drilled to line up with the album posts. The bottom fold-over is placed on the post after the back cover, then the pages of the book. Then the top fold-over is placed over the posts and finally, the top cover is added and the nuts are screwed on. The spine-cover can extend to be endsheets as illustrated on page 132.

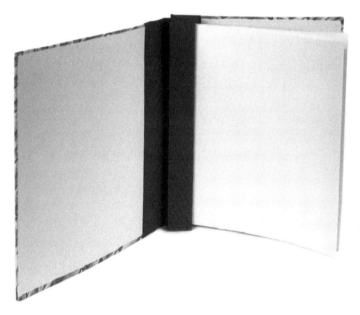

ALBUM BINDING *with Post and Nut* Here, book board is used for the side-covers. Decorative paper is wheat pasted to the outside of the boards and a paste-down on the inside. Book cloth is used on the boards which are turned-in at the spine-edge. It is the same principle of album binding, but uses board, cloth and adhesives.

INSERTING PHOTOGRAPHS

1. Photographs can be attached without adhesives by inserting the corners of the pictures into diagonal slots. See *Slots,* page 82. Position the photo on the page. Mark in both directions, in from the corners of the photo, so that when the dots in each corner are connected with a slot, the diagonal cut will be at least ³⁄₈" in from that corner of the photograph. This allows the tips of the photos to go through to the verso.

Aeros Keith Lillstrom

2. Rather than a diagonal slot, a curved slot can be made by using a curved wood chisel called a *gouge.* See page 43. At each corner strike the gouge twice closely together making two parallel curved slits. Slice to connect the ends to form a curved slot. Tis is less apt to rip than the first method.

Alpha Gaylord Lillstrom

3. In attaching photographs, a pair of slots is more secure, hides less of the photograph, as well as a more attractive means of attachment. Each slot is the thickness of the photo paper. The slots are parallel and at least ¼" apart. The outside slot is at least ³⁄₈" in from the corner.

Photo by Lynette Pirrung

These sewings are on a continuous paper cover support.　　

LONG STITCH
through SLOTTED WRAPPER COVER

This is an older binding. Gary Frost showed me a slide of an eigh-teenth-century Italian example of this binding. It is a quick binding. A single thread sews each of however many sections onto the cover. The exposed sewing on the spine looks better if the text block is at least ½" wide. This allows the staggered stitches on the spine to be more pro-nounced. The sections, rather than the binder, position the stitches on the spine.

The stitches go in and out of the section, catching the cover with each stitch. This standard in and out procedure requires a variation in stitch-ing at the head or tail of certain sections. I will describe sewing four sec-tions, with four pierced sewing stations. The head and the tail are two wrapping stations.

Bert Weijermars, *Langsteek,* sample of the *Long Stitch through Slotted Wrapper Cover.*

Varying the number of sections or the addition of pierced sewing stations will alter how
the book must be sewn. The important thing to
remember how to properly sew this binding is
to keep in mind that *every section* will have a *single thread* wrapped around the head and the tail
of the section, onto the spine. This gives support since it ties the head and tail of each section to the cover. Also it is an attractive edging,
reminiscent of endbands.

If, when sewing, you find you have not made
a wrap around the edge of the top or bottom of
the section onto the spine, back up and correct
the sewing. If you find you have wrapped
around the head or tail twice in sewing any one
section, again, back up to correct.

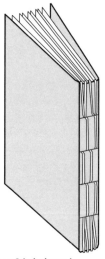

Long Stitch through
Slotted Wrapper Cover

PREPARATION

Sections

The sections must be created by assembling folios within folios. You
cannot fold down sections for this binding, as the head and tail cannot
be trimmed after sewing. The thread is wrapped around each section
onto the spine-cover at the head and tail.

To achieve a thick text block, place four folios within each other to
create a 16 page section. Or, create octavos of heavy stock. Make four
such sections. The diagram shows how to sew four sections, each with
four sewing stations.

Measure the spine by very slightly compressing the depth of the book
block. Make sure the resulting book block will produce a spine of at least
one half inch deep, to show the spine stitching.

Cover

The spine of this binding holds it shape better if it is two or three-ply.
A good cover for this binding is *Flat Back with Fixed Foredge Turns-In*. See
page 285.

HEIGHT of cover must be precisely same height of the sections, since the
thread is wrapped around the head and tail of each section onto the
cover. A slightly larger cover would be crimped by the wrapping. A
cover shorter than the height of the sections would not protect the
surface of the first and last page of the book.

WIDTH of the total cover equals:
width of the front cover foredge turn-in, if any,
plus width of the book block (front cover),

plus depth of the book block when slightly compressed,
plus width of the book block,
plus width of the back cover foredge turn-in, if any.

If you use foredge turns-in, you can allow for an overhang on the foredge. Slightly increase the width of the turn-in and the side-covers.

Optional Concertina Guard

Endsheets with spine-pleats might be fitted between the sections and the cover. This would hide cracks seen in between sections, as the pages are turned. See *Concertina Guard,* page 319.

Sewing Stations

The illustration is for six sewing stations. The head and tail are wrapping stations and four stations are pierced on each section. The cover has a horizontal slit across the spine positioned at each pierced station of the book block.

Measure and mark one section. Station 1 is the head, so the first pierced station is number 2. The tail is station 6.

Placement of the pierced stations can be equidistant, dividing the height of the backbone by five. Usually I leave more space between the bottom station and the tail of the book than the distance between the other stations. This suggests a base to the spine, denoting which end is up and therefore, differentiates the front from the back cover. After marking one section, use it as a guide for the remaining three. Pierce the stations.

Marking the Cover Stations

Lay the unfolded cover open on the table with the inside facing up. Lay a section on the cover, lining up the fold of the section with one hinge-fold. Mark the four sewing stations on the hinge-fold, using the section as a guide. Move the section over, lining up the fold of the section with the other hinge-fold. Mark the stations on the hinge-fold.

Place the cover on your cutting surface. Connect the dots at each station with a horizontal slit. Be sure not to cross the hinge-folds or you will cut onto the side-covers.

Thread

Length of thread depends upon height of the backbone and the number of sections. For four sections, cut a piece of thread seven times the height of the back. Heavier thread makes a better looking exposed sewing on the spine. I suggest #12 thread. It must be heavily waxed. I use pre-waxed linen thread which is available in various colors. Thread needle pulling through about ⅓ the thread.

THE ELABORATED SEWING PROCEDURE
Sewing the First Section

Place in the first section to be sewn onto the spine at the hinge-fold.

1. Start on the inside of the section at station 2. Go through the section, guiding needle through the slit on the cover, at the hinge-fold. Pull the thread to the outside, leaving 4" of thread dangling within the section.

   Proceed along the spine, keeping the thread close to the hinge-fold, but on the spine, not on the side-cover. Wrap around the head to the inside of the section to sewing station 2. Pull thread taut until the dangling thread is shortened to about 1½". Tie a Square Knot at station 2 on the inside of the section. Pull towards the tail to tighten knot. Make sure it is tight and precisely at the station. If it is tied low, it can slip to the station later, loosening the stitch.

2. Proceed on the inside of the section to the third station. Take the needle through the section, through the slit on the spine close to the hinge-fold.

3. Proceed on the spine to the fourth station, which is a slit. Take the needle through the slit on the spine, close to the hinge-fold and through the corresponding sewing station of the section, to the inside.

4. Proceed on the inside of the section to station 5. Take the needle through the fifth station, through the slit, close to the fold, to the outside of the spine. Take the thread along the spine, close to the hinge-fold. Wrap around the tail to the inside of the section to station 5. Take the needle though the section and slit to the outside.

You have completed sewing one section. The second will have a variation in how it is completed. At this point examine the sewing. There should be three stitches on the spine of the cover. The pattern of the stitches for each section will vary on the spine and within the section. Alignment and distance between the stitches of the cover will be positioned by the thickness of the sections, themselves. You will not have to adjust where the stitches fall on the spine. It is only necessary to control placement of the stitches with the first and last section. These spine stitches should be kept close to the hinge-fold, on the spine. Do not allow any stitches at the head and tail to loop over onto a side-cover.

Finally in examining the first sewn section, notice your spine stitch at the head wraps around to the inside of the section. At the tail there is also one thread which comes from the section, around the tail, across the spine to station 5.

Sewing each section, the main thing is to make sure that you have wrapped around the head and tail, connecting the section to the cover. If there is no wrap around or two, you have sewn incorrectly. Back up and correct.

Sewing the Second Section

Close the first section and place the second beside it on the spine. The second does not go inside the first, but is adjacent. Open the second section to the center folio. If the sewing is not on the bench, but hand-held, grasp the side-cover, first section and half the second section with thumb and forefinger, prepared to sew.

Remember to space sections across the spine using the same compression with which the spine was measured. If you sew the sections compressed tighter than measured, you will end up with the spine on the cover much wider than the sewn text block.

5. Lay the thread along the spine, wrap around the tail to the inside of the second section to the fifth sewing station. Take the needle through the station, through the cover slit and pull the thread outside. Remember not to squeeze the sections, to obtain the proper spacing across the spine. The first two sections should take up half the width of the spine.

Proceed along the spine to the next slit. Go through station 4 into the section. Pull thread inside.

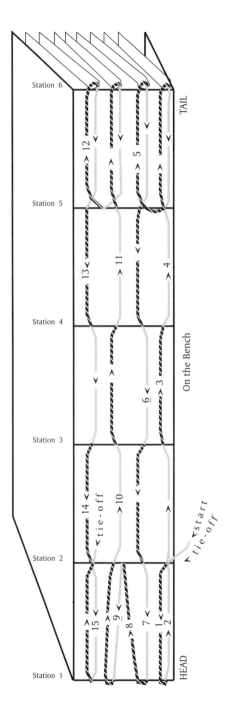

6. Proceed inside to the third station. Go through section and cover slit to outside.

    Proceed along the spine to station 2. Go through the slit and the section to the inside. Pull thread taut.

7. Proceed inside the section to the head. Do not wrap around. At this point there is a variation in procedure to insure only one wrap around the head of the second section.

    Instead of making a wrap around, pull thread beyond the head, so that needle and all the thread are hanging out of the head of the second section.

Sewing the Third Section

Close the second section and place the third section in position. Open the third section to center folio.

8. Wrap around the head of the second section, proceed along the spine to the bottom slit. Go through the slit into station 2 of the third section. This makes the wrap around for the second section.

9. Proceed inside the third section to the head. Wrap around the head. Proceed along the spine to the slit at station 2. Go through slit and into station 2 of the third section. This makes the wrap at the head of the third section.

10. Proceed inside the section to station 3. Go through station 3 and slit to the outside.

    Proceed along the spine to the slit at station 4. Go through station 4 to the inside.

11. Proceed inside the section to station 5. Go through station and slit to the outside. Pull to tighten all the stitches of the third section.

    Proceed along the spine, wrap around tail, proceed inside to station 5. Go through station and slit to the outside. Pull thread taut.

Sewing the Fourth Section

Set the fourth section in place and open.

12. Go along the spine, wrap around tail into the fourth section. Proceed inside the section to the fifth station. Go through station and the slit, close to the hinge-fold. Pull thread to outside, making sure wrap remains on the spine and does not slip onto the side-cover.

13. Proceed along the spine to the next slit. Go through slit at the hinge-fold, through the section to the inside of the fourth sewing station. Proceed within the section to station 3. Go out station and slit.

14. Proceed along the spine to the next slit. Go through sewing station 2 to the inside of the section.

15. Proceed inside the section, wrap around the head, proceed along the spine to the slit.

Go through the slit, through station 2, to inside of section. Pull thread tight. Tie a *Half Hitch,* page 73, on the inside of the section, at the second sewing station, by passing the needle behind the inside stitch between the second and third sewing stations. Tighten knot by pulling downward. Cut excess thread to ¾".

CONDENSED DESCRIPTION of SEWING PROCEDURE
Sewing the First Section

1. Start on inside at station 2. Go to outside at the hinge-fold. Proceed close to the hinge-fold. Wrap around the head. Proceed inside of section to station 2. Tie a Square Knot at station 2.
2. Proceed on inside to station 3. Go out 3 near the hinge-fold.
3. Proceed to station 4. Go through slit close to the hinge-fold, into station 4 of the section.
4. Proceed to station 5. Go out 5, close to the fold, to the outside. Wrap around the tail to the inside to station 5. Go through 5 to the outside.

Sewing the Second Section

5. Place the second section in position. Proceed along the spine, wrap around the tail to the inside of the second section to station 5. Go through to outside. Proceed along the spine to station 4. Go through to inside.
6. Proceed inside to station 3. Go through to outside. Proceed along the spine to station 2. Go through to inside.
7. Proceed inside to the head. Do not wrap around. Close the second section, place the third section in position.

Sewing the Third Section

8. Wrap around the head of the second section, proceed along the spine to the slit. Go through the slit into station 2 of the third section.
9. Proceed inside the third section to the head. Wrap around the head. Proceed along the spine to the slit. Go through slit and into station 2 of the third section.
10. Proceed within the section to station 3. Go through to outside. Proceed along the spine to station 4. Go through to inside.
11. Proceed within the section to station 5. Go through to outside. Proceed along the spine, wrap around the tail. Proceed inside the section to station 5. Go through to the outside.

Sewing the Fourth Section

12. Set the fourth section in place and open. Proceed along the spine, wrap around the tail into the fourth section. Proceed inside to station 5. Go through to outside, close to the hinge-fold.

13. Proceed along the spine to station 4. Go through at the hinge-fold to inside. Proceed to station 3. Go to outside.

14. Proceed along the spine to station 2. Go to the inside.

15. Proceed in the section, wrap around the head, proceed along the spine to station 2. Go through to inside, tie-off at station 2 with a Half Hitch.

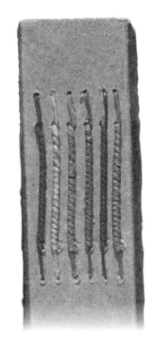

Detail. For *packing*, see *Glossary*.

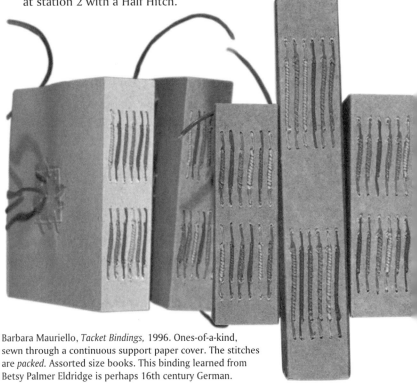

Barbara Mauriello, *Tacket Bindings,* 1996. Ones-of-a-kind, sewn through a continuous support paper cover. The stitches are *packed.* Assorted size books. This binding learned from Betsy Palmer Eldridge is perhaps 16th century German.

VARIATION on the LONG STITCH

This is a variation in sewing of the *Long Stitch through Slotted Wrapper Cover.* As with the previously described long stitch binding, the four stations on the spine-cover are slits. They divide the spine into five parts. Path of sewing has been altered, so that the exposed stitches are located only on the top, middle and bottom divisions of the spine.

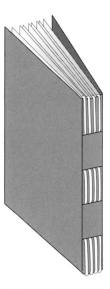

The traditional long stitch binding pinches the stitches resulting in diagonal stitches at the head and tail. I altered the procedure of sewing so that the stitches would always be parallel, rather than *V*-shaped at the head and tail. This variation has a more simplified appearance and secures the sections to the cover in a pleasing alternative pattern of an exposed spine binding.

PREPARATION

The sections, sewing stations, cover and length of thread are prepared the same as for *Long Stitch through Slotted Wrapper Cover.* If you wish to attach the optional *Laced Jacket* A, page 153, sew the book block onto a flat back cover without foredge turns-in.

ELABORATED SEWING PROCEDURE

Sewing the First Section

1. Start on the inside. Proceed through station 2 to outside. Pull all but 4" of thread through to the outside of the spine.
   Go along the spine, wrap around the head near the hinge-fold. Proceed inside of the section to station 2. Pull thread taut until the dangling thread is shortened to about 1½" or just enough to tie a knot. Tie a Square Knot at the station, pulling towards the tail to tighten.

2. Proceed on the inside of the section to the third station. Go through to outside, close to the hinge-fold.

3. Proceed along the spine to station 4. Go through, close to the hinge-fold, to inside of the section.

4. Proceed on the inside of the section to sewing station 5. Go through station 5 to the outside. Proceed along the spine, close to the hinge-fold. Wrap around the tail, proceed inside the section to the fifth sewing station. Take the needle though station 5 of the section only. Do not go through cover slit. Pull thread to outside of section.

Sewing the Second Section

5. Grasp the second section and take the needle through the mountain peak of sewing station 5. Do not go through the station on the cover. Pull the thread to the inside, as you position the section against the inside of the spine-cover. Proceed within the section, wrap over the tail. Proceed along the spine to the top slit in the cover. Take the needle through the slit, through station 5 to the inside.
6. Proceed within the section to station 4. Go through to outside. Proceed along the spine to the next slit. Go through to inside of station 3. Proceed to station 2. Go through the section and cover slit.
7. Proceed along the spine, wrap around the head and proceed inside of the second section to station 2. Take the needle through station 2 of the section. Do not go through the cover slit. Pull thread to the outside of the section.

Sewing the Third Section

8. Grasp the third section and take the needle through the mountain peak of sewing station number 2. Do not go through the station on the cover. Pull thread to inside of section, while you place the section securely against the spine.
9. Proceed inside the third section, wrap around the head and proceed on the outside of the cover along the spine to the slit.
10. Take the needle through the slit and through the station to the inside of the section. Proceed within the section to the third station. Go through station and slit to outside. Proceed along the spine to next slit. Go through to the inside of station 4.
11. Proceed within the section to station 5. Go through to outside. Proceed along the spine, wrap around the tail, proceed inside of the section to station 5. Go through station only. Do not go through cover. Pull thread to the outside of the section.

Sewing the Fourth Section

12. Grasp the fourth section and take the needle through the mountain peak of sewing station 5. Do not go through the station on the cover. Pull thread to inside of the section, pushing the section into position against the spine. Proceed inside of the section, wrap around the tail and proceed along the spine to the slit on the cover at station 5.
13. Go through slit, close to the hinge-fold, through the fifth station to the inside of the section. Pull thread taut, making sure the wrapped stitch remains on the spine and does not slip to the side-cover. Proceed within the section to the fourth station. Go to outside.

14. Proceed along the spine to the next slit. Go through slit, through station 3 to the inside. Proceed within the section to the second station. Go through to outside.

15. Proceed along the spine, wrap around the head, proceed inside of the section to station 2. Before you tie the knot, check to be sure this last stitch on the spine has not slipped over onto the side-cover. Tie a *Half Hitch,* page 73, on the inside of the section, at the second station, by passing the needle behind the inside stitch between the second and third stations. Tighten knot by pulling downward.

CONDENSED DESCRIPTION of the SEWING PROCEDURE
Sewing the First Section

1. Start inside at station 2. Go to the outside, along the spine, wrap around the head, near the hinge-fold. Proceed inside of the section to station 2. Tie a Square Knot at the station.

2. Proceed on the inside to station 3. Go through to outside, close to the hinge-fold.

3. Proceed to station 4. Go through to inside.

4. Proceed on inside to station 5. Go through to outside. Proceed along the spine, wrap around the tail. Proceed inside to station 5. Take needle though station 5 of the section only. Do not go through cover slit.

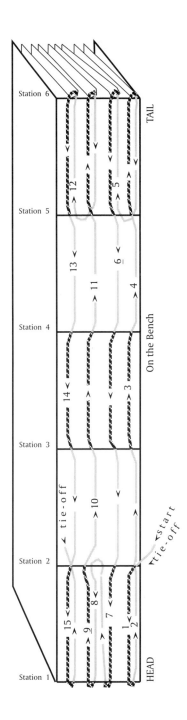

Sewing the Second Section

5. Grasp second section and take needle through mountain peak of station 5. Do not go through the station on the cover. Pull the thread to the inside, as you position the second section against the inside of the spine-cover. Proceed inside of the section, wrap over the tail. Proceed along the spine to station 5. Take the needle through to the inside.

6. Proceed inside the section to station 4. Go through to outside. Proceed along the spine station 3. Go through to inside. Proceed within the section to station 2. Go through to outside.

7. Proceed along the spine, wrap around the head and proceed inside to station 2. Take needle through station 2 of the section. Do not go through the cover slit. Pull thread to the outside of the section.

Sewing the Third Section

8. Grasp the third section. Take needle through mountain peak of station 2. Do not go through the station on the cover. Pull thread to inside of section, while you place section securely against the spine.

9. Proceed inside, wrap around the head and proceed along the outside to station 2.

10. Go through station 2 to the inside. Proceed within the section to station 3. Go through to outside. Proceed along the spine to 4. Go through to the inside.

11. Proceed within the section to station 5. Go through to outside. Proceed along the spine, wrap around tail to the inside of the section to station 5. Go through station only. Do not go through cover.

Sewing the Fourth Section

12. Grasp the fourth section and take the needle through the mountain peak of sewing station 5. Do not go through the station on the cover. Pull thread to inside of the section, pushing the section into position against the spine. Proceed inside, wrap around the tail and proceed along the spine to station 5.

13. Go through to the inside. Proceed within the section to station 4. Go to outside.

14. Proceed along the spine to station 3. Go through to the inside. Proceed to station 2. Go through to outside.

15. Proceed along the spine, wrap around the head, proceed on the inside of the section to station 2. Tie a Half Hitch as described on page 73.

LACED JACKET *A*

Optional for Variation on the Long Stitch Binding

An optional jacket can be laced onto the binding called *Variation on the Long Stitch.* This second cover of the same heavy stock is placed over the first, woven onto the sewn cover. The foredge turns-in of the jacket are placed around the sewn cover.

If the jacket is added, do not use foredge turns-in on the sewn cover and do not reinforce spine. The jacket will provide these.

The jacket tabs under the second and fourth divisions. The result is a woven spine, with the sewing hidden, except for the small amount of stitching wrapped over the head and tail, reminiscent of head bands.

Dimensions of Jacket

Measure and cut the jacket the same height as the sewn cover. Exact width is determined by fitting and marking, rather than measuring. Width of the jacket is that of the sewn cover and slightly more at each fold to accommodate the thickness of the paper of the outer cover. The jacket is also wider by the amount of the foredge turns-in, which wrap around the foredges of the inner cover.

Cut jacket to height of the sewn cover and total width of sewn cover and with enough for two foredge turns-in. Fold one foredge hinge-fold on the outer cover. Place the jacket in place over the sewn cover and mark the position of the second hinge-fold on the inside of the spine. Remove and fold. Again, place jacket snug against the spine of the sewn cover. Mark the positions of the foredge folds on the inside of the jacket. Remove and fold.

Making the Spine-Tabs

Stand the folded jacket to the left of the sewn book, with the spines tangent. Mark the positions of the slits of the sewn spine onto the right hinge-fold of the jacket. Stand jacket on the right of the sewn book, spines tangent and mark the positions of the slits on the sewn spine on the left hinge-fold of the jacket. Do not cut four slits on the jacket.

Cut along left hinge-fold of the jacket connecting the top two marked positions. Cut along left hinge-fold between the bottom two positions. Do the same on the right hinge-fold of the jacket.

Cut the second division horizontally from one hinge-fold to the other, midway between the first and third division. Cut the fourth division horizontally from one hinge-fold to the other, midway between the third and bottom division.

This creates four tabs. Fold the tabs. The four horizontal folds across the spine mark the divisions of the spine.

Adjusting and Pointing the Tabs

Measure and cut each tab to ⅜" in length. Next, the width of the horizontal cut edges of the tabs must be made narrower than the width of the spine. This will allow easier insertion of the tabs under the second and fourth divisions of the sewn cover.

Place a dot ¼" in from both sides on the horizontal cut edge of all the tabs. At the top tab, make one cut at an angle from the point where the fold of the tab meets the left side-cover to the left dot on the horizontal cut edge of the tab. Do the same on the third tab.

On the first tab, cut from the point where the fold of the tab meets the right side-cover to the remaining dot on the horizontal cut edge of the tab. Cut the third tab in the same manner. Turn the jacket upside down. Cut the two remaining tabs.

Bert Weijermars, *Langsteek met jas.*
Sample binding of the *Variation on the Long Stitch* with *Laced Jacket* A.

Attaching the Jacket

Place the jacket over the sewn cover, with the foredge turns-in around the sewn cover. Insert the first tab under the second division of the sewn cover. Use the tip of a bone folder to pry open the top slit on the sewn spine. Insert the the fourth tab, then the second and third.

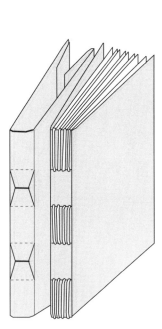

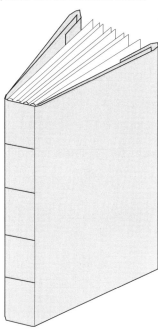

Marking the Spine   Jacket *A* Attached

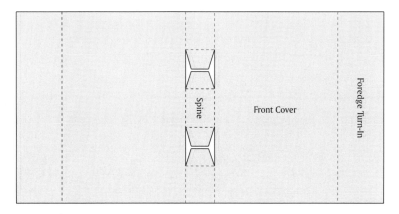

Layout of Jacket *A*

LONG STITCH
with WOVEN SPINE-TAB

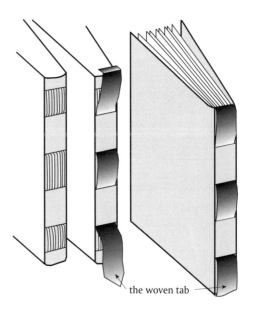

the woven tab

In the previous binding, *Variation on the Long Stitch,* the second and fourth divisions of the spine are free-floating, not attached to the backbone. This presents the opportunity of weaving a single tab in and out of the five divisions of the spine to hide the stitches. A cover weight paper tab, the height of the backbone and a little narrower, could be woven behind the second division of the spine, lay on top of the third and woven underneath the fourth division.

This binding variation would be sewn with the rapidity of the long stitch, have a single flat back cover with foredge turns-in but offer the option of an interesting paper-woven motif on the spine with no thread visible on the cover.

However, the tab would not be attached at the head or tail and could easily be bent. To correct this short-coming, the *Variation on the Long Stitch* has been modified so that a spine-tab can not only be woven, but tucked inside at the head and tail between the spine-cover and the book block. This modified binding will be referred to as *Long Stitch with Woven Spine-Tab.*

PREPARATION

Sections and cover are prepared the same as for *Long Stitch through Slotted Wrapper Cover.* If you wish to attach the optional *Laced Jacket B,* described on page 162, sew the book block onto a flat back cover without foredge turns-in.

Sewing Stations

Measure and mark the first section:

1. There will be 4 sewing stations which are equidistant, dividing the height of the back into five divisions. Mark these four stations.
2. There are two more pierced stations. One is about $\frac{5}{16}$" from the head. The other station is about $\frac{5}{16}$" from the tail. Mark these two additional stations on the first section.

These two additional stations take the place of wrapping around the head and tail. Since the sections will not be attached to the spine at the first $\frac{5}{16}$" at the head and tail, this gives room to tuck the woven tab around the head and tail, to rest between the inside of the spine-cover and the book block. The station closest to the head is number 1, the station closest to the tail is 6.

Now that the first section has 6 stations marked on the fold, use it as a guide to mark the remaining three sections. Pierce the stations. Lay the unfolded cover open on the table with the inside facing up. Place the first section on the cover, lining up the fold of the section with one hinge-fold. Mark the six sewing stations on the hinge-fold, using the section as a guide. Move the section over, lining up the fold of the section with the other hinge-fold. Mark the stations on that hinge-fold.

Place the cover on your cutting surface. Make a horizontal slit from the top dot on one hinge-fold, across the spine to the other top mark. Do the same with the five remaining stations. Be sure not to cut onto the side-covers.

Thread

Length of thread depends upon height of the backbone and number of sections. For four sections, thread is seven times the height of the back. Use heavily waxed #12 thread.

ELABORATED SEWING PROCEDURE
Sewing the First Section

Lay the first section within the cover, tangent to the proper hinge-fold. Start on inside.

1. Proceed through station 2 to outside. Pull all but 4" of thread through to the outside of the spine.

    Proceed along the spine, towards the head to the slit on the spine. Go through station 1 to inside. Proceed inside the section to station 2. Adjust the thread until the dangling thread is shortened to about $1\frac{1}{2}$". Tie a Square Knot at the station. See page 72.
2. Proceed on the inside of the section to station 3. Take the needle through the section and the slit, close to the hinge-fold.

Proceed on the spine to station 4. Take the needle through the slit, close to the hinge-fold, through the sewing station to the inside of the section.

3. Proceed on the inside of the section to station 5. Go through the station and the slit, close to the fold, to the outside of the spine.

    Take the thread along the spine, close to the hinge-fold. Take the needle through the slit on the spine, through the sixth sewing station, to the inside of the section.

4. Proceed inside the section to station 5. Take the needle out through the section only. Do not go through cover slit.

Sewing the Second Section

5. Grasp the second section, take needle through the mountain peak of station 5 of the new section. Do not go through cover. Pull thread to inside of this section. Holding the thread taut, slide the section back into position with its fold against the inside of the spine, tangent to the first section. Proceed inside the section to station 6.

6. Take the needle though section and the cover slit. Proceed along the spine to station 5. Go through the slit and section to the inside. Proceed to station 4. Go through the section and slit to the outside. Proceed along the spine. Go through the next slit and section to the inside of station 3.

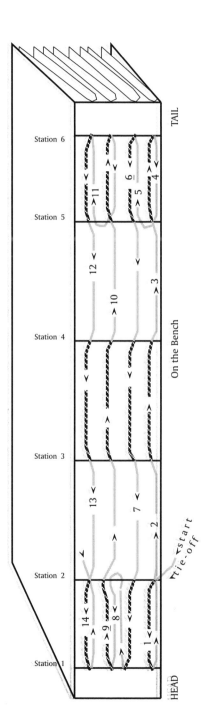

7. Proceed inside the section, go out station 2 and the slit. Proceed along the spine to the next slit. Go through slit and section to inside. Proceed inside to station 2. Go out the section, but do not go through the cover slit.

Sewing the Third Section

8. Grasp the third section, take the needle through the mountain peak of station 2 of the section, only. Pull the thread through. Holding the thread taut close to the section, back the third section along the thread until the mountain peak rests against the inside of the spine-cover, tangent to the second section. Proceed inside the section to the first sewing station. Go through the section and cover slit to the outside.

9. Proceed along the spine to the second slit. Go through slit and section to the inside. Proceed inside the section to station 3. Go through to the outside. Proceed along the spine to next slit. Go through station 4 to the inside.

10. Proceed within the section to station 5. Go through section and slit to outside. Proceed along the spine to the slit.

   Go through slit and section to inside of station 6. Proceed along the inside to station 5. Take the needle out through the section only. Do not go through the cover slit.

Sewing the Fourth Section

11. Grasp the fourth section, take needle through the peak of station 5 of the new section. Pull thread to inside. Place the peak against the inside of the spine tangent to the third section. Proceed inside to station 5. Go out the station, through slit to outside. Proceed along the spine to the fifth slit. Go through the slit and section to the inside.

12. Proceed within the section to the fourth station. Go out section and slit. Proceed along the spine to the next slit. Go through the third station to the inside of the section.

13. Proceed within the section to the second station. Go through the station and slit.

14. Proceed along the spine to the bottom slit. Go through to the inside. Proceed inside the section to the second sewing station. Tie a Half Hitch on the inside of the section at the second station by passing the needle behind the inside stitch between the second and third stations. Tighten knot by pulling downward. The *Half Hitch* is described on page 73.

REVIEW, or CONDENSED SEWING PROCEDURE
Sewing the First Section

Illustration starts on the inside of the section.

1. Go through station 2 to outside. Pull all but 4" of thread to the out-side. Proceed along the spine, to station 1. Go through to inside. Proceed on to station 2. Pull, reducing loose end of thread to 1½".
2. Proceed to station 3. Go through to the outside, close to the hinge-fold. Proceed to station 4. Go through, close to the hinge-fold, to the inside.
3. Proceed to station 5. Go through close to the fold, to the outside. Go through station 6, to the inside.
4. Proceed to station 5. Go through the section only. Do not go through cover slit.
5. Grasp the second section. Take needle through the mountain peak of station 5. Do not go through cover. Pull thread to inside of this section. Slide section back into position, tangent to the first section. Proceed inside the section to station 6.
6. Go though to the outside. Proceed to station 5. Go through to the inside. Proceed to station 4. Go through to the outside. Proceed to station 3. Go through to the inside.
7. Proceed inside to station 2. Go to outside. Proceed along the spine to bottom slit. Go through station 1 to inside. Proceed to station 2. Go out station 2 of the section, but do not go through the cover slit.
8. Grasp the third section. Take needle through the mountain peak of station 2. Do not go through cover. Pull the thread through. Back the third section along the thread until the mountain peak rests against the inside of the spine-cover. Proceed inside to station 1. Go through the section and cover to the outside.
9. Proceed to station 2. Go through to the inside. Proceed to station 3. Go through to the outside. Proceed to station 4. Go through to the inside.
10. Proceed to station 5. Go through to the outside. Proceed to the slit at station 6. Go through station 6 to the inside. Proceed inside to station 5. Take the needle out through the section only. Do not go through the cover slit.
11. Grasp the fourth section. Take needle through the peak of station 5 of the new section. Pull thread to the inside. Place the peak against the inside of the spine, tangent to the third section. Proceed to sta-tion 6. Go out section and slit to the outside. Proceed along the spine to station 5. Go through to the inside.
12. Proceed to station 4. Go out section and slit. Proceed to station 3. Go to the inside of the section.

13. Proceed to station 2. Go through to the outside.
14. Proceed along the spine to the bottom slit. Go through to the inside. Proceed to station 2. Tie a Half Hitch on the inside at the second station, by passing the needle behind the inside stitch between the second and third stations. Tighten knot by pulling downward.

SPINE-TAB

Cut a piece of cover stock 3" longer than the height of the spine. Width of the tab is $\frac{1}{16}$" less than width of the spine. Actual length needed is $\frac{5}{8}$" longer than height of the spine, but the additional length will function as a needle and may be bent during the weaving. Cut the leading edge of the tab to a point. After tab is woven, it will be trimmed to extend $\frac{5}{16}$" over the head and $\frac{5}{16}$" below the tail.

Gently insert tip of bone folder down from the head into station 5 slit to open it for the tab. Weave the pointed end of the tab underneath the 4th division of the spine. Pull tab down across top of third division. If you have a two ply cover, weave under the outer spine only.

Insert tip of bone folder, coming down, into the slit at station 3. Weave the tab behind the second division. Pull tab down across the bottom division. Pull the point and crumpled areas, if any, $\frac{5}{16}$" beyond the tail. Trim head and tail overhang to extend $\frac{5}{16}$" beyond the cover.

Fold tab at head and tail and tuck the ends around the spine, between the cover and the sections.

If you have trouble pushing the tab under a division, it may be too wide. If that is not the problem, thread a darning needle with #18 thread. Stitch onto the point of the tab. Start the weaving by taking the needle under the fourth division and pulling.

Bert Weijermars, *Langsteetvariatie met strap,* sample binding of the *Long Stitch with Woven Spine-Tab.*

LACED JACKET *B*

Optional for Long Stitch with Woven Spine-Tab

Instead of weaving the spine-tab directly onto the sewn cover for the binding *Long Stitch with Woven Spine-Tab*, the tab or tape, can be used to weave a laced jacket on top the sewn cover. The tab can be the same paper of the same or different color or the tab can be a cloth ribbon.

If the jacket is added, do not use foredge turns-in on the sewn cover and do not reinforce spine. The jacket will provide these as a 2-ply cover.

Dimensions of Jacket

The jacket is measured in the same manner as *Jacket* A, See page 153.

Spine Cuts

Stand the folded jacket to the left of the sewn book, with the spines tangent. Mark the positions of the slits of the sewn spine onto the right hinge-fold of the jacket. Stand jacket on the right of the sewn book, spines tangent and mark the positions of the slits on the sewn spine on the left hinge-fold of the jacket.

Cut the four slits on the jacket, creating five divisions. Cut along both hinge-folds starting at the end of the first division, down to the beginning of the third. This will remove the second division from the spine of the jacket. Cut along both hinge-folds starting at the end of the third division, down to the beginning of the fifth. This will remove the fourth division.

Spine-Tab

The tab will be cut at least ⅛" narrower than the width of the backbone. If the tab is made of paper, it will be cut 3" taller than the spine of the jacket. This is because the leading edge may become crumpled while weaving and will be trimmed down to size after woven. If a cloth ribbon is used, it, too, should be a little longer than the final height of the tab.

Weaving

A needle and thread are attached to the leading edge of either the paper or cloth tab to guide it under the divisions. Needle should be longer than the height of a spine division.

1. Sit the jacket in place. Gently insert the tip of a bone folder at the top of the second division of the sewn cover, to open the slit.

2. Slide needle under the second division and pull the tab under the second and half way over the third division of the jacket.

3. Insert tip of bone folder at the top of the fourth division of the sewn cover, to pry open the slit. Slide needle under the fourth division of the sewn cover and pull the tab under that division and half way over the fifth division of the jacket. Clip the thread.

4. Pull the tab down until it extends over both head and tail. Trim both extensions to ¼".

5. Fold the tab at head and tail and tuck the ends under, between the sewn cover and book block.

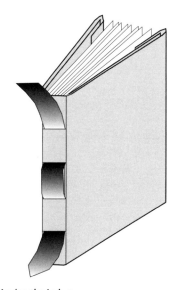

Lacing the Jacket

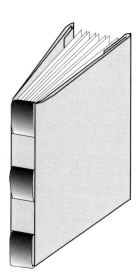

Jacket *B* Attached

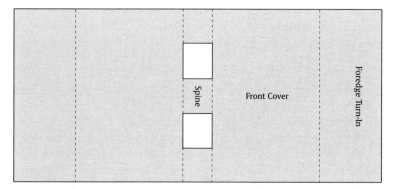

Layout of Jacket *B*

LONG STITCH with CHAIN

This binding is similar to the *Variation on the Long Stitch,* with the addition of link stitching across the second and fourth divisions to form a chain. This gives another means of securing the book block as a unit; the spine has an added decorative element.

Since the second and fourth divisions of the spine are not free-floating but attached to the backbone, exploration of a woven tab or jacket is not possible.

PREPARATION

The sections, cover and length of thread are prepared the same as for *Long Stitch through Slotted Wrapper Cover.*

Sewing Stations

Placement of four pierced sewing stations will be equidistant, dividing the height of the backbone into five divisions. Mark these four stations on one section as a guide.

There are an additional two pierced stations, where the link stitch occurs. One of these is at the center of second division from the tail. The other is midway in division 4. Mark these stations.

Now there are a total of six pierced sewing stations marked on the section. With the head and tail as wrapping stations, there is a total of 8 stations. Station 1 is the tail and station 8 is the head. Stations 3 and 6 will be where the link stitches are made.

Mark the remaining three sections, use the first as a guide. Pierce all the stations.

Cover Sewing Stations

Lay the unfolded cover open on the table with the inside facing up. Lay the first section on the cover, lining up the fold of the section with one hinge-fold. Mark the six pierced stations on the hinge-fold, using one section as a guide. Move the section over, lining up the fold of the section with the other hinge-fold. Mark the stations on the hinge-fold.

Lay aside the section, place the cover on a cutting surface. At stations number 2, 4, 5 and 7, make a horizontal slit from the dot on one hinge-fold, across the spine to the corresponding mark.

Stations 3 and 6 on the cover spine are pierced, instead of slit. At station 3, pierce four holes horizontally across the spine. Each hole corresponds with a section. Do not place the two extreme holes directly on the hinge-fold. Space the holes equidistantly across the width of the spine. Mark and pierce the four holes at station 6 in the same manner.

ELABORATED SEWING PROCEDURE
Sewing the First Section

Lay the first section within the cover, tangent to the proper hinge-fold. Start at sewing station 2 on the inside of the section.

1. Proceed through the station and slit. Pull all but 4" of thread through to the outside of the spine. Proceed along the spine, close to the hinge-fold.
2. Wrap around the head of the spine to the inside of the section. Proceed to station 2. Pull thread taut until the dangling thread is shortened to about 1½" or just enough to tie a knot. Tie a Square Knot at station 2, pulling towards the tail to tighten. Make sure the stitch on the spine has not crept over onto the side-cover before knot is tied. See page 72.
3. Proceed on the inside of the section to station 3. Take the needle through the section and cover station. Pull thread to outside.

    Place the needle back into sewing station 3 on the spine, into station 3 of the section. Pull most of thread to inside, leaving a small loop of thread on the spine at station 3. Insert a small darning or curved needle into the loop. Continue to pull thread on inside of section until it holds the needle snugly. This will adjust the loop to a very small size. Later the needle will be removed and the loop, when bent sideways on the spine, should not extend beyond the next pierced station. In the meantime, the extra needle will insure you do not pull the tiny loop to the inside of the section and lose it.

On the Bench

Proceed on the inside of the section, to sewing station 4. Go through the station of the section, through the cover slit, to the outside of the spine.

4. Proceed on the spine to the next slit. Take the needle through the slit, close to the hinge-fold, through the fifth sewing station to inside of the section. Proceed on the inside of the section to the sixth sewing station. Take the needle through the section and cover of station 6. Pull thread to outside. From the outside of the spine, place the needle back into sewing station 6, through the cover and the section. Pull most of thread to inside the section, leaving a small loop of thread on the spine at station 6. Insert another small darning needle or curved needle, into the loop and continue to pull thread on inside of section until it holds the darning or curved needle snugly.

Proceed on the inside of the section to sewing station 7. Go through the station of the section, through the cover slit, to the outside of the spine.

5. Proceed on the spine, close to hinge-fold, to the tail. Wrap around the tail. Proceed inside the section to station 7. Take the needle though the section only. Do not go through cover slit. Pull thread to outside of the section.

Sewing the Second Section

6. Grasp second section and take needle through mountain peak of station 7.

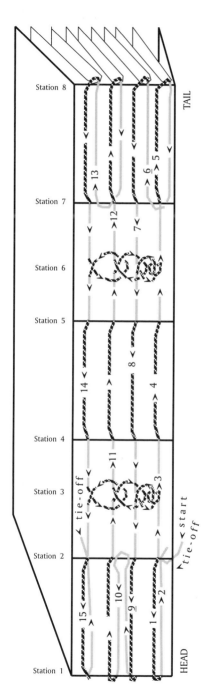

Do not go through the station on the cover. Pull the thread to the inside, as you position the second section against the inside of the spine-cover. Take the thread on the inside of the section, wrap around the tail. Proceed on the spine to the next slit at station 7. Go through the slit and section of station number 7 to the inside.

7. Proceed inside the section to station 6. Go through section and cover slit to outside. Remove darning needle from the adjacent loop. Take the threaded needle through the loop, which will anchor the linking. Pull the thread tight. Then, drop forward. Take the threaded needle back into station 6 on the spine, through the cover and section to the inside.

   Each time you create a link, it is important to be consistent in the direction. Dropping forward forms a *locking link stitch*. Dropping backwards would form a *lapping* U *stitch* as chain which lies flatter but there is more danger of tearing. The locking link stitch is stronger. Consistent pressure in the links controls the size and shape of each segment in the chain. Proceed inside the section to station 5. Go through the section and cover slit to outside.

8. Proceed along the spine to station 4. Go through slit and section to inside. Proceed inside the section to station 3. Go through the section and cover to outside. Remove the darning needle from the adjacent loop. Take the needle down through the loop. Pull thread tight. Take the threaded needle back into second section at station 3, through the cover and section to the inside. This has formed a link stitch on the spine. Proceed inside the section to station 2. Go through the section and cover slit of station 2 to outside spine.

9. Proceed along the spine and wrap around the head. Proceed inside the second section. Go through the section only. Do not take the needle through the cover slit. Pull thread to outside of the section.

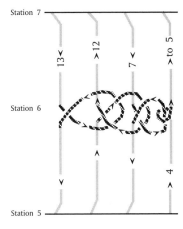

Detail of the Link Stitch for Division 4

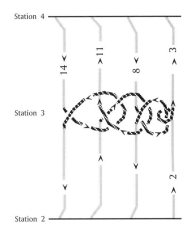

Detail of the Link Stitch for Division 2

Sewing the Third Section

10. Grasp third section and take needle through mountain peak of station 2. Do not go through the station on the cover. Pull the thread to the inside, as you position the third section against the inside of the spine-cover.

    Proceed inside the section, wrap around the head to the outside. Proceed on the spine to station 2. Take the needle through slit at station 2, through the section to the inside.

    Proceed on the inside of the section to station 3. Take the needle through the section and cover station. Pull thread to outside. With the needle above, go down behind the two threads of the adjacent link to form a chain. Take the needle back up into station 3, through the cover and section to the inside.

11. Proceed inside the section to station 4. Go through the section and cover slit to outside. Proceed along the spine to the next slit. Take the needle through the slit, through the fifth sewing station to inside of the section.

    Proceed on the inside of the section to the sixth sewing station. Take the needle through the section and cover of station 6. Pull thread to outside. From above come down behind the two threads of the adjacent link to form a chain. Take the needle back into sewing station 6, through the cover and section to the inside.

12. Proceed inside the section to station 7.

    Go through the section and cover slit to outside. Proceed along the spine to the tail. Wrap around the tail and proceed inside the section to station 7. Go through the section only. Do not take the needle through the cover slit. Pull thread to outside of the section.

Sewing the Fourth Section

13. Grasp fourth section and take needle through mountain peak of station 7. Do not go through the station on the cover. Pull the thread to the inside, as you position the fourth section against the inside of the spine-cover. Proceed inside the section, wrap around the tail. Proceed along the spine to the next slit in the cover.

    Take the needle through the slit and section of sewing station number 7 to the inside. Proceed inside the section to station 6. Go through section and cover slit to outside. Pull thread tight.

    From above come down behind the two threads of the adjacent link to form a chain. Go back into sewing station 6 on the spine, through the cover and section to the inside.

    Proceed inside the section to station 5. Go through the section and cover slit to outside.

14. Proceed along the spine to station 4. Go through slit and section to inside. Proceed inside the section to station 3. Go through the section and cover to outside. Slip the needle down behind the adjacent link to form a chain. Go back into sewing station 3 on the spine, through the cover and section to the inside.

Proceed along the section to station 2. Go through the section and cover slit of station 2 to outside.

15. Proceed along the spine and wrap around the head. Proceed inside the section to station 2. Before you tie the knot, check to be sure this last stitch on the spine has not slipped over onto the side-cover.

Tie a Half Hitch, page 73, on the inside of the section, at the station, by passing the needle behind the inside stitch between the first and second stations. Tighten knot by pulling towards the head.

REVIEW, or CONDENSED SEWING PROCEDURE
Sewing the First Section

1. Start on the inside at station 2. Go through station 1. Pull all but 4" of thread through to the outside.
2. Proceed on the spine, close to the hinge-fold. Wrap around the head and continue on the inside to station 2. Pull, reducing loose end of thread to 1½". Tie a Square Knot.
3. Proceed on the inside to station 3. Go through to the outside. Go back into station 3, pulling most of thread to inside, leaving a small loop on the spine. Insert a darning needle into the loop. Pull thread until snug. Proceed on inside to station 4. Go through to outside.
4. Proceed to next slit. Go through station 5 to inside. Proceed to station 6. Go through to outside. Go back into station 6, to inside, leaving a small loop on spine. Insert another darning needle into the loop. Pull until snug. Proceed to station 7. Go through to outside.
5. Proceed on the spine, close to the hinge-fold. Wrap around the tail, proceed on the inside to station 7. Go through the section only.

Sewing the Second Section

6. Grasp the second section. Take the needle through mountain peak of station 7. Do not go through the cover. Pull thread to the inside. Position the section in the spine-cover. Proceed within the section, wrap around the tail. Proceed on the spine to station 7. Go through station 7 to the inside.
7. Proceed to station 6. Go to outside. Remove the darning needle. Proceed down through the anchoring loop. Go back into station 6 to the inside. Proceed to station 5. Go through to the outside.
8. Proceed to station 4. Go through to the inside. Proceed to station 3. Go through to the outside. Remove the darning needle.

Go down through the loop. Go back into station 3 to the inside. Proceed to station 2. Go through to outside.

9. Proceed to the head and wrap. Proceed inside, out station 2 of section only. Do not take the needle through cover slit. Pull thread to outside.

Sewing the Third Section

10. Grasp third section. Take needle through mountain peak of station 2. Do not go through cover. Pull thread to inside. Position section against spine-cover. Wrap around the head. Proceed on the outside to station 2. Go through station 2 to inside. Proceed to station 3. Go through to the outside. Slip needle down behind the two threads of the adjacent link to form a chain. Go back into station 3 to the inside.

11. Proceed to station 4. Go through to the outside. Proceed to next slit. Go through station 5 to the inside. Proceed to station 6. Go through to the outside. Pull thread to outside. Slip needle down behind adjacent link to form a chain. Go back inside at station 6.

12. Proceed to station 7. Go through to outside. Proceed to the tail. Wrap around to inside, go through station 7 of section only. Do not take the needle through cover. Pull thread to outside.

Sewing the Fourth Section

13. Grasp fourth section. Take needle through mountain peak of station 7. Do not go through cover. Pull thread to inside. Position section against spine-cover. Proceed inside, wrap around the tail. Proceed along the spine to station 7. Go through station 7 to inside. Proceed to station 6. Go through to outside. Slip needle down behind adjacent link to form a chain. Go back into station 6 to inside. Proceed to station 5. Go through to outside.

14. Proceed to station 4. Go through to inside. Proceed to station 3. Go through to outside. Slip the needle down behind adjacent link to form a chain. Go back into station 3 to inside. Proceed to station 2. Go through station 2 to outside.

15. Proceed along the spine. Wrap around the head. Proceed inside to station 2. Tie-off with a Half Hitch.

Bert Weijermars, *Langsteek met ketting,* sample binding, 1994, Long Stitch with Chain.

BUTTONHOLE STITCH

One of the beauties of this binding is the repetition of wrapping the spine at the head and tail, which echoes vertical folds of the exposed sections.

The *Buttonhole Stitch* forms a bead which tightens the wrapping as well as giving a decorated border. Simply taking the needle down through the loop does not give a locked stitch. Using the standard stitch used to sew on buttons as a locked stitch and forming a bead was suggested by Valerie Mayse at Penland School[9]. Valerie said the twist was referred to as the *buttonhole stitch*. I thought that would be a good name to describe the binding. My thanks to Valerie.

SECTIONS

The sections must be created by assembling folios within folios. You cannot fold down sections for this binding, as the head and tail cannot be trimmed after sewing. Thread is wrapped around each section onto the spine-cover at the head and tail.

This binding should have at least 8 sections, because the wrapping on the spine looks better with a number of repetitions.

COVER

Width of the spine-cover is the depth of the book block while applying slight pressure. Remember this thickness when sewing. If you space the sections too far apart, you will not be able to get all the sections into the cover. If sewn tightly compressed, the spine will be wider than the total of the sections.

HEIGHT of the cover is exactly the same as the book block, since the sewing wraps around the sections onto the spine.

WIDTH of the total cover is the sum of the width of one foredge turn-in, *plus* the front side-cover, *plus* the spine, *plus* the back side-cover, *plus* its foredge turn-in.

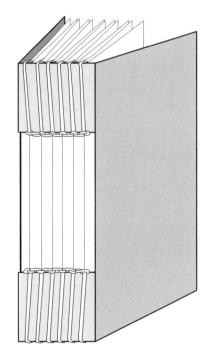

Spine Supports

The *Flat Back* has been specifically modified for this binding. The center division of the spine is slit and folded back towards the head and tail to form two supports. This requires three cuts on the spine.

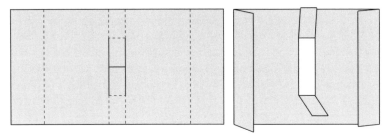

The economy of this design is the opening on the spine folds back to make 2-ply supports which are not pasted, but held in place by the sewing.

1. Cut horizontally, in from the hinge-fold at one side-cover, across the spine to the other hinge-fold. This cut is equidistant from the head and the tail.
2. Cut vertically, on each hinge-fold from a point ¼ the way down from the head, to a point ¼ the way up from the tail. The length of each vertical cut is ½ the height of the spine and centered on the spine.

The three cuts create two tabs in the form of an *H*. Fold the top tab up and in, behind the top ¼ of the spine. Hold the bottom tab down, in behind the bottom ¼ of the spine. Tabs are on the inside of the spine-cover. The spine has now been altered to become a 2-ply support at the head and tail. The book block is sewn onto the reinforced supports. For an elaborate cover for this binding see page 82.

Variations on the Spine Supports

After completing this binding, you may wish to bind another and vary the size and proportion of the spine supports. The bottom support might be taller than the top to suggest a base.

You might remove more of the center of the spine. For a book with a spine less than 6", each support can be as small as ⁵⁄₁₆" in height. Making the tabs larger than ½ the height of the spine will require trimming them at the head and tail, once they have been folded behind the supports.

For larger books, 6 to 10" tall, supports must be at least 1" in height to bear the weight of the book block. The Button-hole binding is not practical for a book taller than about 10". The spine opening can continue onto the side-covers.

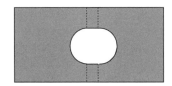

This allows a small portion of the first and last page to be seen at the center of the spine-edge. The title, author and date could be printed in these locations on the first and last page. It saves the expense of having to print the covers.

Sew the sections onto a *Layered Cover,* page 84. Prepare the inner cover as above. Remove the tabs on the spine on the outer cover. Sandwich the two covers and bind as one. Layered covers can be cut away in areas, to reveal levels and colors of one or two covers beneath the outer cover.

The drawing to the left is a layered cover with book block, prior to sewing. The lighter outer cover is shorter in height. It has a larger rectangular opening, which allows a border of the inner cover to show. In addition, the outer cover has a large foredge turn-in with zig-zag edges, which appears as the third layer. Behind that appears the fourth layer, the first page of the book block.

Optional Pleat

A book block pleat with endsheets might be fitted between the sections and the cover. This would serve its purpose of not having cracks seen in between sections, as the pages are turned. Its effect would be more a visual one on the outside of the spine. Since the peaks of the sections are exposed on the spine, a book block pleat of a different color might be a means of elaboration of design and color. See *Book Block Pleat,* page 319.

Keith Smith, *Drawn From Reality,* Book Number 123, 1989. Edition of 300. There is no book block pleat on this binding. Cover is not printed. Title, date and author printed on first and last page of the book is seen with the covers closed. 18 x 14 x 3 cm.

SEWING STATIONS

Each section will have two pierced sewing stations. The head and the tail serve as wrapped stations. Sit the book block into the cover. The pierced stations on the sections will be level with or preferably, $\frac{1}{32}$" underneath the bottom edge of the top spine support and the top edge of the bottom.

Mark the stations on the mountain peaks of the sections using the edge of the spine supports as a guide. Remove the sections from the cover and pierce the book block stations. There are no sewing stations pierced or slit on the spine-cover. The thread will wrap the support at the head and the tail.

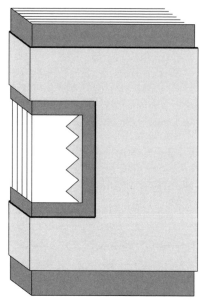

Book block and layered cover ready to sew. This layered cover has an outer paper smaller than the primary cover and in a lighter contrasting tone. Only the outer cover has a foredge turn-in. Both covers are sewn at once.

Thread

Start with 6' of heavily waxed thread. Amount of thread needed depends on the height of the support and number of sections. If more is needed, add inside the section with a Weaver's Knot.

SEWING PROCEDURE

The sewing at the head is done first. Then turn the book upside down so the head of the book is sitting on the table. Use the same procedure and sew the remaining set of sewing stations around the other support.

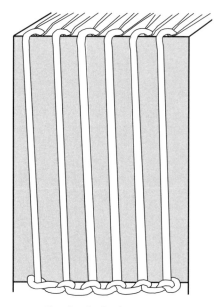

Forming the Bead

Sewing the First Section

Sit the first section into place against the hinge-fold. Start on the inside of the section at the pierced station.

1. Go through to the outside, leaving four inches inside the section. Proceed up the outside of the support, close to the hinge-fold. Wrap around head then come down the inside of the section to the pierced station.

    Pull to adjust the dangling thread to 1½". Tie a Square Knot at the station. Make sure the wrapped stitch has not slipped off the support onto the side-cover. Tighten knot by pulling towards the tail.

2. Take the needle out of the pierced station to the outside. To start the beading, slip the needle under the stitch on the outside of the spine support, towards the initial side-cover. The needle will be heading in the reverse direction in which the sewing is progressing.

Sewing the Second Section

3. Sit the next section into position. Take the needle through the mountain peak of the new section to the inside. Pull most of the thread to inside, leaving a small loop outside, about the size of the diameter of a pencil. Proceed up the inside, wrap around the head and proceed down the support.

Forming the Bead

4. Take the needle through the loop from underneath to form the bead. Pull downward to tighten.

Alternative Beading

Another method of creating the beading is to omit step number 4 and replace it with step number 4A.

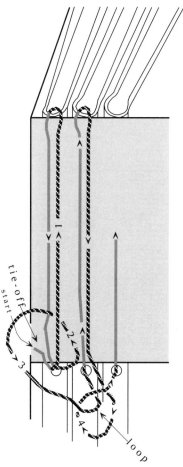

Sewing the first and second sections

4A. Proceed up the inside of the spine and wrap around the head and proceed down the support, taking the needle down through the loop, which first has been twisted 180° to the left. Pull the thread through in a downward movement to tighten. Adjust shape of the bead if necessary. Loop can be twisted to the right each time for a different shaped bead.

Remaining Sections

5. To sew the remaining sections follow steps 3 and 4 or in the alternative, 4A. After sewing the final section, go back into mountain peak to inside.

Valerie Mayse, Buttonhole Stitch, 1989. Sections are pamphlet sewn onto the pleat.

Tie-Off with a half Hitch by taking the needle under the stitch on the inside of the section and then looping through that loop. Tighten this overhand knot by pulling down towards the tail. Repeat the overhand to form a square knot. Thread the needle again. Flip the book over and make a separate sewing at the other end of the book.

Bert Weijermars, *Knoopsgatensteek,* sample binding of the Button Hole Stitch.

LONG STITCH / LINK STITCH

Langstitch und Kettenstitch

This is an eight-section binding with exposed vertical stitches on the spine, with a row of chaining at the head and tail. A single thread is used to sew the sections into the paper cover. It is an older German book style. Pamela Spitzmueller, Conservator at the University of Iowa, researched it and uses a version of this binding for conservation. She has taught the binding at many workshops and you and I are now indebted to her.

PREPARATION

The top and bottom row of stations on the cover, stations 1 and 6, are for the link stitches, creating a row of chains at the head and tail. Stations 2 through 5 on the cover create the long stitches. The sections double up, sharing the long stitch stations. Paired sections are called a set. Cover stations 2*A*, 3*A*, 4*A* and 5*A* are used to sew the first two sections or *Set 1*. All the 2–5 *B* stations on the cover are shared by the third and fourth sections, called *Set 2*. The letters determine how many pairs of sections or sets are used in the book block. Since this binding will be described for 8 sections,

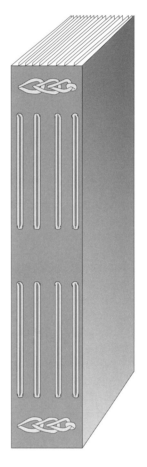

cover stations 2–5 have 4 pairs of shared stations, *A*, *B*, *C* and *D*. It is a binding of 4 sets.

If a 5 set binding, yielding 10 sections, is desired, a fifth set lettered as *E* would be placed on the spine for stations 2 through 5. In addition, cover stations 1 and 6 would need an additional lettered station. Stations 1 and 6 always contain one more pierced position for linking than stations 2 through 5, the long stitch stations.

As described, this binding requires an even number of sections.

The overhang cover for this binding is *Flat Back with Borders*, page 287. Construct the cover with 2" turns-in at head, tail and foredges. Make the square of the book ¼".

Depth of the spine-cover is measured with the book block only slightly compressed, much looser than the sections for the previous *Long Stitch* bindings. This is because the stations on the cover are pierced, rather than slit, no closer together than ⅛" or they may rip, perforating during sewing.

Since the cover stations are at least ⅛" apart, the book block must consist of thicker rather than thinner sections. If the sections are not thick, they still can be used. However, the pierced sewing stations on the spine-cover determine the spacing of the sections, resulting in a small gap between thinner sections.

Heavy thread should be used to better show the link stitches. Start with 4' of heavily waxed thread. If more is needed, add inside the section with a Weaver's Knot.

Sewing Stations for the Sections

Create 8 sections. Each section will have six sewing stations, numbered from the head to the tail. Mark one section:

The first station will be ¼" from the head.

The sixth station is ¼" in from the tail.

The second station is ½" from the first station.

The fifth station is ½" from the sixth station.

The third and fourth stations are equally spaced between the second and fifth stations.

Mark the remaining sections and pierce the sections only.

Sewing Stations for the Cover

Open the constructed cover and place it on the table with the inside of the cover facing up. Lay a folded section with the mountain peak tangent to the left hinge-fold. Center the section on the fold, since the cover is taller than the section. Mark the six sewing stations of the section along the hinge-fold.

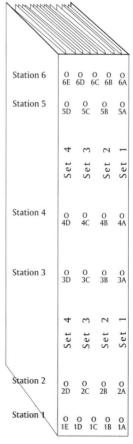

Move the section over, with the mountain peak tangent to the right hinge-fold and center it. Mark the six sewing stations of the section along that hinge-fold. This is to position only the rows of the sewing stations which the sections and cover have in common, not the number of pierced positions. The cover has fewer number of stations than the total of the stations of the book block. This is because the sections are sewn in sets, sharing the long stitch stations, 2 through 5 on the spine-cover.

At the row or level of the first sewing station on the cover, pierce 5 horizontal holes equidistantly across the spine. Do not pierce on the hinge-folds. The two extreme positions of the row of holes should be ⅛" in from the hinge-folds.

These 5 holes will be used for the link stitches at the head. The 5 holes will be assigned letters to assist in the pattern of sewing. With the inside of the cover facing up, the hole on the far left is sewing station 1, hole A. The next hole is sewing station 1B, 1C, 1D and at the far right, station 1E.

At the sixth sewing station, pierce 5 horizontal holes equidistantly across the spine. The two extreme positions are ⅛" in from the hinge-folds. These 5 holes are assigned letters. At the far left is station 6A. At the far right, station 6E. Stations 6A through 6E will be used for the link stitch at the tail.

At the second sewing station on the inside of the spine-cover, pierce 4 holes horizontally across the spine. The first and last hole is not on the hinge-folds. Position of the holes are at the center of each set. The holes are assigned letters. At the far left is station 2A. At the far right, station 2D.

Pierce 4 holes in the same manner at the third, fourth and fifth stations across the spine. These stations will also be referred to as A through D.

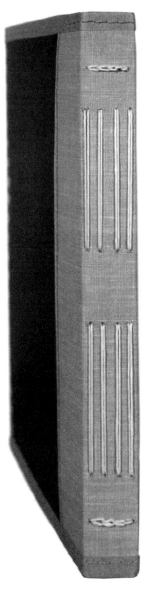

Long Stitch/Link Stitch. A paper cover with foredge turns-in is reinforced by machine sewing book cloth around the spine prior to binding. Cotton bias tape is machine sewn along the head, tail and the turn-in.

SEWING PROCEDURE

Looking at the inside of the spine, this sewing will be described starting at the left hinge-fold and proceeding to the right. Sewing proceeds to the tail, then back across to the head with long stitches sharing stations as a set. The first and sixth stations are turn-arounds for sewing back and forth across the spine. They will also lock the sets with link stitches.

Sewing the First Section

Hold the cover with the inside facing you.

1. Put the first section in place at the hinge-fold. Open the section to the middle. Start the sewing from the inside of the section, at the *second* sewing station.

    Take the point of the needle through the section at station 2. Extend the point of the needle into the cover sewing station 2A, on the far left of the spine. Pull thread to the outside of the spine, allowing 4" of loose thread to dangle on the inside of the section.

    Turn the section/cover with spine facing you. Proceed on the spine along hinge-fold.

2. Go through spine station 3A and through mountain peak of the third station of the section. Pull thread inside, reducing the amount of loose thread dangling at station 2 until it is 2".

SEWING THE FIRST SET
Outside view of the spine-cover

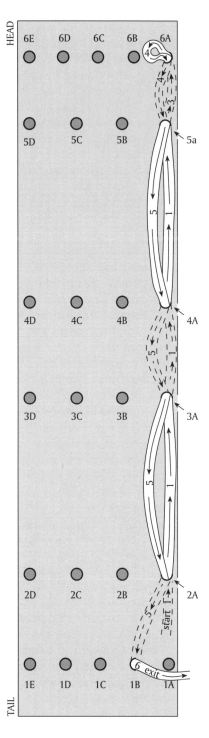

Proceed to station 4 on the inside. Go through 4 and cover station 4*A* to the outside.

Proceed to station 5*A*. Go through 5*A* and 5 of the section.

3. Proceed on the inside to station 6. Go through station 6 and cover station 6*A*. Pull the thread to the outside.

Place the point of the needle back into cover station 6*A* and stop. Do not take needle into the section. Close the first section. See detailed illustration on page 184.

Sewing the Second Section

Add the second section, moving the mountain peak back onto the point of the needle at station 6.

4. Pull most of the thread to the inside of section, leaving a small loop on the spine at station 6*A*. Insert a small darning needle into the loop. Pull the thread on the inside until the loop snugly holds the darning needle. This will adjust the loop to a very small size. Later the darning needle will be removed. When bent sideways the loop should not extend beyond station 6*B*. In the meantime, the darning needle will insure you do not pull the tiny loop to the inside of the section. Proceed inside the second section to station 5. Go through 5 and 5*A* to the outside.

5. Proceed to station 4*A*. Go through 4*A* and 4 of the section, to the inside. Proceed to 3. Go through station 3 and 3*A* to the outside. Proceed and go through 2*A* and 2 to the inside. Proceed to 1. Go though station 1 and 1*B* to the outside.

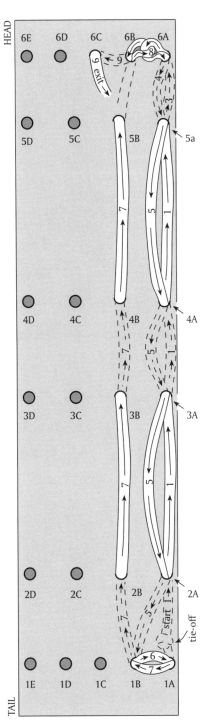

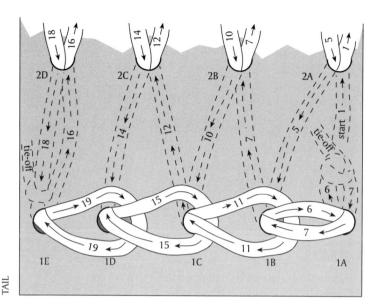

Detail of the sewing at the tail. The sewing starts at Station 2A, not iA. Tie-off is inside the first section step 6.

6. Proceed to station 1*A*. Go through 1A of the spine into station 1 of the first section. Tie a square knot on the inside at station 1 with the dangling thread. Clip the dangling thread to ¾". Do not clip the thread on which the needle is attached. See diagram above.

    Take the needle out through station 1 of the first section and station 1*A* of the spine. Proceed across the spine. Insert the needle part way into station 1*B* of the spine and stop. Do not take the needle into the second section.

Sewing the Third Section

    Add the third section, moving the mountain peak back onto the point of the needle at station 1.

7. Pull the thread to the inside of section. Do not leave a loop on the spine. Proceed inside the third section to station 2. Go through 2 and 2*B* to the outside. Proceed to and through station 3*B* and 3 to the inside. Proceed to and through station 4 and 4*B* to the outside Go through 5*B* and 5 to the inside. Go though station 6 and 6*B* to the outside.

8. Remove darning needle. Take the threaded needle through the loop which is protruding from station 6*A* to create a link stitch. Proceed on the spine to 6*B*. Insert the needle part way into the spine at 6*B* and stop. Do not go into the third section.

9. Instead, proceed on the inside of the spine-cover. Take the needle through spine station 6C, from the inside of the cover to the outside. Proceed across the spine to station 6B. Drop the needle back behind the chain at 6B and proceed to 6C on the spine. Insert the needle part way into the spine at 6C and stop. Do not go into the third section. In making the link stitch, keep the direction and pressure consistent in order to obtain uniformity in the chain. See diagram on page 184.

Sewing the Fourth Section

Add the fourth section, moving the mountain peak back onto the point of the needle at station number 6.

10. Pull the thread to the inside of section, adjusting the chain. Proceed inside to station 5. Go through 5 and 5B to the outside. Proceed along the spine. Go through 4B and 4 to the inside. Proceed to 3. Go through 3 and 3B to the outside. Proceed on the outside. Go through 2B and 2 to the inside. Proceed inside. Go though station 1 and 1C.

11. Proceed on the spine to 1B. Drop the needle back behind the two horizontal stitches at station 1B. Proceed to station 1C, forming a link stitch. Insert the needle part way into station 1C and stop. Do not take the needle into the fourth section.

Sewing the Fifth Section

Add the fifth section, moving the mountain peak back onto the point of the needle at station 1.

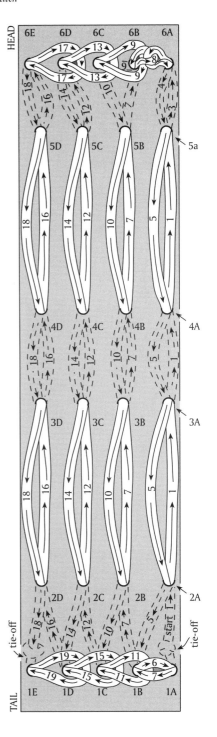

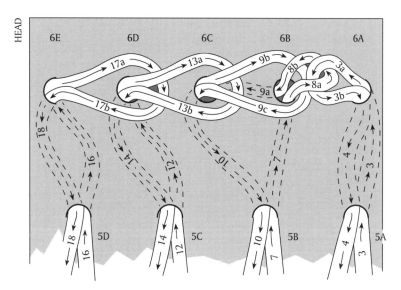

HEAD

Detail of the sewing at the head. Step 3a exits the first section and cover. Step 3b goes back into cover station 6A, but into station 6 of the second section. A needle though the loop of thread keeps the loop on the outside until step 8 links the loop. Step 9a enters the cover, only, at station 6B and exits 6C. Step 9b links under the threads and 9c re-enters 6C of the cover into station 6 of the fourth section.

12. Pull thread to the inside adjusting link stitch. Proceed inside section to station 2. Go through 2 and 2C to the outside. Proceed along the spine. Go through station 3C and 3 to the inside. Proceed to 4. Go through station 4 and 4C to the outside. Proceed on the outside. Go through 5C and 5 to the inside. Proceed on the inside. Go through 6 and 6D to the outside.

13. Proceed to 6C. Take the needle behind both threads at 6C and proceed to station 6D on the spine. Insert the needle part way into the spine at 6D and stop. Do not go into the fifth section.

Sewing the Sixth Section

Add the sixth section, moving the mountain peak back onto the point of the needle at station 6.

14. Pull the thread to the inside of the section, until proper size of link is achieved. Proceed on the inside of the sixth section to station 5. Go through 5 and 5C to the outside. Proceed along the spine. Go through 4C and 4 to the inside. Proceed to 3. Go through station 3 and 3C to the outside. Proceed on the outside. Go through 2C and 2 to the inside. Proceed inside. Go through station 1 and 1D to the outside.

15. Proceed on the spine to station 1*C*. Take the needle behind the chain at 1*C*. Proceed to station 1*D* on the spine. Insert needle part way into the spine at 1*D* and stop. Do not go into the sixth section.

Sewing the Seventh Section

Add the seventh section, moving the mountain peak back onto the point of the needle at station 1.

16. Pull thread to the inside adjusting link stitch. Proceed inside section to station 2. Go through 2 and 2*D* to the outside. Proceed along the spine. Go through station 3*D* and 3 to the inside. Proceed to 4. Go through station 4 and 4*D* to the outside. Proceed on the outside. Go through 5*D* and 5 to the inside. Proceed on the inside. Go through 6 and 6*E* to the outside.

17. Proceed to 6*D*. Take the needle behind the chain at 6*D* and proceed to station 6*E* on the spine. Insert the needle part way into the spine at 6*E* and stop. Do not go into the seventh section.

Sewing the Eighth Section

Add the eighth section, moving the mountain peak back onto the point of the needle at station 6.

18. Pull the thread to the inside of the section, until proper size of link stitch is achieved. Proceed on the inside of the eighth section to station 5. Go through 5 and 5*D* to the outside. Proceed along the spine. Go through 4*D* and 4 to the inside. Proceed to 3. Go through 3 and 3*D* to the outside. Proceed on the outside. Go through 2*D* and 2 to the inside. Proceed inside. Go through station 1 and 1*E* of the spine.

19. Proceed on the spine to 1*D*. Take the needle behind the chain at 1*D* and proceed to station 1*E* on the spine. Go through 1*E* and 1 of the eighth section. Proceed on the inside to station 2. Tie a Half Hitch at station 2 by slipping the needle under the stitch above the station, then taking the needle through the resulting loop. Do this again to form the knot. Tighten by pulling downward. See Page 73.

Sample binding of the long stitch/link stitch. Stations 2, 3, 5 and 6 for sections 1, 2, 7 and 8 as well as the cover have been altered to give a variation on the spine.

Pamela Spitzmueller, two samples of Long Stitch/Link Stitch. In these variations of the Long Stitch/Link Stitch, the linking forms chains on the spine with all the long stitches relegated to the inside of the sections. Both books have wooden spines.

SEWING onto TAPES

With Kettle Stitch

PREPARATION

Tapes

Non-adhesive linen tape supports, usually ¼" wide, is made for binding, but generally is only used if the sewing on the backbone is to be covered later. Leather or paper as a tape support might be used, but paper will wear out quickly as a hinge. better is two strips of book cloth glued back to back or book cloth glued to paper and then trimmed into tapes. To construct paper tapes see page 299. Each tape is approximately ¾" wide by 1⅔ times the width of the book block. Make at least two; you may wish more for structure or for appearance. There should not be too great a distance between tapes.

Center the length of each tape on the book block horizontally. Pinch the tape at the edges of the back to mark the hinge-folds.

Sewing Stations

Prepare however many sections desired. Each tape requires two sewing stations on the back, one on each side and tangent to every tape.

In addition there is a station ½" in from the head and a station the same distance from the tail. These are for the kettle stitches. Station 1 is at the head. Pierce the stations on the sections only.

Cover

I would suggest *Flat Back with Foredge Turns-In* or the *Z-Fold Flat Back*. Tapes are attached inside and the sewing is invisible. If you are sewing onto leather or decorative paper tapes, the same cover can be used. Weave the tapes onto the side-covers through slots. See page 82.

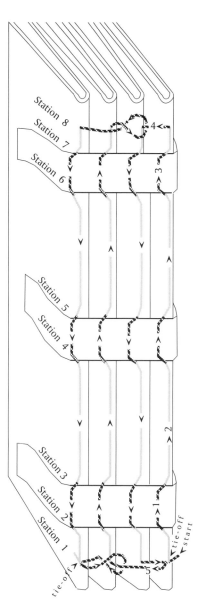

188 PART 2 DESCRIPTIONS OF BINDINGS

You may want separate side-covers. If a Flat Back cover is used the sewing should proceed through stations on the cover. Stations on the Flat Back cover are marked to line up with the stations on the sections. When sewing to the outside of a section, proceed through the cover station as well.

Modifying the Stitches

If the sewing on the spine is exposed you may wish to elaborate on basic sewing procedure. The exposed sewing on the backbone can be modified by use of macramé knots. Another color thread may be looped around the sewing on the back into a pattern of stitches and knots.

Thread

Length of thread required equals height of section times number of sections, adding one additional section height.

SEWING PROCEDURE
Sewing the First Section

1. Start on outside of the first section at sewing station 1. Proceed on inside to station 2 leaving 2″ of cord on the outside. Go out station 2. Place tape in position. Go over tape and into station 3.
2. Proceed inside, go out station 4. Set the next tape in position. Proceed over tape into station 5. Proceed on the inside, go out station 6. Place third tape in position.
3. Go over tape into 7. Come out 8, set next section in place.

Sewing the Second Section

4. Go in station 8 of next section which has been set into position. Go out station 7, over tape, back into station 6. Go out 5, over the middle tape, into station 4. Go out 3, over bottom tape into station 2. Come out station 1. Tie a knot with loose cord extending from the first section. Proceed to station 1 of the next section.

Sewing the Next Odd-Numbered Section

5. Go into station 1 of new section. Go out station 2, up over tape and inside station 3. Go out 4, over the tape, into station 5. Go out 6, over the tape into 7. Go out 8 and link the previous section to this with a *kettle stitch* which does three things: drops backward, links, slips under itself forming a locking stitch, climbs to the next section and enters. To do this, take the needle down under the stitch of the previous section at station 8. Slip under the thread. Climb to the next section and go into station 8 of new section. Kettle stitches are elaborately described in Volume III, *Exposed Spine Sewings*.[9]

Remaining Sections

6. Sew the even-numbered sections as in Step 4, using a kettle stitch at station 1 instead of a knot.
7. Sew the odd-numbered sections as in Step 5, a mirror procedure. tie-off after making the final kettle stitch. Pass the needle under the cord on the outside of the station, then take needle through the loop to form an overhand knot. Repeat the overhand procedure to form a square knot. Attach the covers.

Philip Zimmermann, untitled. Sewn onto split thongs, laced through wooden boards. 1980.

Susan Share, *In Foreign Trade,* board pages sewn onto tape (fabric strap) supports. 1990.

Keith Smith, untitled prototype of stair-stepping pages. Sewn onto tapes, laced through slots in the boards. 1990.

SEWING onto TAPE SUPPORTS

Without Kettle Stitch

PREPARATION

Supports

Use strips of leather or construct paper tapes, as described on page 299. Each support is approximately ¾" wide by 1⅔ times the width of the book block. Make at least two, but you may wish more for structure or appearance. Center each tape on the book block horizontally. Pinch the tape at the edges of the back-bone to mark the hinge-folds.

Sewing Stations

Prepare however many sections desired. Each tape requires two sewing stations on the back, one on each side and tangent to every tape.

For three tapes there are six stations, one on each side of the tapes. Station 1 is at the tail. Pierce the stations on the sections.

Cover

Any of the flat back covers will suffice. Since the tape sewing is not as attractive as the binding *Blanket Stitch with Slit Tape*, I would not suggest separate side-covers with an exposed spine. *Flat back with Foredge Turns-In* or *Z-Fold Flat Back* with foredge turns-in would be better. Tapes are laced through or sewn onto the side-covers.

Thread

Length of thread required equals height of section times number of sections, adding one additional section height.

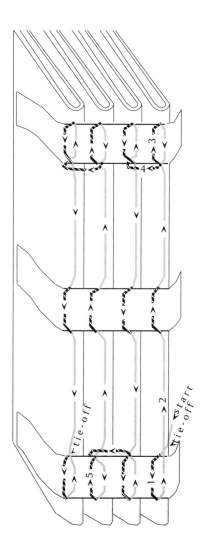

SEWING PROCEDURE
Sewing the First Section

Start on inside of the first section at sewing station 1.
1. Go through station 2 to outside, leaving 2" of cord on the inside. Place tape in position. Go over tape and into station 1.
2. Tie knot at station 2. Proceed inside, go out station 3. Set the next tape in position. Proceed over tape into station 4. Proceed on the inside, go out station 5. Place third tape in position.
3. Go over tape into 6. Come out 5, set next section in place.

Sewing the Second Section

4. Go in station 5 of next section, come out 6, back into 5 pulling the section tightly against the previous. Proceed inside to 4, come out over the tape, into station 3. Go out 2, over the tape into station 1. Come out station 2. Proceed to station 2 of the next section.

Sewing the Next Odd-Numbered Section

5. Go into station 2 of new section. Go out 1, up under the thread into station 2. Go out 3, over the tape, into 4. Go out 5, over the tape into 6. Go out 5, around the thread to the next section.

Remaining Sections

6. Proceed in the same manner, sewing down the even-numbered sections and up the odd.
7. Sew the even-numbered sections as in Step 4. Follow step 5 for the odd-numbered sections. tie-off by passing needle under the cord on the inside of the station, then taking needle through the loop and pull downward. Repeat the procedure to form a Half Hitch as described on page 73. Attach the covers.

Susan Share, *Vivian's Photos,* one-of-a-kind. Sections sewn onto cord. 1984. This book is used in performance. The book is played like an accordion, flapping audibly for rhythm. Xerox, board, cloth, acrylic, etching. 15.7 x 12.5 x 9 cm.

RAISED CORDS

Very little will be said in this book about sewing onto tapes and cords, since that is covered in *Exposed Spine Sewings* and *Bookbinding for Book Artists*. Sewing onto continuous paper supports is explored in Volume II of *Non-Adhesive Binding, 1–, 2– & 3–Section Sewings*.

Supported sewing is sewing onto tapes, cords or into a continuous support, such as a paper or vellum cover. Unsupported sewing is a structure based solely on the thread, such as the many Coptic bindings.

Whereas tapes require a sewing station on each side and tangent to the tape, sewing onto cords uses one station under the single or double cord. Tapes and cords almost always use a station at the head and tail for kettle stitches as the turn-around is sewing all along the spine.

Raised thong sewing of the twelfth and thirteenth century was an early supported sewing similar to this cross-section pattern of double raised cord.

Double Raised Cords

Later, to give a smooth look to the spine, sewing recessed cord became popular. The cord is pulled inside the book in tightening the sewing along the length of the section.

Sewing Recessed Cords

For non-adhesive bindings, raised cord sewing is better than recessed, as the section will not slide. In the late nineteenth century Cobden-Sanderson and Cockerell, Dove Bindery and Dove Press, revived the use of raised cords.

Sewing Raised Cords

For more information for sewing onto tapes and cords I refer you to my other books mentioned above.

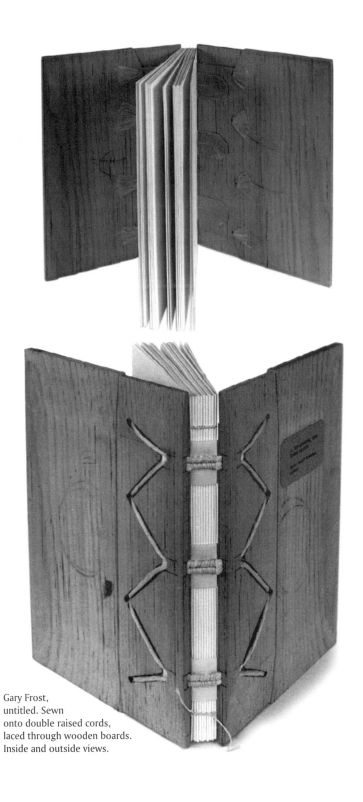

Gary Frost,
untitled. Sewn
onto double raised cords,
laced through wooden boards.
Inside and outside views.

Gary Frost, untitled. Sewn onto split leather thongs which are woven through wooden side-covers.

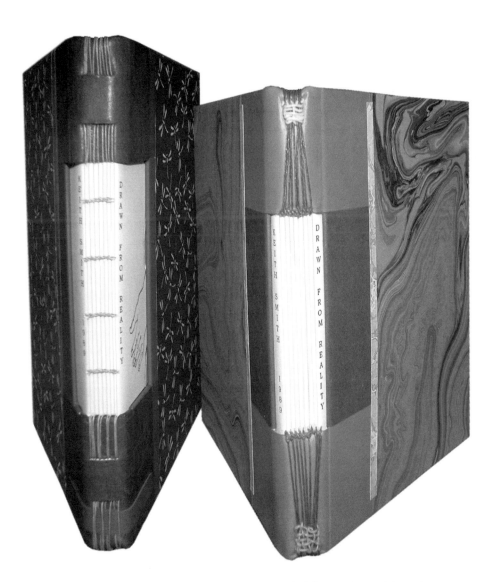

HARD COVER QUARTER LEATHER BINDINGS: On the left is a variation of the sewing
Variation on the Long Stitch, described on page 149. On the right is a variation of the
Buttonhole Stitch, page 171. These kangaroo leather bindings were made in March
2003, sewing copies of *Drawn From Reality,* Book 123. No paste or glue was used, fol-
lowing ideas presented in Non-Adhesive Binding Volume V, *Quick Leather Bindings.*
The illustration above is added to this edition to stress that any sewing described in
Volume I or Volume II Non-Adhesive Binding can be hard cover. You are not limited to
paper covers.

BLANKET STITCH with SLIT TAPES

This is a rapid and attractive sewing with an exposed spine. Each tape support is sewn individually. Separate side-covers are then attached.

PREPARATION

Sections

There must be an even number of sections. Use at least six, preferably more, in order for the suggested blanket stitching on the spine to show its pattern.

Supports

There are two tapes, each 1" in height. Length of the tapes should be at least 1⅓ times the width of a page. Tapes can be leather, reinforced paper or book cloth. See *Tape Supports and Hinges*, page 299.

Sewing Stations

Place the tapes across the back of the book block. One tape should be within an inch of the tail and the other an inch from the head. Mark, *but do not pierce* a row of stations at the top and bottom of each tape. Run a pencil across the sections using the top and bottom edge of each tape as a guide. This will make 4 sewing stations on each section, each tangent to the bottom or top of a tape. Remove the tapes.

Mark another station on each section, ½" above the first row of stations at the tail. These will be centered in the middle of the lower tape. Mark an additional station on each section, ½" below the top row of stations. These will be centered in the middle of the top tape.

Sewing Stations

Each section is now *marked* with six sewing stations, but *do not pierce* all the marks. The first station is at the head and number 6 is at the tail. Only some stations will be pierced and used on each section:

First Section pierce all six sewing stations.

All Even-Numbered Sections pierce sewing station numbers 1, 2, 4 and 5.

All Odd-Numbered Sections, Except Number 1 pierce stations number 2, 3, 5 and 6.

Center each tape across the backbone. Crease each tape at the edges of the back to make hinge-folds on the tapes. Make a horizontal slit centered on each tape from one hinge-fold to the other. The slits will be the width of the spine.

The slit on the bottom tape corresponds to sewing station 2 on the sections. The slit on the top tape is station 5.

Thread

Allow 2" of thread per section, for each tape.

Cover

Separate side-covers are attached.

SEWING PROCEDURE

Sewing procedure is the same for both tapes. The following describes the bottom tape. To sew the top tape, substitute 4 for station 1; 5 replaces 2; and 6 replaces 3.

Sewing the First Section

1. Start inside the section. Go through sewing station 2, through the slit on the tape. Pull all but 2" of thread to outside. Make sure the needle is positioned at the end of the slit on the tape, so that you can make full use of the width of the slit as sewing progresses. With each additional section, position of the thread through the slit will be determined by the thickness of the section. Proceed along the tape. Go through station 1. Tie a Square Knot on inside at station 2.

2. Proceed inside. Go out through station 3. Close the first section and add the second.

Sewing the Second Section

3. Go along the tape, through slit, into station 2 of new section.

4. Come out station 1. Close this section, add the next.

Third Section

5. Proceed on the tape, through slit and station 2 of this section.

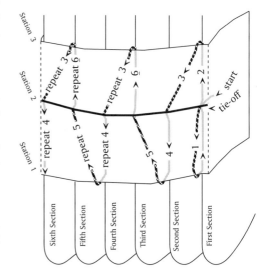

6. Proceed on the inside. Go out through station 3. Close the section and add the next.

Remaining Sections

For each additional even-numbered section, repeat steps number 3 and 4. For each additional odd-numbered section, repeat steps 5 and 6.

For the final section, go along the tape, take needle through slit, into station 2 of the last section. Proceed on the inside of the section and go out station 1. Close the section and you are ready to begin the beading.

Sewing will end with step 6 repeated, if the book block has an odd number of sections. Repeated step 4 will end the sewing, if there are an even number of sections.

Beading

7. Proceed across the back, past the second vertical stitch at the bottom edge of the tape. Slide the needle underneath the second stitch, heading in the direction of the first.

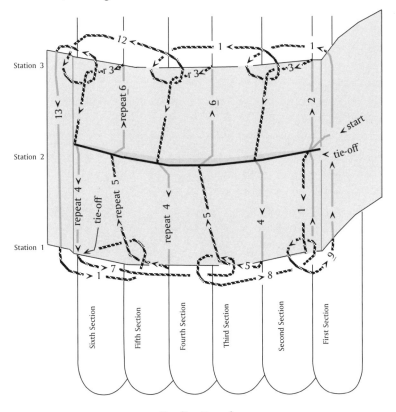

Beading Procedure

Pull thread until there is a tight loop at the bottom of the second stitch and push the loop down off the tape, just onto the section. This is the first bead, reminiscent of a blanket stitch in embroidery.

8. Proceed just beyond the next vertical stitch at bottom of the tape. Backtrack under this stitch, towards the second. Pull thread tight and push the bead down onto the section.

Proceed in this manner until you bead all the remaining vertical stitches at the bottom of the tape. As the beads are tightened they will yield an almost horizontal, zigzagging line.

9. Then go onto the side-cover, behind the tape, up to the top of the tape. Now the blanket stitching will proceed along the top, back to the first section.

10. Proceed from the side-cover, across the sections at the top of the tape. Go beyond the immediate vertical stitch at the top of the tape. Proceed backwards, under that stitch. Pull the thread tight, pushing the bead up, off the tape onto the section.

11. Proceed towards the next section, beyond the next vertical stitch.

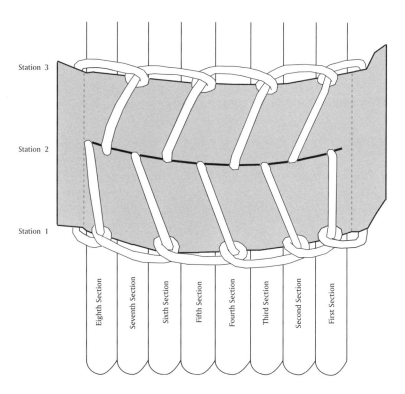

Exposed Spine Sewing and Beading

Proceed backwards, un-der the stitch. Pull thread tight, pushing the bead up, off the tape onto the section.

12. Continue until you have looped under the final vertical stitch at the top, completing zigzag line of beading along the top.

13. Take the needle behind the tape to the bottom of the tape. Proceed across the sections, next to the bottom of the tape.

14. Go beyond the first vertical stitch at the bottom of the tape. Backtrack under the stitch. Pull thread tight and form the bead.

Take the needle into sewing station 1 of the first section. Tie a Half Hitch, page 73, on inside of the section, at the second sewing station, by looping under the stitch that extends from station 2 to station 3, then take needle through the loop. Tighten by pulling downward. Repeat. Clip excess thread to ¾". Attach separate side-covers.

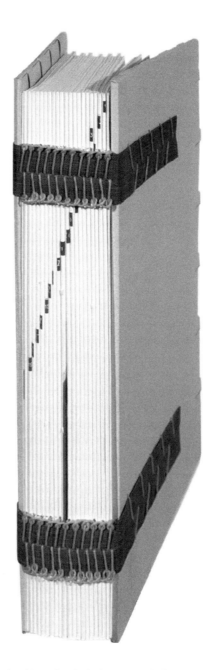

Keith Smith, *Books without Paste or Glue*, hand bound with *Blanket Stitch with Slit Tapes*, 1992. Boards were wrapped with paper which was elaborately tabbed to form a border of tabs along the head, tail and foredge. 23.5 x 16 x 5 cm.

Keith Smith,
prototype sewn with
Blanket Stitch with Slit Tapes, 1990.

Bert Weijermars,
blank binding of the
In-Tape Sewing
sewn on transparent strips of plastic.

IN-TAPE SEWING

PREPARATION

Sections

Use a minimum of 6 sections.

Tapes

Make 3 tapes, each ¾" wide by 1⅔ times the width of the book block. See *Tape Supports and Hinges*, page 299.

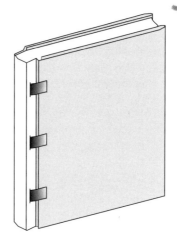

Thread

Length of thread required equals height of section times number of sections, adding one additional section height.

Sewing Stations

The sections have 6 sewing stations in 3 sets of pairs. Station 1 is ¾" in from the head. Station 2 is ½" above the first. Stations 3 and 4 are at the center of the backbone ½" apart. Station 5 is 1¼" in from the tail; station 6 is ¾" in from the tail. Pierce the stations on the sections.

Center the length of each tape on the back. Crease the tape at each spine-edge to denote the hinge-folds. Cut 2 horizontal slits on each tape from one hinge-fold to the other. Slits should be centered ½" apart to accommodate the sewing stations.

COVER

This binding has a cover which emphasizes the spine paper which extends ½" onto the side-covers. Remainder of side-covers is a separate paper reminiscent of a traditional quarter-leather binding.

The paper that is seen across the spine and extending slightly onto the side-covers is called the *outer paper*. It must be cover weight. The *inner paper* can be text or cover weight. It may be a decorative paper. The inner cover is seen on the inside and out of the side-covers.

Measurements for Outer Paper

HEIGHT is the same as the book block. Total width of the outer paper
    equals:
WIDTH of the book block minus ¾",
plus width of the book block minus ⅝",
plus width of the book block,

plus width of spine,
plus width of the book block,
plus width of the book block minus ⅝",
plus width of the book block minus ¾".
Cut and fold outer cover.

Measurements for Inner Paper

HEIGHT of the inner paper is the same as the book block. Total width of
the inner paper equals:

1½" (turn-in at spine)
plus width of the book block minus ⅝", (outside of front side-cover)
plus width of the book block, (inside of front side-cover)
plus width of spine,
plus width of the book block, (inside of back side-cover)
plus width of the book block minus ⅝" (outside of back side-cover).

Measurements for the inner paper are for cutting purposes only. Do
not fold the inner paper by measurements, but by fitting it within the
spine and around the foredge and spine-edge folds of the outer paper.
This will insure it does not buckle from not being wide enough between
folds or sag from being too large. Slit the covers for the tapes after the
sections are sewn onto the tapes.

SEWING PROCEDURE

Sewing the First Section

1. Start on the inside at sewing station 2. Go out through section and
   top slit in the tape. Take needle through bottom slit, into sewing
   station 1.
2. Proceed to station 2 and tie a knot. Do not clip the longer thread.
3. Proceed on the inside to station 3. Go out through 3 and the bottom
   slit of the center tape. Take the needle through top slit of tape, into
   station 4.
4. Proceed to station 5. Go out through 5 and bottom slit of the top
   tape. Go through the top slit of tape, into station 6. Proceed inside
   to station 5. Go out through station 5 and the bottom slit. Close the
   first section and add the second.

Sewing the Second Section

5. Proceed on the outside to sewing station 5 of the second section.
   Go through bottom slit of tape, into station 5.
6. Proceed inside to station 6. Go out 6 and top slit of tape. Proceed to
   station 5. Go through bottom slit and section to inside.
7. Proceed to station 4. Go out 4 and top slit of center tape. Proceed
   outside to station 3. Go in bottom slit to inside of section.

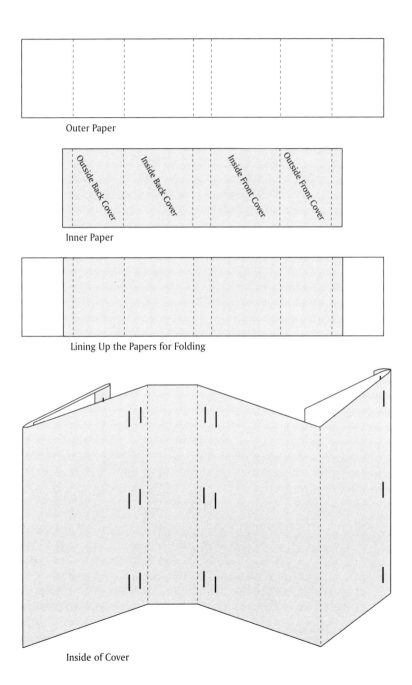

Outer Paper

Inner Paper

Lining Up the Papers for Folding

Inside of Cover

8. Proceed in-side to station 2. Go to outside to station 1. Go in bottom slit of tape to inside of section.

9. Proceed in-side to station 2. Go out the station, through the top slit of the tape. Close the section and add the next.

Remaining Sections

Proceed in the same manner sewing back and forth. Tie-off the last section with a Half Hitch.

ATTACHING THE COVERS

Sit the text block into the cover. Open front cover to mark where to make the slits to accommodate the tapes. Do the same with the back cover.

On the inside of each side-cover, make a ⅞" vertical slit which is ½" in from the spine at each tape position. The cut will go through to the outside on the outer paper.

On the inside, make a ⅞" vertical slit which is 1¼" in from the spine at each tape position. This will show on the outside of the side-cover on the decorative or inner paper.

Cover slits must be made with the cover folded, so that the slit goes evenly through the many layers of the side-cover.

Lace the tapes onto the cover. Tips of the tapes will end on the inside of the covers. Slots are not necessary and the tightness of the slits hold the book block to the cover without tabs or sewing. Since 1½" of the inner paper is turned under near the spine, the weaving of the tapes will hold the two cover papers in place.

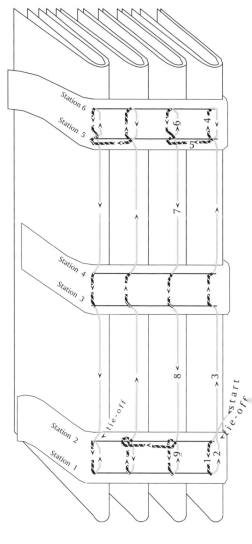

COPTIC SEWING

Various forms of this ancient binding evolved from the fourth century. The simplicity of the exposed sewing across the backbone, sewn onto the boards is appealing. Pages open flat. As with any unsupported sewing, boards must be flush, so that book block rests upon the shelf during storage. Otherwise the book block would sag to the shelf since support from tapes or cords or a continuous support is lacking.

The Coptic described here is sewn all along the spine. There are nine other Coptic sewings described in *Exposed Spine Sewings, Non-Adhesive Binding* Volume III. Some of those are sewn *along* the spine. Others are sewn *across* the spine. All of them were learned from the generous Betsy Palmer Eldridge.

PREPARATION
Sections

A minimum of five sections should be sewn to give a pattern of the links formed by the sewing across the back.

Cover

The sewing is exposed, as there is no spine-cover. Separately wrapped boards can be paper-covered, without the use of adhesives.

It is better to use flush side-covers, especially if the depth of the text block is large otherwise the book standing on the shelf will sag, since it is an unsupported binding. If there aren't too many pages in the book, you may want to use an over-hang cover. Cut the boards to size.

Sewing Stations

Stations for the sections are suggested at less than 1" intervals down the back. Station 1 is at the head. It is important that the end stations are fairly close to the head and tail to keep the book tighter. The stations adjacent to the head and tail should be ½" to ⅝" away to strengthen the end stations, which are the weakest.

Gary Frost, detail of a Coptic

The coptic sewing will be described and illustrated with a chain formed by a locking loop stitch, as opposed to using a chain formed by a *U* stitch, which lies flatter, but tears out easily.

Cover Sewing Stations

Each cover has one sewing station for each row of sewing. This station is no less than ⅛" in from the spine-edge and level with the corresponding station on the book block. Pierce the cover after board is wrapped, using a marked section as guide. Do not take the bradawl too deeply or it will rip to the edge. Hole should be slightly smaller in diameter than the needle for snugness.

Mary Maynor, *From Rocks,* 1998. One-of-a-kind. Covers are "jade-look" polymer clay with hand drilled holes. 8.5 x 8.5 x 2.3 cm.

Thread

Start with 4 feet of heavily waxed thread. If more is needed, add inside the section with a Weaver's Knot. See page 74.

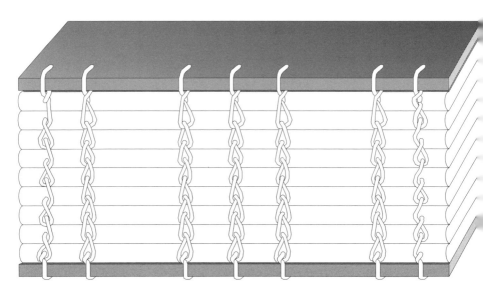

COPTIC BINDING
sewn on the bench, all along the spine

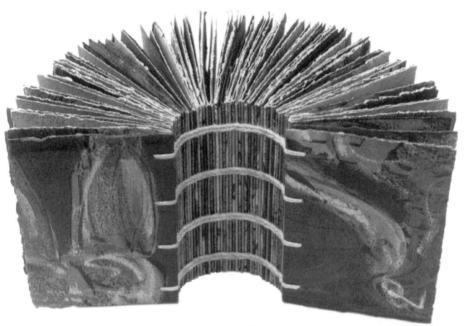

Helen Sanderson, drawings, Adéle Outteridge, Greek binding variation, one-of-a-kind, 1997, 10.5 x 8 x 6 cm. Notice how the spine of an unsupported sewing arcs open.

Adéle Outteridge, *Rusted Papers,* hinged perspex (plexiglass) cover, Arches Velin treated with rusting solutions, linen thread, Coptic sewing with concertina, one-of-a-kind, 1997. 7 x 2.5 cm.

SEWING PROCEDURE *starting at the head*
Sewing the First Section and Board

If you sew from the head to the tail, you must start with the back side-cover and end section. If you wish to start sewing from the front cover and beginning section, sew from the tail to the head.

1. A single thread sews the sections and the boards. Start at the head on the inside of the section. Proceed to outside, leaving 3" thread inside the section. The "first" section here is the end section.
2. Proceed around the spine-edge onto the outside of the side-cover. Go through the station on the cover, exiting between the cover and the first section, away from the spine. Pull thread snug, bringing cover and section together.
3. Take needle from above the head and slip it behind the thread which connects the section and board. Pull thread through and away from spine. Go into station 1 of the first section and tie a knot.
4. Proceed along the inside of the section towards the tail. Take the needle out the next station. Proceed around the spine-edge onto the outside of the side-cover. Go through the cover station exiting between the cover and the first section. Tighten thread bringing cover and section together. Cross under the thread between cover and section before going back into the section.

Remaining Stations on the First Section and Cover Repeat step 4, until you have sewn the station at the tail of the first section, but do not take the needle back into the sewing station on the section.

After you go through the cover sewing station at the tail, come out onto the spine, taking the needle under the thread between the section and board. Tighten thread. If it is not sewn on the bench, you will need to switch to a curved sewing needle.

Sewing the Second Section

5. Place the next section into position. Take the needle through the sewing station nearest the tail of the new section.
6. Proceed inside the section to the next station. Take the needle to the outside.
7. Proceed across the spine, take needle under the threads connecting the board and first section. Pull tight. Then take the needle back into the second section.

Remaining Stations on the Second Section Repeat steps 6 and 7 until you have sewn all the stations of the second section, but do not take the needle back into the end station of the second section.

SEWING the FIRST SECTION and BOARD

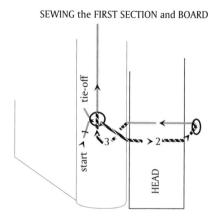

Starting the sewing at the head

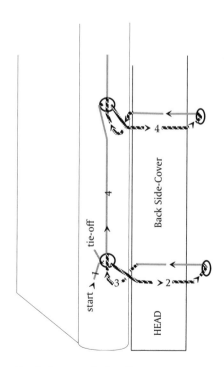

Continuing towards the tail

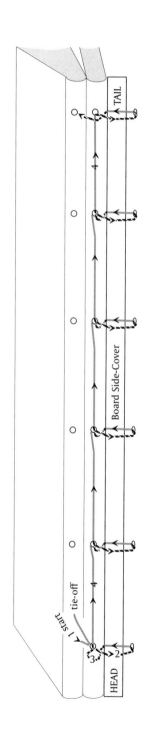

SEWING the SECOND SECTION

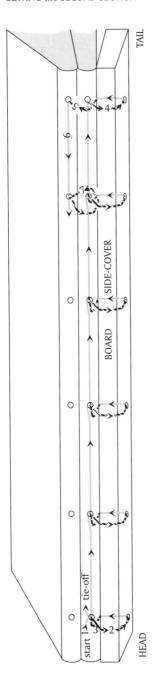

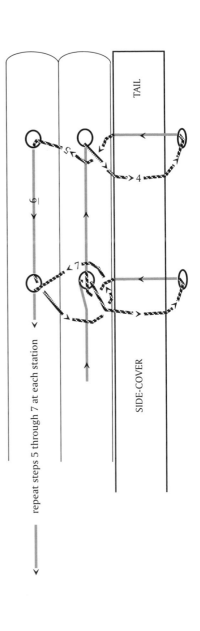

Sewing on the Bench

This binding is an excellent example of the ease of sewing on the bench. Not only are both hands free to sew, but forming chains is much easier. If the book is sewn hand-held, a curved needle must be used to hook under the two threads of the previous

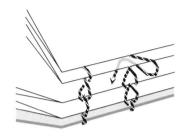

section to form a chain. On the bench, simply lift the section being sewn and the previous. Slide the straight needle in and bring it out.

Sewing the Next Odd-Numbered Section towards the Tail

8. Take the needle across the end station of first section, under the threads connecting board and first section, then under thread between first and second sections. Go into the sewing station nearest to the head of the new section.

9. Proceed inside the section to the next station. Take the needle to the outside. Form a kettle stitch:
    Drop back across the spine, take the needle behind the threads connecting the two previous sections. Take the needle above the station and slip behind the thread connecting the current and the previous adjacent section. Pull thread taut, but not tight. Take the needle back into the station on the current section.

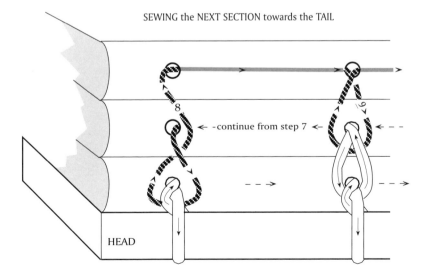

SEWING the NEXT SECTION towards the TAIL

←‑continue from step 7 ←

HEAD

Remaining Stations on This Section Repeat step 9 until you have sewn all the stations of this section, but do not take the needle back into the end station of this section.

Sewing the Next Even-Numbered Section towards the Head

10. Place the next section into position. Drop back to the station of previous section, go under both threads of the previously two connected sections. Slip under thread between previous and current section. Go into the station of the new section.
11. Proceed inside the section to next station.
12. Go to the outside. Drop back to the station of previous section, go under both threads of the previously two connected sections. Slip under thread between previous and current section. Go into the station of the current section. Pull thread tight. Take the needle back into the station on the current section.

Remaining Stations on This Section Repeat steps 11 and 12 until you have sewn all the stations of this section, but do not take the needle back into the end station of this section.

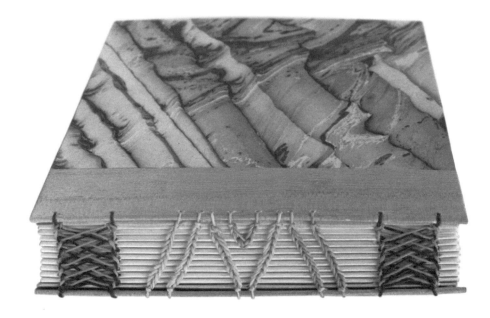

Keith Smith, sample binding, 1995. The letter *M* is a Coptic sewing across the spine. The sewings at each end are Celtic Weave, described in *Exposed Spine Sewings.* The wood at the spine-edge is wood veneer paper from the *Japanese Paper Place,* Toronto.

SEWING the NEXT SECTION towards the HEAD

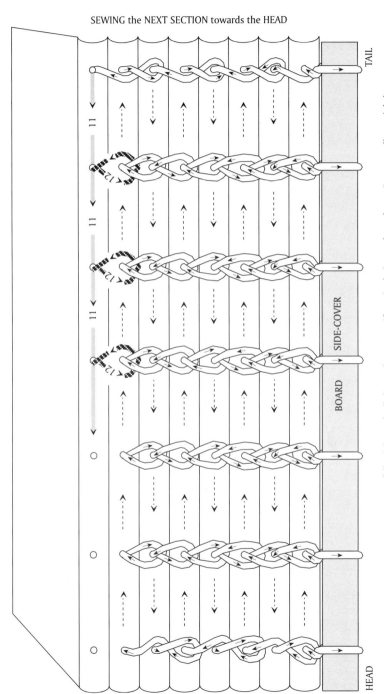

TENSION IN SEWING: Carefully tighten the links so they are uniform in their teardrop shape. Do nor pull too tightly or the rounded bottom of the teardrop will become two straight threads.

Sewing the Remainder of the Book Block

Alternate sewing sections towards the tail (steps 8 and 9) and towards the head (steps 10, 11 and 12). The final section is an exception. The other side-cover is sewn along with the stations on the final section.

Sewing the Final Section and the Board

If the book block has an even number of sections, the final section will be sewn starting at the tail. With an odd number of sections, sewing the final section starts at the head. The following description is for an even number of sections. The next to the last section was sewn. Steps 10, 11 and 12 were repeated, but the needle is not taken back into the end station of the next to the last section. Neither is the needle taken into the last section.

13. Set the final section in place. Proceed beyond the final section around the spine-edge of the cover. Take the needle through the outside of the cover to the inside. Pull thread through and tighten the stitch from the next to the last section, extending across the peak of the final section to the cover.

14. Proceed up over the outside of this stitch and take the needle down behind it, between the cover and the last section. Pull thread down to tighten the cover again.

15. Take the needle into the end station of the last section. Again, tighten the sections and the cover at this end station.

16. Proceed inside the section to the next station. Take the needle to the outside.

17. Proceed across the spine-edge to the outside of the cover. Take the needle through to inside of the cover, pulling the thread out beyond the spine. Tighten the stitch from the section to cover at this station.

18. Take the needle up under the thread that extends from section to cover at this sewing station. Cross over the final section above this station, taking the needle down between the next to last section and the third from the last, behind the thread that connects them. Pull thread down. Tighten the cover and last section at this station.

19. Take the needle into this station on the final section.

Remaining Stations on the Final Section and Cover Continue sewing the remaining stations by repeating steps 16, 17, 18 and 19.

At the final station when you complete step 19, taking the needle to the inside of the end station. Tie-off with a Half Hitch as described on page 73.

SEWING the FINAL (even-numbered) SECTION and the BOARD

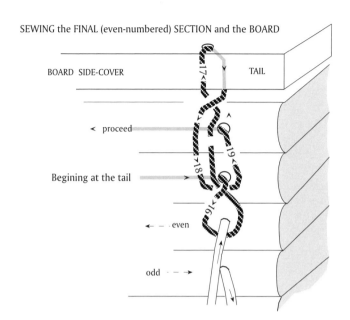

BOARD SIDE-COVER   TAIL

17

< proceed

19

Begining at the tail   18

16

← – ·even

odd · – →

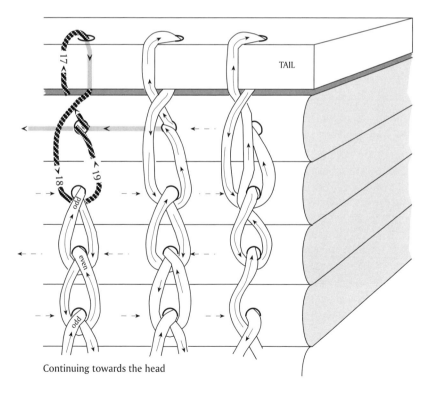

17

TAIL

18   19

odd

<   <

← – ·

even

– →

odd   – →

Continuing towards the head

Susan E. King, *Say, See, Bone: Lessons from French*, Paradise Press, 1988.
Coptic sewing with paste papers made by Susan King. Binding by
Shelley Hoyt.

Bert Weijermars, *Dekensteek*,
Unsupported Blanket Stitch.

UNSUPPORTED BLANKET STITCH

In terms of embroidery, this is a true blanket stitch, unlike *Blanket Stitch with Slit Tapes,* which is only suggestive of the blanket stitch. The two blanket stitch bindings differ in that the latter is a supported binding, sewn onto tapes.

This binding is an unsupported sewing, attached to boards, similar to the Coptic sewing.

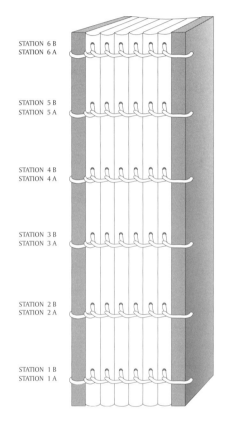

STATION 6 B
STATION 6 A

STATION 5 B
STATION 5 A

STATION 4 B
STATION 4 A

STATION 3 B
STATION 3 A

STATION 2 B
STATION 2 A

STATION 1 B
STATION 1 A

PREPARATION
Cover

The side-covers are separately wrapped boards. Sewing across the back is exposed.

Sections

Use at least 6, for some repetition of the blanket stitches.

Sewing Stations

stations for the book block Numbering of the stations starts at the head and proceeds to the tail. They are at intervals of about 1⅛" along the back.

Each numbered row of stations needs two sewing positions on the section, ⅜" apart. Station *A* is nearer the head.

Station 1*A* will be in from the head ¾". Station 1*B* is 1⅛" from the head. Mark the two positions of each numbered station on the first section. Use it as a guide to mark the remaining. Jog and pierce the sections.

cover sewing stations Each cover has only one position for each numbered sewing station. This is level with station *A*. Cover stations are ⅛" in from the spine-edge. Pierce the cover after board is wrapped. Do not take the bradawl too deeply or it will rip to the edge. Hole should be slightly smaller in diameter than the needle for snugness.

Thread

You will need 1½" per section for each individual sewing. Cord should be heavily waxed.

SEWING PROCEDURE
Sewing the First Section and Cover

1. Start on the inside of the first section at station 1A. Take the needle out through station 1A, leaving 2" cord inside. Take the needle through the sewing station on the cover from the inside of the side-cover. Pull thread to outside of the side-cover, pulling the side-cover a-gainst the first section.

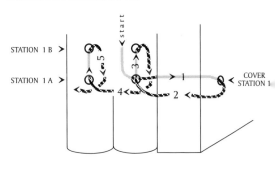

STARTING the BLANKET STITCH

2. Proceed around the spine-edge of the cover. Take the needle back into station 1A of the first section. Tighten the stitch on the side-cover and form it at a right angle to the spine-edge. Tie a Square Knot inside the section at station 1A.

3. Proceed inside, go out through station 1B. Slip the needle underneath the thread connecting the side-cover and first section. Pull thread snugly in an outward direction away from the spine.

Sewing the Next Section

4. Place the next section in position. Go in station 1A of the new section. Proceed inside, going out through station 1B of this newly added section.

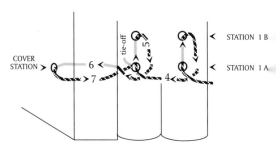

ENDING the BLANKET STITCH

5. Slip the needle under the thread connecting this and the previous section. Pull thread snugly in an outward direction away from the spine. Tighten by pulling downward to form a blanket stitch.

Remaining Sections

Repeat steps 4 and 5 to sew the remaining sections.

Attaching the Remaining Cover

6. After sewing the final section, take the needle through the single position for that numbered sewing station on the cover. Enter from the inside to the out. Pull thread tight, lining up cover. Proceed around the spine-edge of the cover towards the final section.

7. Slip the needle under the thread connecting the side-cover and final section. Pull the thread tight.

    Proceed to station A of the final section. Go to the inside. Tie a Half Hitch by looping under the stitch between positions A and B on the inside. See *Half Hitch,* page 73.

    Each numbered row of stations is sewn separately, following the same procedure.

Peter Madden, *35 Days in Greece.* One-of-a-kind. 1997. Stab binding with found wooden boards as covers with metal hinges. The pages are stitched around the head, foredge and tail. It is not a blanket stitch, but a simple spiral.

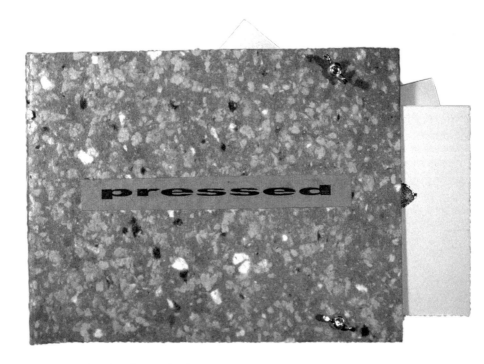

Nancy Brandt, *Pressed,* Polymer plate and Solarplate on Rives BFK. 1997, Edition of 15. Binding is the Spring Action. 21.5 x 29.2 x 4 cm.

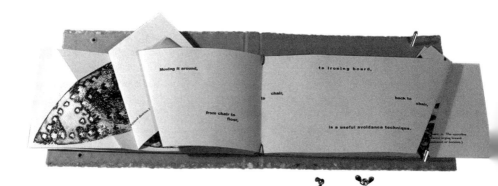

SPRING ACTION

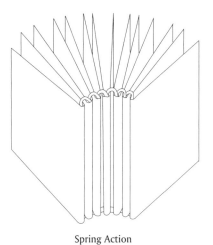

Spring Action

This binding will not stay closed. It pops open, with sections equidistantly apart. If stood upright, it fans open as a cylinder.

Some would see it as a novelty or worse, poor design. I see it with the potential of not only for display, perhaps as a children's book, but for spatial investigation, as well. The spring action can be complemented by webbed pages of tissue paper, pleated through slits in the stiffer sections. Webbed pleats could be parallel, perpendicular or diagonal to the foredge of the book block. Concept of webbed pages has intrigued me since first viewing a book titled *The Lively Dance*.[11]

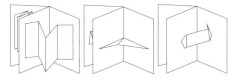

Webbing is like a veil or sheer curtain, partially hiding, yet bidding the viewer to peak. It can be mysterious or alluring, suggestive or repressed. The format is heavily laden with emotional potential.

Psychologically, I see the webbing as a fragile barrier and passive. It is the opposite of the expanding, aggressive binding.

Sculpturally, the binding stands on its own, literally. Coupling the binding with opposing planes sets up a most pleasing three dimensional format, capable of collapsing into a closed book.

PREPARATION
Sections

Use very stiff cover weight paper or use card stock. Fold into sections or folios.

Sewing Stations

There are 2 pierced sewing stations. Station 2 is ½" up from the tail. Station 3 is ½" down from the head. The head and tail are passive stations. Tail is station 1 and head is station 4. The sewing at the head into station 3 is separate from that at the tail into station 2.

SPRING ACTION
Inside view

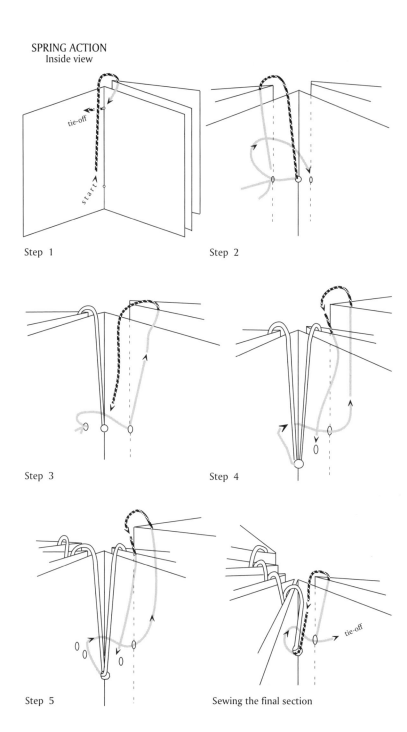

Step 1   Step 2

Step 3   Step 4

Step 5   Sewing the final section

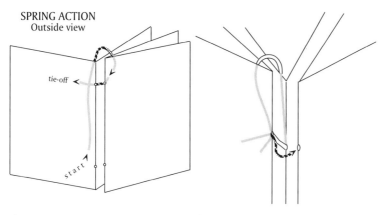

Step 1   Step 2

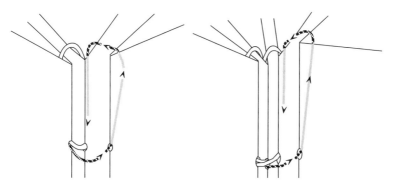

Step 3   Step 4

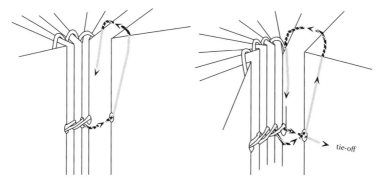

Step 5   Sewing the final section

Thread

Each sewing will require 2" of thread, times the number of sections.

Cover

First and last page of the book block are the side-covers. Since the book must be capable of opening to a cylinder, covers must be downplayed structurally. Visually, as well as conceptually, "covers" would interrupt, posing a beginning and end to the cylindrical, cyclical form.

SEWING PROCEDURE

The procedure starts at the head.

1. Lay the threaded needle inside the first section along the gutter from the tail to the head. Go over the head of first and second section, into the valley of the second. Proceed on the inside of the second section to station 3. Go through station 3 to the outside. Go into station 3 of the first section from the mountain peak to the valley. Tie a Square Knot at station 3 with the loose thread.

2. Go out station 3 of first section across the spine to the third section. Go through station 3 of the third section to inside.

3. Proceed up to the head. Wrap over the head of the third and second section, down to station 3 of the second section.

4. Exit station 3, across the spine to the fourth section. Go through station 3 to inside. Proceed to the head. Wrap over the head of the fourth and third section, down to station 3 of third section.

5. Proceed out station 3, across the spine past the adjacent section to a new section. Go through station 3 of the new section to inside. Proceed up to the head. Wrap over the head of this and the previous section, down the gutter to station 3.

Remaining Sections Continue in this manner, repeating step 5 for remainder of the sections, except for the final section.

Final Section Proceed out station 3 of the next to last section, proceed across the spine to the final section. Go inside at station 3. Tie-off at station 3 by slipping the needle under the stitch above the station, then taking the needle through the loop. Do this again to form a Half Hitch. Tighten by pulling down towards tail.

Sewing the Tail

A separate sewing is done at the tail. Turn the book upside down and proceed as with sewing the head. Substitute tail and station 2, wherever procedure calls for head and station 3.

PIANO HINGE BINDING

This unusual binding was devised by Hedi Kyle. Like so many others, it has an inspired presence. It is sculptural, with an unique combination of paper and rods. Glass or wooden rods as hinge pins should be the same height as the book block, if you wish the book to stand on a shelf. Rods could extend up from head and still set square. Rods can be extremely long, extending above and below the book block. The book will not sit on a shelf, but be stored in a box. Opening the book reveals a lovely detail of the dovetailing of the sections at the gutter.

Keith Smith,
sample Piano Hinge Binding
with alternating black and white sections.
Rods are skewers. Note the dovetail effect in the gutter between sections.

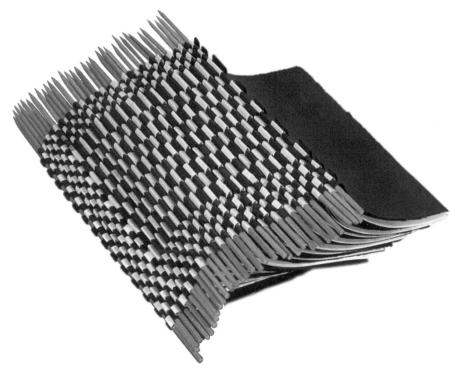

View of the spine of the book on the previous page. Alternating colors of sections gives a checker board effect. Varying the size of the loops alters the spine design.

Emily Martin, *Wish You Were Here,* one-of-a-kind, 1996. "A commemorative book of postcards, tickets and 21 envelopes collected and mailed home from a trip to the United Kingdom. Piano Hinge binding using sharpened pencils, all materials collected on the trip. 17.6 x 22.8 x 20.4 cm.

Grasping the covers, the spine can be stretched like an elastic belt, returning to its original width when released.

Preparing the Sections

Sections are not creased in half.

1. Center each section around the hinge pin to determine width of the horizontal slits. Determine the number of slits desired and mark the position and width of the slits lightly with a pencil. Test a section to see if slits proper width before slitting all the sections.
2. Lay the section flat on cutting surface. Slit each station. Use this as a guide to slit the remainder of the sections.
3. Gently bend every other hinge-loop to the right and the others to the left. Be careful not to crease the center of the section. The spine looks best without a center crease on the sections. Prepare each section in the same manner.

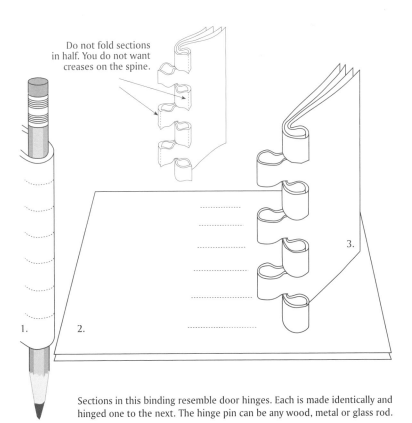

Do not fold sections in half. You do not want creases on the spine.

Sections in this binding resemble door hinges. Each is made identically and hinged one to the next. The hinge pin can be any wood, metal or glass rod.

PIANO HINGE BINDING

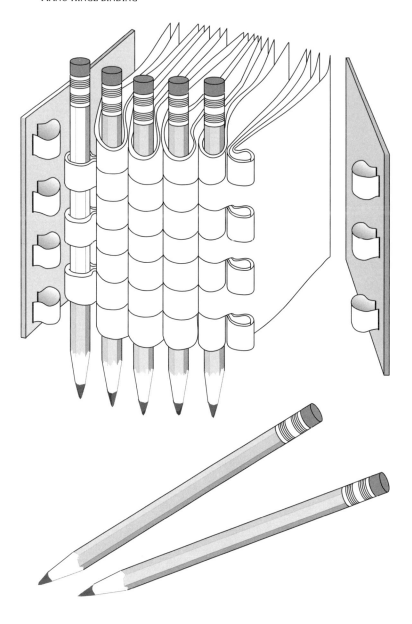

Sections are not creased so there are no folds on the spine. Wooden dowels, skewers, pencils or glass rods are used as hinge pins to connect one section to the next. Each separate book board side-cover is attached with the same kind of hinge pin.

BOOK BOARD SIDE-COVERS

There are two approaches to covers. The second is by far the easier, not needing tabs. This first description permits book board side-covers.

Lacing the Book Board Side-Covers

Number of loops on the board covers depends on number of hinge-loops slit on the sections. If there are an odd number of hinge-loops, there will be an additional loop on one of the side-covers. See illustration on the facing page. Position of the paper tape loops must line up with the extended loops on first and last sections.

The side-covers might be *Separately Wrapped Boards,* see page 293; or *Bordered Paper Side-Covers,* page 289.

Any number of slits can be made for decoration. At least four slits are needed structurally to form the loop and tuck the tabs at each edge. The slits are made horizontally across the cover for each needed loop. The paper tape is woven through, following the six steps shown below.

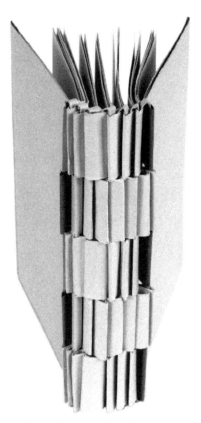

Strips of paper as hinge pins

LACING a BOOK BOARD SIDE-COVER

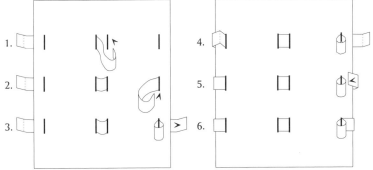

Inside of separate board side-covers. Six steps in lacing each tape to form a loop. For finishing off the tab at the foredge and tail, see *Tucking the Tab,* pages 309–310.

Flat Hinge Pins

The Piano Hinge Binding may be hinged by other than cylindrical pins. Sections are folded in the middle *with a crease*. A second fold is made in from the spine-fold slightly wider than the strips of vellum or strong paper used as hinge pins to connect one section to the next. The spine takes on a louvered look. See example on the previous page.

Paper hinges were trimmed to extend ½" above the head and below the tail. Ends of the strips were then inserted into the adjacent section. This finishes the binding with the appearance of a laced head and tail.

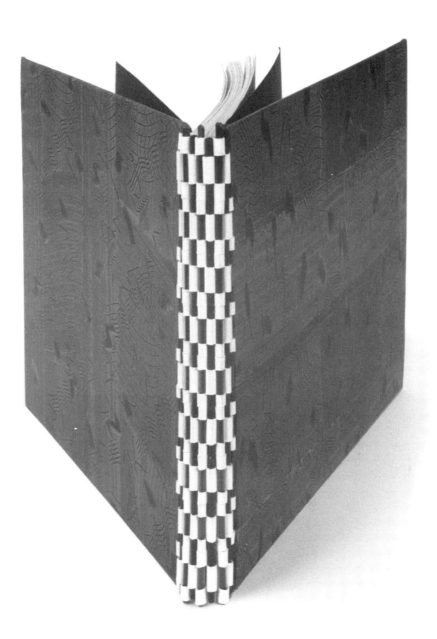

ABOVE
Julie Leonard, untitled, 1989. Piano Hinge Binding of a photo album. Every other loop
on the section was cut off. This allowed the dark glass rods to show on the spine.
TO THE LEFT
Jane Cameron, untitled Piano Hinge Binding, 1992. This floor-displayed book is fairly
long. Plant stems are used for the hinging.

PAPER SIDE COVERS

Using separate paper side-covers instead of book board avoids the use of tabs. A folio of cover weight paper is folded in the same manner as the sections. One such folio would be added to the first section by inserting a hinge pin. Since only every other loop is used in inserting a pin, the bare pin will appear on the outside of the cover; it will not look finished.

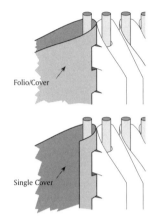

Eliminating the Double Cover

If you find the two sheets of paper objectionable the folio can be modified in two ways:

1. Cut off the second half of the folio close to spine-edge and the loops. This leaves only the outer part. Opening the book, you will see the stub of the inner cover, which was cut off.

2. Fold the folio off-center, so the outer part is wider than the book block. Fold the excess along the foredge as a turn-in. Attach it to the inner part of the folio. Use either a tab or glue it.

1. Cut off the second part of the folio/cover.

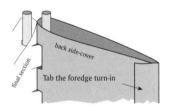

2. Form a foredge turn-in. Tab the turn-in to the second part of the folio to make a 2-ply cover.

Eliminating the Extra Loops

The bare hinge pin showing on the paper cover is easily eliminated. The solution came from Kitty Spangler during one of my workshops: Slits for the pins in the cover/folio will be cut only half the width of the slits used for the sections. See example on page 236.

Dimensions of the Cover Paper

HEIGHT of the cover is the same as the sections.
WIDTH of the sheet of paper for the cover should be the same as the sheets used for the sections,
plus width of the foredge turn-in, if any,
plus 1½".
1. Cut the covers to the dimensions stated above.
2. Mark the width of the cover slits on the stencil used for the sections.

Slits for the cover will be only half the width of the slits used for the sections. These smaller slits for the cover can be centered on the previous stencil.

3. Lay the flat sheet for the cover on a cutting surface. Place the stencil used for slitting the sections onto the cover, lining it up 1" in from the foredge on the left. The overhang on the right will be greater, mostly for the foredge turn-in.

4. Make the slits in each side-cover.

5. With the cover flat, insert a pin into the cover, only. This will help shape the cylinders of paper, alternating on each side of the pin. Fold the cover, along the left edge of the slits, next to the left of the pin. The outside of the cover will not show the slits or the pin.

6. Remove the hinge pin.

7. Set the front cover onto the loops of the book block and join the first section and front cover with the pin. Do the same for the back cover and the final section. You will probably have to trim the width of the top layer of the cover. This is why an extra inch was left on the left foredge. With the right or bottom layer, to form the foredge turn-in.

Roberta Lavadour, *Gathering Fall,* 1998. One-of-a-kind. Handmade paper and birch twigs. Piano Hinge Binding devised by Hedi Kyle. 37.5 x 15.2 cm.

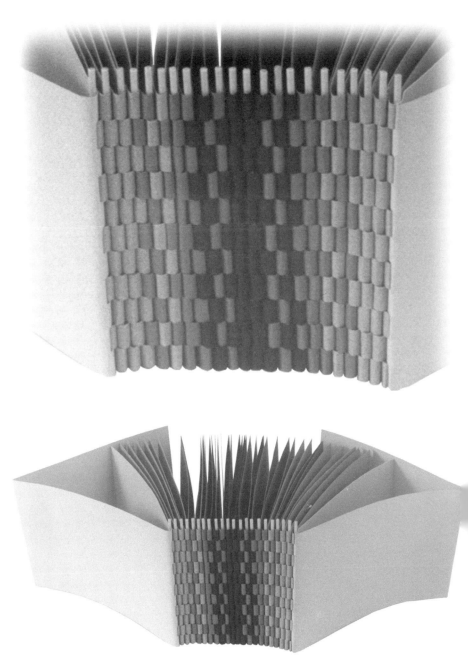

Kitty Spangler, untitled Piano Hinge Binding devised by Hedi Kyle with the cover attachment Kitty Spangler devised, 1993. By slitting the cover only half as wide as the sections, the wooden dowels do not show on the outside of the covers.

PIANO-HINGED COLLAPSIBLE STAR

This variation on the *Piano Hinge Binding* was also devised by Hedi Kyle. In order that I might dismantle and describe the binding, she kindly sent this example.

A long sheet of paper is folded down as described on page 243, *Folding an Oriental Fold Book*.

The two folds, one at each end of the book block are hinge-folds. To attach the book block to separate side-covers, each hinge-fold will be slit to form piano hinges. See below.

At each end of the book block, six horizontal slits have been made with the hinge-fold closed. The slits extend ½" in from the spine-edge on both sheets of the folio. See illustration on the following page.

Hedi Kyle, sample of *Piano-Hinged Collapsible Star* for demonstration purposes. 1990.

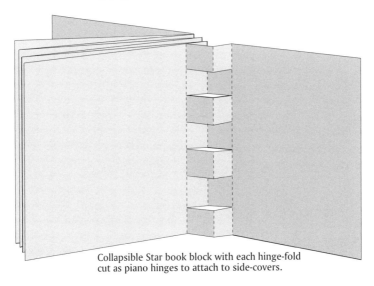

Collapsible Star book block with each hinge-fold cut as piano hinges to attach to side-covers.

At the front of the book with the book block closed, the even-numbered hinges are folded outward. At the back of the book the odd-numbered hinges are extended.

Separate Side-Covers

Each side-cover is folded with a foredge turn-in. The other extreme of the width of the cover is the *inside cover sheet*. This can be considered as an endsheet. Opening the cover it is the first page seen. It is the same color and weight as the cover stock. The inside cover sheet is turned to reveal the book block.

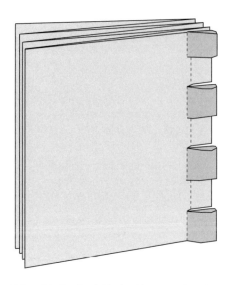

Collapsible Star book block with every other piano hinge extended ready to attach to side-covers.

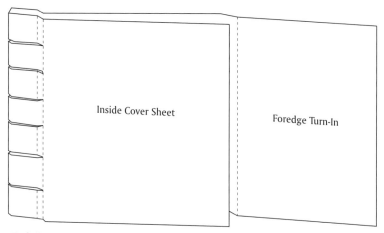

Inside Cover Sheet

Foredge Turn-In

Back Cover

HEIGHT of the side cover is the same as the book block.
WIDTH of each side-cover equals:
width of the foredge turn-in
plus width of the book block (outside of the side-cover)
plus ½" as half of the piano hinge
plus ½" as the other half of the piano hinge
plus width of the book block (inside cover sheet).

Prepare the front side-cover by folding the turn-in and folding the odd-numbered piano hinges to the inside. Prepare the back cover by folding the turn-in and folding the even-numbered piano hinges to the inside.

Even numbered hinges on the front cover dovetail into the odd-numbered hinges on the back cover and are fixed in position with a spine-tab.

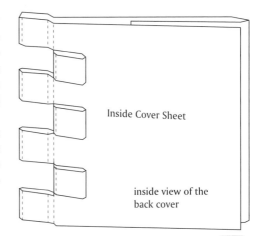

Inside Cover Sheet

inside view of the back cover

Spine-Tab

Cut three spine-tabs from cover weight paper or vellum. Each tab will be mitered at the bottom for easy insertion.

HEIGHT of the spine-tab is same as the book block.

WIDTH is slightly less than ½" so that it will fit snugly within the piano hinges and not slip out.

The first tab attaches the separate side covers on the spine. The second attaches the odd-numbered hinges of the front side-cover to the even-numbered hinges at the beginning of the book block. The third tab attaches the even-numbered hinges of the back cover to the odd-numbered hinges at the end of the book block.

All the hinges on the side-covers are utilized. Only the even-numbered hinges at the beginning of the book block and odd-numbered at the end are used. The unused book block hinges will not be seen.

Spine-Tab

Mary Ellen Long, *Pagings,* 1998. One-of-a-kind fold book. "Stamped titles and authors from books in the 'library' on copper. Collaged pages from books on site in the forest 'library'". 15.2 x 38 x 48 cm. opened.

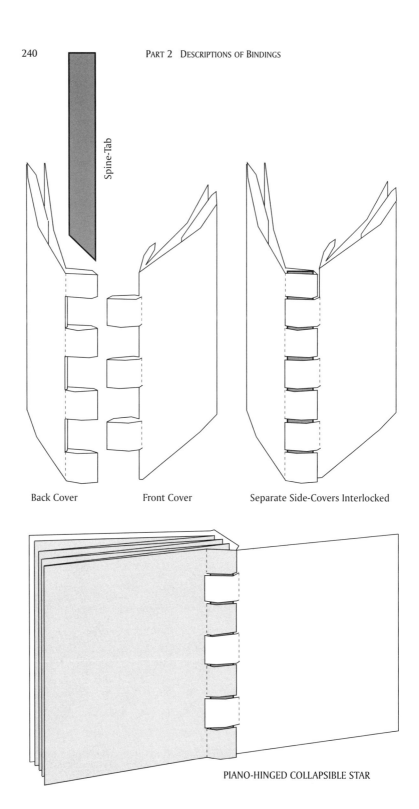

Back Cover   Front Cover   Separate Side-Covers Interlocked

PIANO-HINGED COLLAPSIBLE STAR

At the bottom of the facing page the illustration shows the final page of the book block has been dovetailed into remaining hinges of the back cover and secured with a spine-tab.

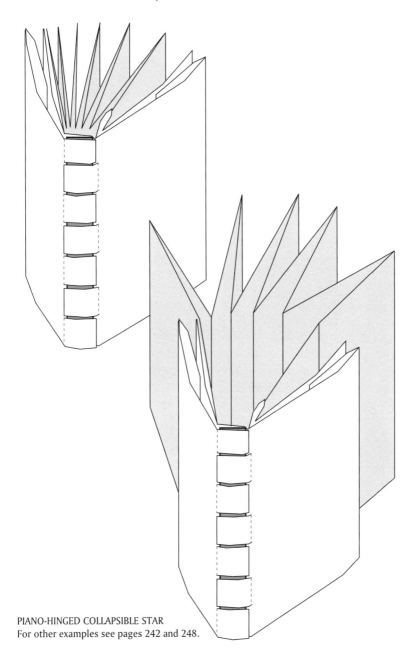

PIANO-HINGED COLLAPSIBLE STAR
For other examples see pages 242 and 248.

Excerpt from the text:
  kheth
  cheth
  heth
  he
  h

a fence ~ a gate ~ an enclosure
defining the inside and the outside.

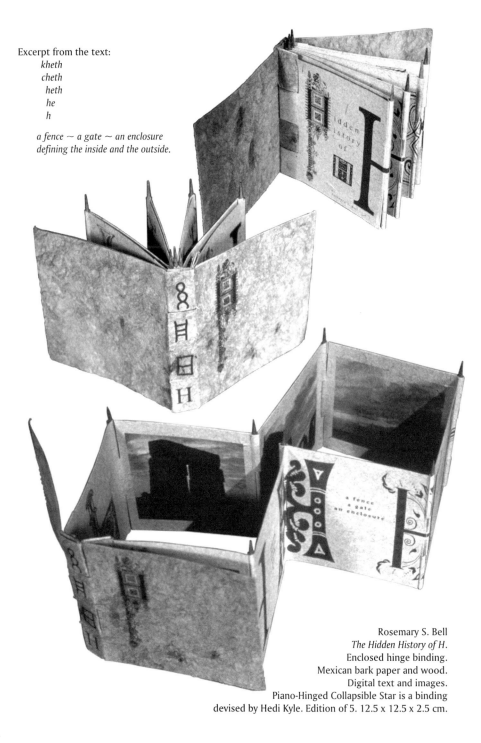

Rosemary S. Bell
The Hidden History of H.
Enclosed hinge binding.
Mexican bark paper and wood.
Digital text and images.
Piano-Hinged Collapsible Star is a binding
devised by Hedi Kyle. Edition of 5. 12.5 x 12.5 x 2.5 cm.

FOLD BOOKS

The Oriental fold book differs from the other types of books—the fan, the blind and the codex, in that the book is constructed without sewing. Folding creates the structure and, thus, can create or alter the content.

A sheet is cut to the height of the pages. Width of the pages is made by simply folding a sheet back and forth in page-width increments.

I say simply, but it can be quite frustrating to create a book with pages of identical widths, each page of which, when closed, sits precisely on top of the next. If you accurately mark off the width of each page, your folds may be sightly off, resulting in the depth of the book not being at right angles to the surfaces. The closed book is askew.

I have tried marking the page widths by walking off a divider which has been adjusted to the width of the page. This pricks an indentation smaller and more uniform than finding each page measurement individually with a ruler and pencil. A 90° triangle is then placed at every other mark and a line is scored. These are folded against the score. On the reverse side, the divider indentations which have not been scored are located and similarly scored and folded. Even this method can yield poor results.

Someone finally taught me a fool-proof method and, not surprisingly, the most simple approach requiring no tools. Of course the person was Hedi Kyle. She devised the system and has innovated so many binding. She is the binder's binder. This is the procedure:

FOLDING an ORIENTAL FOLD BOOK

1. Cut the paper to the desired height of the book by the total width of all the pages. The paper should be grain short.

grain direction

2. Fold in half with the grain, very carefully lining up the front edge of the height of the book with the back. If one height varies from the other, the paper was not cut precisely at right angles.

Re-cut to adjust, as the error in angle will be compounded with the folding. Once step two is completed, the exact center of the book is located and the fold is at a right angle to the horizontal edges of the sheet. What is more, this initial fold is the guide with which all remaining folding will be lined up.

3. The top half of the sheet will be completely folded first, before the paper is lifted and turned over to make all the folds on the second half. While folding the first half, allow the bottom half of the paper to remain flat on the table.

    Pick up the top half of the sheet by the edge opposite the fold, which is the foredge. Line it up with the initial fold. Once it is perfectly aligned, hold it in place with one hand. With the other hand, brush the top paper from the alignment back, to make the second fold. The top half of the paper now has two pages, each ¼ the width of the total sheet.

4. Grasp this second fold at each end (the head and tail), allowing the bottom half of the sheet to remain on the table.

5. Reverse the direction of the second fold from a valley to a mountain peak.

6. Take this newly directed mountain peak to the initial fold and line it up. Hold the alignment in place with one hand. With the other hand, press the top paper, pushing away from the initial fold to create the third fold.

7. Bring the foredge to the initial fold. Line it up, hold it in place. Brush back to create the fourth fold.

8. The top half of the sheet now is folded into four pages, each ⅛ the total width of the sheet. At this point the top half can be opened flat, the sheet can be flipped and the entire procedure of folding can be done to the o ther half of the sheet. Again, the center fold is the edge with which to align.

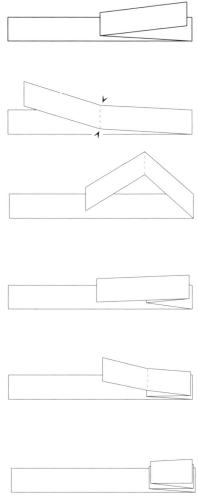

8 A. Or, instead of proceeding to step 8, you can continue to fold the
   first half of the sheet to pages each of which will be $\frac{1}{16}$ the width of
   the sheet.

This is done by reversing the fold closest to the center fold into a
mountain peak. Bring it to the center fold. Then bring the next fold,
which is already a mountain peak, to the initial fold. Continue toward
the foredge, bringing each fold to the initial fold. Each valley must first
be reversed to a mountain peak before it is brought to the initial fold.
Then, open and flatten the first half of book, leaving the center fold. Flip
the book over and fold the second half in the same manner.

ITINERARIES through the FOLD BOOK

Itineraries through this book can be created by how it is displayed.

1. The fold book can be seen a page at a time,
   in the fashion of a codex.
2. Fully extended, the fold book reverts to
   the single picture format. The physical act
   of turning pages is not necessary. Everything is seen at once.

3. Not only turning pages, but physically manipulating the format
   offers avenues of expression unique to the book format. Fully
   extending the book and then collapsing several pages as a unit gives
   an abbreviated reading. Perhaps pages 3 through 6 are secondary.
   They can be by-passed. The book reads page 1, 2 and then 7, 8, 9 10.

If the book is conceived in this manner, the viewer must be clued to
this itinerary by visual code or written instructions.

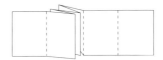

Visual Code

4. Page 2 can contain the left half of an object. Page 5 will show the
   remainder of that picture. When viewed a page at a time or fully
   extended, the book reads one way.

5. However, the artist visually suggests to the reader that the halved image appearing in different parts of the book could be physically united by manipulating the folds of the book.

When collapsed to an abbreviated itinerary, pages 2 and 5 are tangent. This confronts the viewer with the fact that a book is more than visuals, as in the single picture format. The book is a physical object with which both the author and reader must contend.

Written Instructions

The same use of abbreviated itineraries can be constructed with text. The reader is literally told of intended alternative readings or perhaps only subtly clued.

6. Fully extended, the format reveals the unabridged text.

| NOW | I AM SI CK OF | OBSERVING | LENT. | I LONG FOR SU MMERING | AGAIN | S |

7. Slightly collapsing the book, the format shows an intended abbreviated text when we pages 3 and 4 are not in view.

8. As the days are abbreviated, so is the text. A shorter text comes into being by manipulating the book so that only the first two and last two pages are in view.

The reader is confronted with the final letter in the book. Does the *S* stand for the author's name? Is it

only a sound as in *ssss* for sizzling, simmering. Perhaps it recalls *ssshh* in beckoning silence.

9. Another possibility is suggested by the fact that an oriental fold book is an implied cyclical format. Indeed, it is literally a cycle when the form is manipulated.

The end of the text suggests a return to the beginning. Since the reader is actively manipulating the pages, they may discover that the last page can be bent around to connect to the first. Now, the *S* connects with *NOW* to develop into *snow,* confirming the cycle, literally as well as seasonally.

Folding a sheet of paper not only constructs a binding, it can create the content.

Christine A. Forsythe, *Roadways: Message & Meaning,* Fall, 1995. One-of-a-kind, two fold books in a box. Mixed materials. 12.5 x 12.5 x 12.5 cm. Extends to two meters.

If an Oriental fold book has both ends attached to covers, it can be seen in the manner of a codex, page by page. It cannot be fully extended. Stretched opened, it sits upright as a many-sided cylinder.

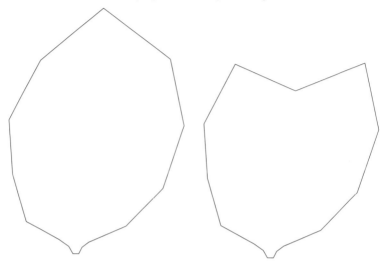

As the folds are reversed, closing the pages creates peaks.

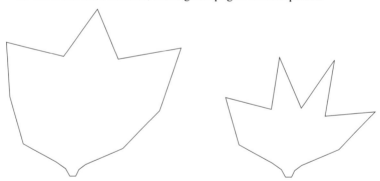

This modification of the fold book makes an unique format. It is known as *Collapsing Star*. See *Piano Hinged Collapsible Star*, page 237.

All bindings can be broken down into four classifications. These are the four *types of books*, determined by how they are bound.

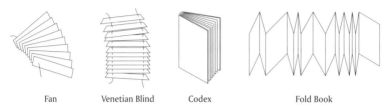

Fan   Venetian Blind   Codex   Fold Book

Fan Singles sheets attached at one point.
Venetian Blind Separate sheets strung from two cords.
Codex Sheets or sections attached along one edge creating a spine.
Oriental Fold Book A sheet folded back and forth upon itself to create pages. It has a mechanical rather than sewn binding.

The four types of books can be compounded. A compound binding is a format that incorporates two or more of the same or different types of books. Two separate bindings are incorporated as a single format.

There are two traditional compound bindings, the *Concertina Binding* and the *dos-a-dos*. Most compound bindings are rare. There has of yet been little investigation of the possibilities of these hybrids.

Any combination of fans, blinds, codices and/or fold books can suggest possible formats for investigation.

Compound or combined books are complex in structure, often permitting permutations of reading with no set order for the various possible itineraries. Their display invites play.

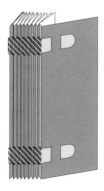

The *Concertina Binding* is a codex with the sections pamphlet sewn onto a pleat, which is essentially a fold book. The *dos-à-dos* is two codices of any kind of binding with a common back cover.

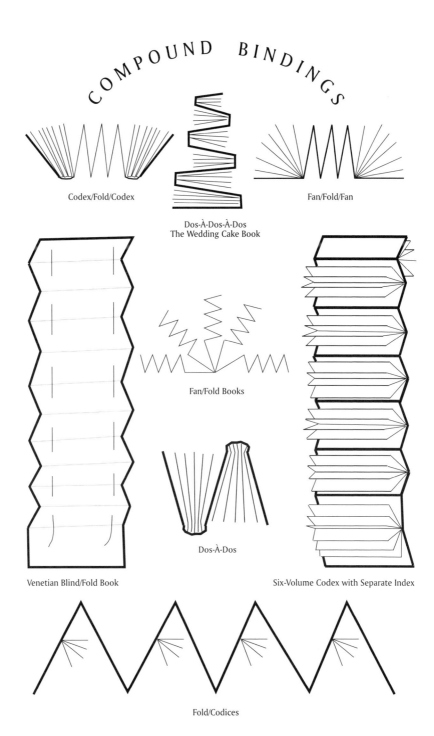

COMPOUND BINDINGS

Codex/Fold/Codex

Dos-À-Dos-À-Dos
The Wedding Cake Book

Fan/Fold/Fan

Fan/Fold Books

Dos-À-Dos

Venetian Blind/Fold Book

Six-Volume Codex with Separate Index

Fold/Codices

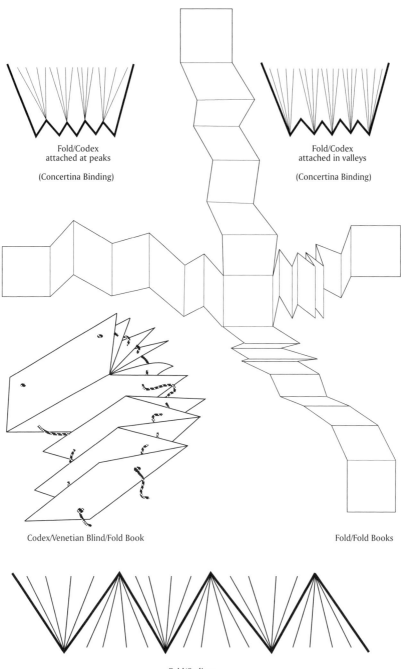

Fold/Codex
attached at peaks

(Concertina Binding)

Fold/Codex
attached in valleys

(Concertina Binding)

Codex/Venetian Blind/Fold Book

Fold/Fold Books

Fold/Codices
(Concertina/Dos-À-Dos)

Scott McCarney, *Intersection/Communication*, 1990. Piano-Hinged Collapsible Star. This binding is viewed as a codex. Removing the spine-tab, the codex is transformed into a fold book. Scott's book is a very lengthy compound fold book. The smaller pages of the fold book are translucent. The larger pages contain transparencies in various cut out shapes. This codex/fold book/fold book is a compound binding.

DOS-À-DOS

One of the oldest compound bindings is a codex attached to another codex. The dos-à-dos places two separate texts with two separately sewn backs within close proximity since they share a back cover in common. Yet, since they are back to back, they cannot be viewed simultaneously, since the front cover of one book faces the viewer while the front of the other does not.

This compound binding was more popular in past centuries when two related volumes would be so bound: the *New* and *Old Testament, The Iliad* and the *Odyssey* or other related works such as Milton's *Il Penseroso* and *L'allegro.*

The dos-à-dos is a format, not a binding. Any of the bindings described in this book can be bound in two copies with a common back cover to form a dos-à-dos. Although I have never seen an example, you could combine two different bindings as a dos-à-dos.

After viewing the first volume you must turn the object over to begin the second. The first page of each segment is on the outside. Both volumes end at the middle of the object.

Julie Leonard, untitled Coptic sewing dos-à-dos, 1990.

WITH Z-COVER

The quickest binding of a dos-à-dos would be two single section booklets pamphlet sewn.

Preparation

Fold the cover in thirds, forming a Z.
Prepare two sections of the same dimensions, each to fit inside one of the valleys of the cover.
Place one section inside one of the folds of the cover. Mark the spine and pierce the cover and section simultaneously. Pamphlet sew the cover and section. The procedure is described on page 89.
Sew the other section inside the remaining cover fold.

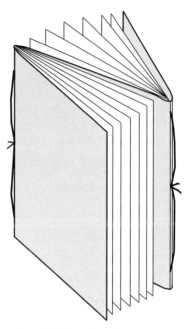

Pamphlet Sewn Dos-à-Dos

WITH PLEATED SPINE-COVER

Each volume can have several sections, each pamphlet sewn to a pleat. This can be made quickly by sewing two unsupported concertina bindings with a common back cover as shown on the bottom of the facing page. Also, see *Concertina Binding,* page 261.

Preparation

Fold a cover sheet in thirds, forming a Z. The two mountain peaks will be the center or initial folds of the pleated spines. See *Cover Pleat* page 320 and *Pleat as Spine and Cover,* page 324.

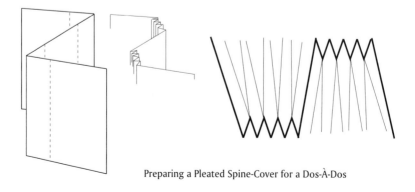

Preparing a Pleated Spine-Cover for a Dos-À-Dos

The *Z*-cover can be modified to accept multi-section volumes by having two folds at each spine.

The two volumes do not have to have the same number of pages. One volume might be a thicker book while the other is a thinner addendum or glossary.

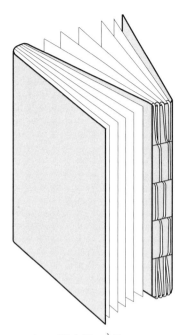

Long Stitch / Dos-À-Dos

Sample unsupported Concertina Binding / Dos-À-Dos.

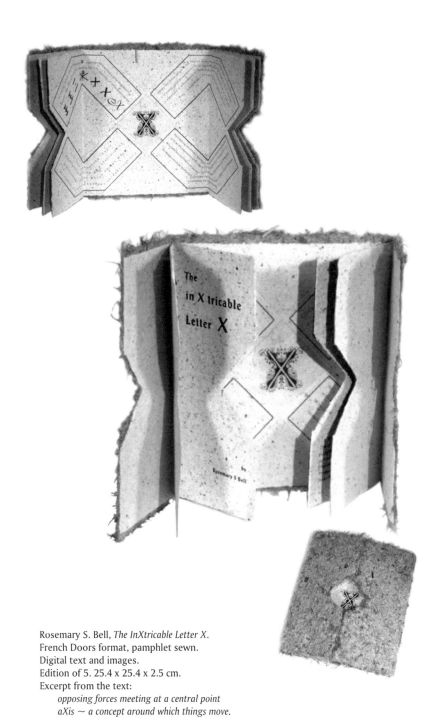

Rosemary S. Bell, *The InXtricable Letter X*.
French Doors format, pamphlet sewn.
Digital text and images.
Edition of 5. 25.4 x 25.4 x 2.5 cm.
Excerpt from the text:
  opposing forces meeting at a central point
  aXis ~ a concept around which things move.

FRENCH DOORS

Two Tangent Facing and Connected Codices

French Doors is a format not a specific type of binding. Any binding can be used to construct the French Doors. They are bound separately except for a common back cover. The example to be described has two codices consisting of a single section each, pamphlet sewn to its corresponding fold on the cover. See *Pamphlet Sewing*, page 89 through 106.

Dimensions

HEIGHT of the cover and the two text blocks are the same. You may use an overhang cover, but the foredges must be flush.

WIDTH of the back cover must be twice the width of one book block, with a slight amount more, so the volumes will not dovetail and can open easily. Cut the width a little long and it will be trimmed to size when fitted.

WIDTH of the two front covers is the same as the sections.

Folding Procedure

The cover is folded as each section is added, rather than being pre-folded. This insures a proper fit.

Fold one hinge-fold to make one front cover. Pierce the stations and pamphlet sew that section.

Lay the other section into position to mark where to fold the other hinge-fold on the cover. Fold the remaining hinge-fold. Pamphlet sew the second section. Trim excess from front cover foredge.

Variations

You could make a list of variations on this format to see if any suggest an avenue you might like to explore.

1. Think about the movement of turning pages in both books simultaneously as well as alternately. Will the book make sense if the viewer turns one or more pages first from one book then the other?
2. Make the tangent gap between the two text blocks other than a vertical. It might be an irregular shape.
3. The gap between the facing book blocks might be tangent, then veer apart exposing part of the back cover. This would constantly reveal text, image or titles of the two-volume book no matter to which pages the books are opened.
4. The gap may be diagonal.

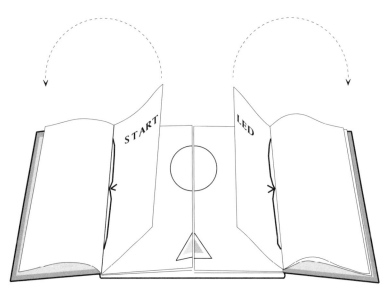

1. Exploring Logistics of Movement

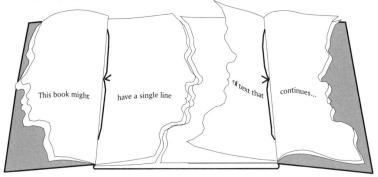

2. Irregularly Shaped, Tangent Foredges

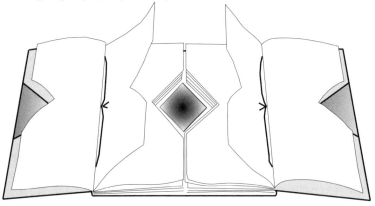

3. Veering from Tangential Foredges

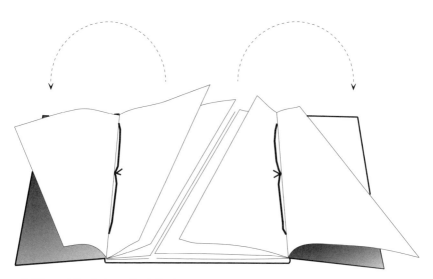

4. Diagonal Gap between Book Blocks

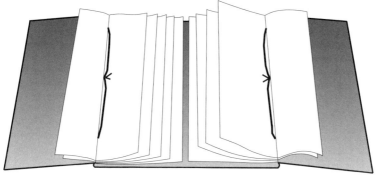

5. Variable Page Size

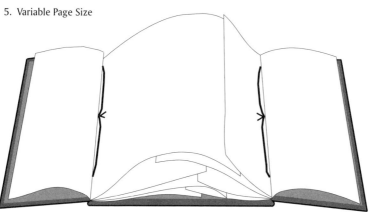

6. Overlapping Pages

5. Each successive page slightly longer, until the final page of each book is tangent. The two volumes are symmetrical. The movement down the left closed volume goes down the staircase, the movement then goes up the other closed book. (Seven steps to heaven, seven steps to hell.) A small amount of content on every page is seen with both volumes closed.

6. Overlapping, rather than tangent pages. Opening a page on one book may flip one or more pages on the other. The action is inspired by shuffling a deck of cards.

7. French Doors could be a two-volume fold book.

8.–? Continue the list on your own while taking a walk or doing the dishes. The best part of binding does not transpire in the bindery, but while doing the chores or lying in bed or watching a western.

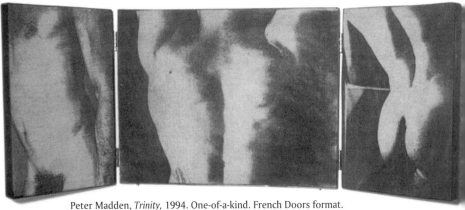

Peter Madden, *Trinity*, 1994. One-of-a-kind. French Doors format.

CONCERTINA BINDING

The concertina is the most widely used compound binding. Sections (the codex) are sewn to an accordion pleat (the Oriental fold).

Each section is pamphlet sewn to the pleat, either on a mountain peak or in the valley or a combination. Any of these is an *unsupported concertina binding*. Without the supported sewing of tapes across the spine, the book opens extended and the spine remains flexible.

Barbara Mauriello, *Gaudy Nights*, one-of-a-kind sewn to a pleated spine, 1988.

The spine can be fixed into position by *tape supports* of paper, book cloth or leather sewn and wrapped on the outside of the spine. Amount of wrapping determines the fixed expansion of the spine, described on page 271. This separate sewing creates a *supported Concertina Binding*. Examples are shown on pages 262, 272, 280 and 298.

Compound Hinging

Both the supported and unsupported concertina bindings open easily and pages turn freely because of the double hinging of the folds of the section and the folds of the pleat. Changing from sections to folios, the compound action insures that pages of any thickness even with items attached will lie flat at any open position.

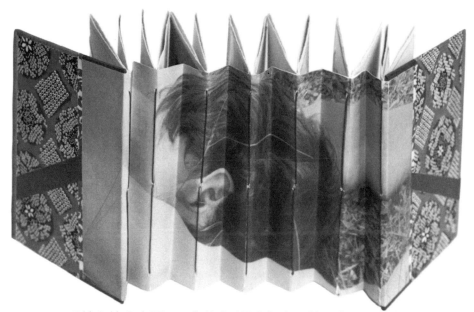

Keith Smith, *Book 121,* one-of-a-kind, 1987. Collection of the Tokyo Metropolitan Museum of Photography. Pamphlet sewn unsupported Concertina Binding with leather inlays and a photographic pleat. 17.5 x 15.3 cm.

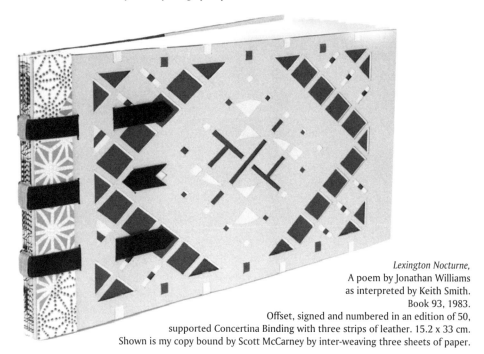

Lexington Nocturne,
A poem by Jonathan Williams
as interpreted by Keith Smith.
Book 93, 1983.
Offset, signed and numbered in an edition of 50,
supported Concertina Binding with three strips of leather. 15.2 x 33 cm.
Shown is my copy bound by Scott McCarney by inter-weaving three sheets of paper.

Compound Hinging: The hinging takes place with the pleat as well as the section.

Potential of the Format

The spine-pleat is the chief variable that makes this binding so appropriate for varying the approach to formatting. See *Cover Pleat*, page 320. Pleat and sections may be the same or differing heights.

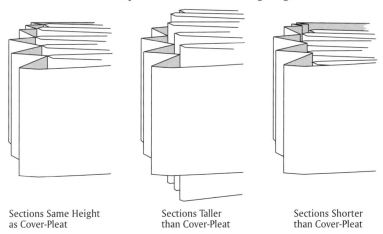

Sections Same Height   Sections Taller   Sections Shorter
as Cover-Pleat   than Cover-Pleat   than Cover-Pleat

The supported and unsupported concertina bindings easily offer the most potential for variation of any bindings.

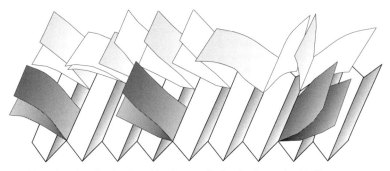

More than One Section Pamphlet Sewn to Peaks of a Concertina Binding

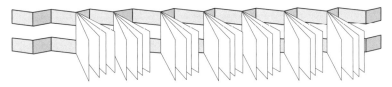

Sections Attached to more than One Spine-Pleat as a Concertina Binding

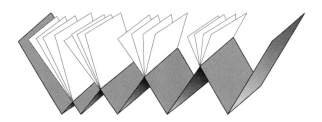

Inversely Proportional Variable Size Pleat and Sections for a Concertina Binding

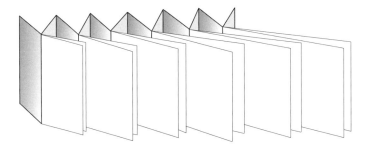

Variable Size of Sections for a Concertina Binding

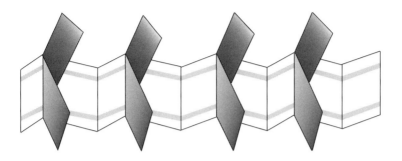

Sections or Folios Folded at other than a 90° Angle

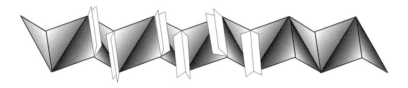

Spine-Pleat Folded at other than a 90° Angle

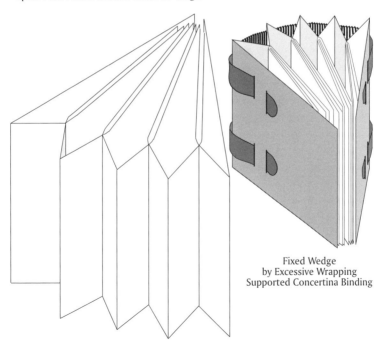

Fixed Wedge
by Excessive Wrapping
Supported Concertina Binding

Pie-Shaped Unsupported Concertina

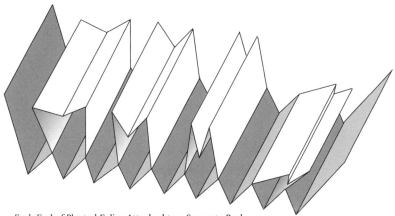

Each End of Pleated Folios Attached to a Separate Peak

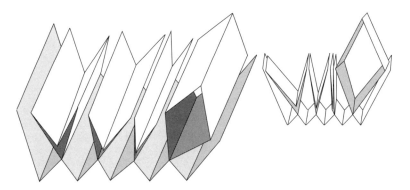

Pop-Up Folios Attached to Same Pleat

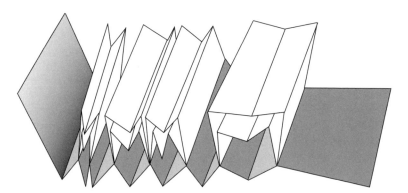

Pulling the Spine Reveals Webbed Translucent Sections

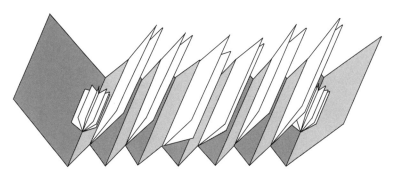

Codices in Cover Hinge-Folds of a Concertina Binding

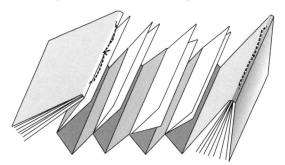

Pamphlet-Sewn Codices as Covers for a Concertina Binding

Fold Books-as-Sections for a Concertina Binding

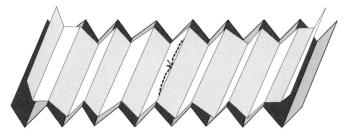

Fold Book-as-Book Block for a Concertina Binding

Number of Supports

The supported con-certina binding may have any number of tapes on the spine.

A single tape may be wrapped and beaded. In the sample to the right, wrapping within the tape without beading suggests other variations. Two or more wrappings might exist within a single tape.

The supported con-certina binding almost always has two or three tapes wrapped and bead-ed on the spine. Each wrapping/beading uses a separate thread.

In this sample, a single paper tape is attached by wrapping through the sections and through slits within, rather than around, the tape. This allows wrapping, but no beading. End of the tape is sewn to the cover near the foredge.

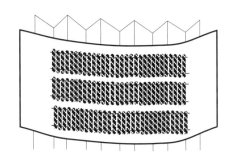

Several wrappings within a single tape support.

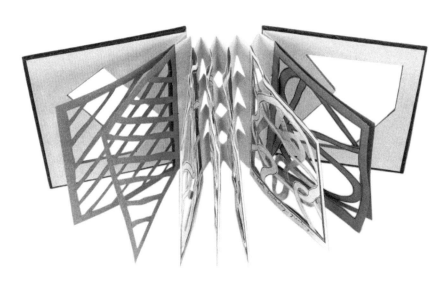

PROCEDURE FOR THE UNSUPPORTED SEWING
Pleat

Determine use and look of the pleat and construct your pleat.

1. For a spine-pleat to which separate board covers will later be attached see *Folding an Oriental Fold Book*, page 243 and *Pleat as Spine*, page 323.
2. For a pleat folded as spine and endsheets, with separate side-covers attached see *Pleat as Spine and Cover*, page 324.
3. For a pleat folded as spine and side-covers, separate side-covers are not needed.
4. A decorated pleat can be constructed from certain photo mural papers which will take a crease. Water color paper can be imaged, making use of compression and extension of the imaged pleat. See *Book 121,* illustrated on page 262.
5. For decorating the pleat, it can be imaged by piercing and slitting. Parts of the pleat can be folded back to create openings or areas removed, as long as integrity of the structure is maintained, as in the book shown below. Also, see drawn illustrations of cut and folded pleats, page 327.

Sections

Fold the sections. Usually the pleat is the same height as the sections, which will be pamphlet sewn onto the pleat. Mark, but don't pierce the sewing stations on the sections. Decide if you want each section attached to a mountain peak or valley, on the inside of the spine-pleat. You need not mark the stations on the pleat.

Remember, compound hinging action is achieved by sewing the sections on the mountain peak on the inside of the concertina pleat.

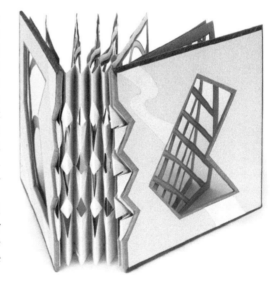

Keith Smith, *Book 145,* 1989. Cut paper. 10.7 x 10 cm. Birthday book for Scott.
The slit and folded pleated spine of this book is the *diamond* pleat, described on page 327. Open view of this book is on the facing page.

SEWING the SECTIONS

The sections are pamphlet sewn to the pleat to construct the unsupported concertina binding and as the first part of constructing a supported concertina binding. Each section is pamphlet sewn to a pleat on the inside of the spine.

Mountain Peak Stations and Sewing

Stations on the sections are marked on the mountain peaks. If you are going to pamphlet sew each section to a mountain peak on the inside of the spine, proceed as follows: Lay the valley of the section over the inside peak of the pleat. Pierce the stations of the section and the pleat at once. Turn section around, so pleat and section are peak to peak for sewing. Pamphlet sew each section separately to the pleat.

Valley Stations and Sewing

If you are going to pamphlet sew the sections to the valleys on the inside of the spine, proceed as follows: locate the inside valley of the pleat. On the outside of the spine, that position is a mountain peak. Lay the mountain peak of the section over the outside mountain peak, which is the position of the inside valley. Pierce the stations of the section and the pleat at once. Bring the section to the inside and pamphlet sew to the valley.

Ties-Off

Start the sewing on the inside of the section if you wish the ties-off inside. If you are going to make a supported sewing on the spine, the pamphlet sewing can start on the outside. The ties-off will not show on either side since the tapes can be positioned to hide them.

Sections have been pamphlet sewn to the pleat as an unsupported concertina. Tapes will be used for the second sewing which is a supported spine sewing.

SUPPORTED SPINE SEWING, *Wrapping and Beading*
Wrapping

The optional sewing around tape supports on the outside of the spine creates a *supported* Concertina Binding. Sewing stations are always on the mountain peaks of the spine. Wrapping the leather or book cloth tapes between the stations fixes the distance the pleats are held apart. Thicker thread or the use of cord requires less wrapping. The wrapping is done from one end to the other, then the beading proceeds in the other direction back to the initial station. One edge of the tape will have a double bead, the other a single bead. See illustration on page 277.

SUPPORTED SPINE SEWING

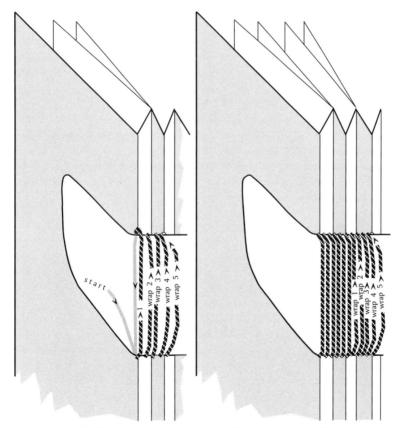

Wrapping the First Section   Wrapping the Second Section
For purposes of showing the wrappings, the threads wrapped around the support in the drawings above are not touching. They must be tangent when you wrap so that the tape support does not show through between the threads.

Expanding the Spine

Determine the width of the spine desired to calculate the number of wrappings necessary. This calculation is learned by trial and error. The spine is expanded as the pleats are fixed however far apart desired, similar to swelling a backbone.

The spread of the pleats is achieved by the number of wrappings around the tape between each pleat prior to sewing through station on the next pleat. The thickness of the thread is another factor. At least a #12 thread is recommended. The book below uses cord.

For Parallel Side-Covers As a guide, if the sections are octavo, 80 lb. text and the thread is #12, three wrappings between stations will probably expand the spine-pleat to the width of the book block. Less than three wrappings will result in a pinched spine. The covers will not fully close against the book block.

For Wedge-Shape More than three wrappings expands the book toward a wedge-shape, as the spine becomes wider than the foredge. The disadvantage is the book cannot be stored on a bookshelf but requires a protective book box, such as a clamshell or slip case.

The wedge-shape can be attractive, as it shows off the pleat. See illustration on page 265. It is also functional. Objects can be collaged to the pages, which will expand the foredge to the depth of the spine. Such a book could be stored on a bookshelf.

For a Crown Spine Excessive number of wrappings with 6 or 8-cord linen twine will alter the spine to a cylindrical shape, which I refer to as a crown spine shown below.[12]

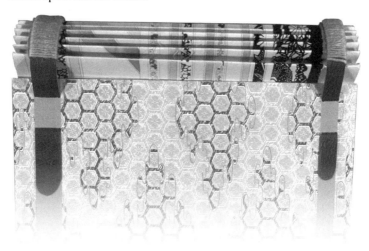

Keith Smith, *Book 96* with an extremely expanded spine, referred to as a *crown*.

Marking the Stations

Construct stiff tapes so the wrapping does not bend them. See *Tape Supports*, page 299. Center the tapes in position horizontally across the spine-pleat. The supported concertina binding usually has two tapes. One is placed about ¾" down from the head. One is placed the same distance up from the tail. Mark the stations using the top and bottom edge of the tapes as a guide. Remove tapes and pierce the stations. Station 2 is the station closest to the head. It also refers to the station close to the tail. Station 1 for the top tape is the second station down from the head. Station 1 for the bottom tape is the second station up from the tail.

If your sections are sewn in the valleys, the supported spine stations will proceed through the sections. If the sections are sewn to inside peaks, the supported spine sewing will appear inside the book in the valleys of the pleats, seen intermittently between sections.

Thread

Length of thread depends on number of wrappings, number of sections and width of tape. Start with 48" and log the amount left over or added on to the thread, for future reference. Cord should be heavily waxed to maintain neat and tangent wrappings around the tape. Linen cord should not be waxed.

Right-Handed Sewing Procedure

If there are three tapes, sew the tape at the head, turn the book over and sew the tail. Sew any middle tapes last. It is easier to hold the book with one hand from above, while sewing is done with the other. Center the tape on the spine, at the sewing stations nearest the head. If you are right-handed, place your left forefinger inside the left hinge-fold pleat.

Place your left thumb on the tape to hold it centered on the spine, as well as between the stations on the first peak. Sewing/wrapping will proceed from the left hinge-fold to the right.

Each tape will utilize only two stations on each peak. The bottom station will be referred to as sewing station 1, the top as station 2.

Start inside, within the pleat, if your sections were sewn on inside peaks. The stations will be within the sections, if the pamphlet sewing was done in the valleys.

You can start at either station. At whichever station you start you will end with a single bead along that edge of the tape. The following description starts at station 1, giving a double bead along the top edge of the tape:

1. Go through station 1, pulling all but 4" of thread to outside. Proceed up the tape, re-positioning your thumb on this first vertical wrap.

    Your thumb and forefinger are now holding the wrap, the tape and the pleat.

2. Proceed into station 2. Make an Overhand Knot. Do not tie a Square Knot, as you will end up at this position, untie this Overhand and tie one Square Knot.

3. Go out station 1, again. Pull thread tight. Tighten the single wrap and again reposition your thumb and forefinger over the wrapping, the tape and the pleat.

4. Wrap the tape several times (a minimum of three) before proceeding to next sewing station. The wraps will go up, over the tape, then down behind, in a clockwise movement. Wraps must be vertical, tangent and tightened as you go, as they cannot be adjusted later, except for the first wrap.

5. Maintaining your left thumb and forefinger grasp, use your middle finger to open the next pleat. Adjust the fold of the next pleat along the tape to the point where the wrapping has ended. Take the needle though sewing station 2 of the new pleat to inside. Proceed out station 1. Pull the thread outside. Make sure you do not pinch this new pleat over against the previous pleat. Let the wrapping determine the spacing of the mountain peaks along the tape.

6. Readjust your thumb and forefinger, grasping the left side of the new pleat. Your thumb will also hold the final wrap in position, while you proceed to wrap between this and the next station. Do not be concerned about the loose thread and first wrap. It can be tightened when you tie-off.

7. Wrap the tape the same number of times before proceeding into next sewing station. Don't pinch the pleat. Allow the wrapping to position the spread between pleats. Keep the wraps vertical, tangent and tightened as you go.

Remaining Stations   Repeat steps 5, 6 and 7 for all additional sewing stations along this tape, except the final pleat.

    After proceeding out station 1 of the next to last pleat, wrap the usual number of times and take the needle into station 2 of the final pleat. Proceed out station 1. Wrapping is now complete. Place a curved sewing needle on the thread and you will be ready to begin the beading, which will proceed from this hinge-fold to the other.

Beading

1. To start the beading, pull the thread snugly to outside and allow the thread coming from station 1 to lay on top of the tape, as if it were another wrap. Take the curved needle behind the tape, between the last two mountain peaks at the far right of the spine. Do not pierce or hook the needle under any of the previous sewing.

BEADING the CONCERTINA TAPE SUPPORT

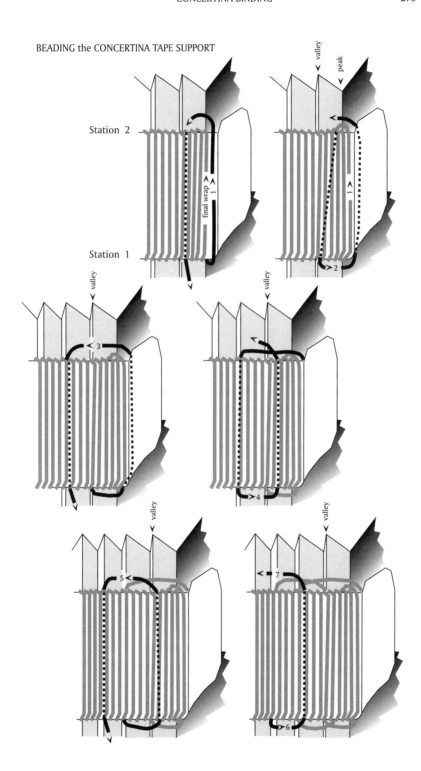

Simply guide the needle from the top, behind the wrapped tape, coming out below the tape. Pull down on thread, tightening the final wrap, make sure it does not become a diagonal, but lays vertically on the tape tangent to the previous wraps.

2. To change directions back to the initial pleat, proceed to the right, take the thread behind the tape at the side-cover. Proceed up the back of the tape. This loop around the bottom edge of the tape is the first single bead. Now you will proceed from the right hinge-fold to the left, back to the initial pleat by beading.

3. The thread is at the top of the tape, at the right of the first mountain peak of the spine-pleat. Proceed across the top of the tape, beyond 2 peaks. Take the needle down behind the tape at that point. This forms the first double bead along the top of the tape. Pull thread down to adjust pressure on the double bead. Look to see if the thread behind the tape at the side-cover is taut. Check to see if the first single bead at the bottom of the tape is not too loose. If you make it too tight, it will disappear underneath the tape.

Pressure on the beads can be fairly loose to fairly tight. It will not affect the wrapping. The important thing to remember is to keep the pressure consistent.

Consistency will give a uniform size and shape in your row of beads. From now on, check the pressure after forming each bead and adjust as you go.

The thread is now extending from behind the tape.

4. Backtrack one position, that is, proceed to the right, past one peak. Take the needle up that valley, behind the tape. This forms the second single bead.

5. Advance two positions. That is, proceed to the left, past two peaks. Take the needle down that valley, behind the tape, forming the second double bead.

6. Backtrack one. Take the needle up behind the tape coming out above the tape.

7. Advance two. Take the needle down behind the tape, coming out below.

Remaining Beading Proceed in the same manner, repeating steps 6 and 7, until in forming a double bead at the top, you take the needle down the final valley.

Next, backtrack one. Take the needle up behind the tape coming out above. Advance two positions. The first position is the final valley, the second is beyond the hinge-fold to the side-cover. Proceed down behind the tape on the side-cover. This forms the final double bead.

Backtrack one. Take the needle up behind the tape in the final valley. This forms the last single bead.

Take the needle into station 2. Untie the Overhand Knot. Tighten the first wrap. Tie the two loose ends of thread with a Square Knot.

Sewing the Tape at the Tail Turn the book over, with the tail at the top. Stand the book on the table to make a separate sewing for the bottom tape, with the same procedure described above. Determine if you want the double bead along the same edge on this tape or if you want the beading symmetrical. Start at station 1, closer to the tail for the former, station 2 for the latter.

CONCERTINA BINDING
with Exposed Spine Sewing

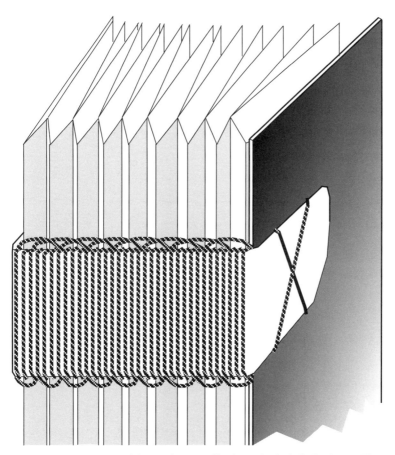

Vertical wraps go around the sturdy tapes of leather or book cloth glued to a stiff paper. Horizontal beads are along the top and bottom of the tape. A double bead is shown at the top, with the single bead at the bottom. Separate board side-covers are attached after the sewing is completed, sewn glued or woven through the boards.

Starting a Sewing at Station 2 If you start any sewing/wrapping, head or tail, at station 2 (the bottom of the tape), instead of wrapping clockwise, proceed down the outside of the tape, around and up behind the tape, wrapping counter-clockwise. After each wrapping, proceed to the next section and go into station 1. Proceed on inside, coming out station 2. Continue wrapping.

Sewing a Middle Tape A third tape in the middle of the spine is optional. All sewing stations on the spine must be pre-pierced before any of the tapes have been wrapped. Tapes at the head and tail can be wrapped using a straight needle to go through the pleats, switching to a curved needle for the beading. However, wrapping, as well as beading will require a curved needle for a third or fourth tape.

Station Variation The top edge of the tape at the head can be placed along the top edge of the spine-pleat and side-covers. The bottom tape can be lowered to the edge of the tail. Each tape would require piercing only along the inside edge of the tape. The head and tail serve as passive stations.

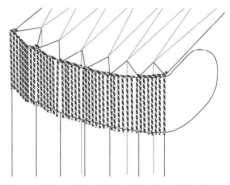

Tape can be positioned along the edge of the pleat. Wrapping should be tangent so that the tape does not show through between the threads.

Sewing station 1 is pierced. Station 2 would be the head itself. Sewing must start on inside, proceeding out station 1. The tape is wrapped as many times as desired.

Then, proceed to next section to station 2. Wrap over the head to the inside of section. Proceed to station 1. Go to outside. Continue wrapping the tape.

Turn book over and use same procedure for the tail. This variation gives a double bead at the very head and tail of the spine.

If you use this variation, you also might want that theme in sewing the sections, using the head and tail as two of your sewing stations. See *5-Hole Variation Pamphlet Sewing*, page 96.

Thread Variation The beading can be a different color thread than the wrapping. After completing the sewing/wrapping and changing to a curved needle, cut the thread and tie on a different color thread. Use a Weaver's Knot to position the knot precisely. The knot is hidden behind the tape, the first time you take the needle behind the tape, just prior to starting the beading.

Cover

Whether you are constructing a supported or unsupported concertina binding, the spine is exposed. Both bindings use separate side-covers, attached after all sewing is completed. If the pleat is folded as spine and side-covers, no other covers need be attached.

If side-covers are needed you can wheat paste decorative papers to book board. If you wish to keep the binding completely non-adhesive, use *Bordered Paper Side-Covers*, page 289 with or without a liner. Or, you might use *Separately Wrapped Boards*, page 293.

To attach the separate side-covers, see *Tape Supports*, page 299; and *Pleat as Spine,* attaching separate covers, page 323.

Keith Smith, *Book 148*, 1990. 38.5 x 32.5 x 3.7 cm. Collection of the New York Public Library Rare Books Collection. The pleat is smaller than the book block, as with the Book 100 on page 298. Boards on this book were shaped to emphasize the difference, making a more interesting spine. The same solution is used on Book 150, page 88.

Shaped board suggests the smaller height of the pleat in relation to the taller sections.

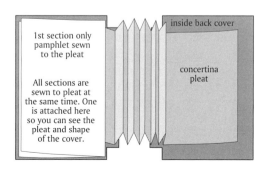

1st section only pamphlet sewn to the pleat

All sections are sewn to pleat at the same time. One is attached here so you can see the pleat and shape of the cover.

inside back cover

concertina pleat

One of the beauties of the Concertina Binding is its compound hinging. This allows heavy weight pages with items attached to lie flat at any opened folio of a supported concertina binding. There is even more flexibility in an unsupported concertina binding.

Another special feature is the pleat can be exaggerated. In the example to the right, the pleat is wider than the pages. In effect, the pleat is a "page" next to the pages of the pamphlet sewn sections.

The pleat-as-page is in view while the entire section is looked at. Turning the final page of the section brings up not only the next page, but the next pleat-as-page.

This is theme and variation. It is like music—the pleat-as-page is holding one note while the pages of the section are singing a melody.

The pleat-as-page could contain text which would be ever-present while the pictures in that section would be viewed. Turning to the next section, a new pleat-as-page might contain a picture always in sight while a section of text is read.

The pleat might contain partial text which is modified or completed by each page turned beside it. Ideas for many projects will come by looking through sections sewn onto various pleats.

Construct various size pleats in relation to the page. Quickly sew on sections for a book-as-sketch. Go through the pages of these blank books. Some will suggest a mood or rhythm or attitude that will be appropriate for a book you have in mind. Others will not. But keep them on hand. Look through these bindings now and then. Blank books are one of your greatest resources for ideas.

PART 3

COVERS AND SUPPORTS

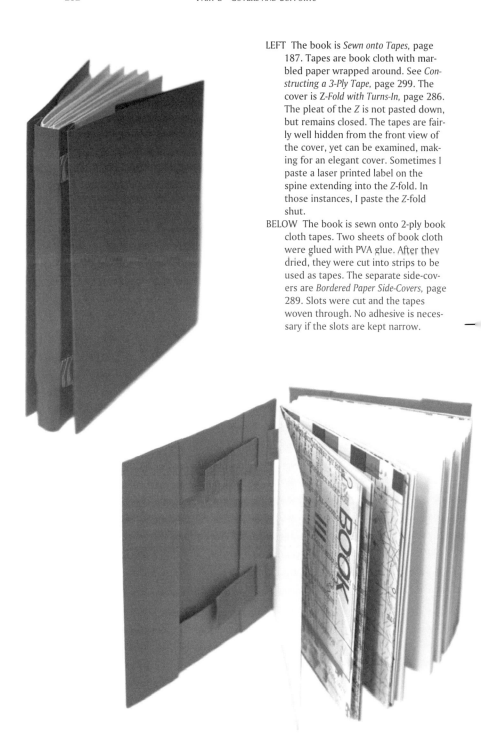

LEFT The book is *Sewn onto Tapes*, page 187. Tapes are book cloth with marbled paper wrapped around. See *Constructing a 3-Ply Tape*, page 299. The cover is *Z-Fold with Turns-In*, page 286. The pleat of the Z is not pasted down, but remains closed. The tapes are fairly well hidden from the front view of the cover, yet can be examined, making for an elegant cover. Sometimes I paste a laser printed label on the spine extending into the Z-fold. In those instances, I paste the Z-fold shut.

BELOW The book is sewn onto 2-ply book cloth tapes. Two sheets of book cloth were glued with PVA glue. After they dried, they were cut into strips to be used as tapes. The separate side-covers are *Bordered Paper Side-Covers*, page 289. Slots were cut and the tapes woven through. No adhesive is necessary if the slots are kept narrow.

Many people will use book board and wheat paste decorative papers to both sides of the boards. These will then be attached to the sewings described in this book. Others will want to keep the entire process non-adhesive. The following is a variety of paper covers requiring no adhesives. Some are ideal for the sewings. I suggest always having a foredge turn-in. A single ply cover will get bent easily. The first cover described is not recommended, but is shown to present an array of possible covers.

FLAT BACK COVER

the 2-fold cover

This limp cover with two folds-as-hinges, it is the simplest flush cover.
It is used on most commercially bound paperbacks.
HEIGHT of the cover is cut first. It is the same height as the text block.
WIDTH of the cover is the sum of the width of the first page,
plus the depth of the book block,
plus the width of the last page.

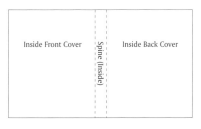

FLAT BACK
with FOREDGE TURNS-IN

the 4-fold cover

The turn-in reinforces the edge of the cover most likely to receive damage. Just as importantly, it dresses up the flat back cover. An added benefit of the turn-in allows printing on the "inside" of the cover, which, when unfolded, is actually the same surface as the outside cover. In production work, this saves the cost of not having to print both sides of the cover sheet.

The foredge turn-in must be wide enough so that it tends to lay flat, unless it is sewn or tabbed. Generally this means it is at least 1" wide. The turn-in may be as wide as the side-cover, but should be trimmed ¼" shorter. Otherwise, careless closing of the cover could cause the edge at the spine to crimp. Design your books as fool proof as possible. Books are only as strong and accident-resistant, as their weakest element.

Measuring Formula

HEIGHT of cover paper equals height of book block.
WIDTH of cover equals width of front foredge turn-in
plus width of first page (front side-cover)
plus depth of book block (spine)
plus width of final page (back side-cover)
plus width of back foredge turn-in.

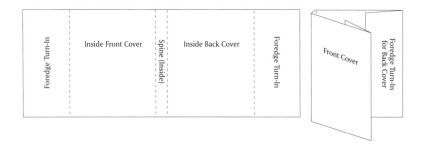

FLAT BACK
with FIXED FOREDGE TURNS-IN

4-fold cover with 3-ply spine

This cover provides a heavily reinforced spine. It is an ideal cover for many bindings and was specifically designed for the long stitch bindings.

Each foredge turn-in is the width of the side-cover, plus the width of the spine. Fold the cover in at the foredge and make a second fold on the turn-in where it meets the spine. The second fold reinforces the hinge-fold as well as the spine.

Fold the other foredge turn-in. The spine portion of the second turn-in goes either on top or underneath the other turn-in, giving a three-ply spine. The turns-in will not open, being fixed in position when the text block and cover are sewn together.

Measuring Formula

HEIGHT of cover equals height of book block.
WIDTH of cover paper equals
width of the spine (front foredge turn-in onto spine)
plus width of the book block (front foredge turn-in)
plus width of the book block (front side-cover)
plus depth of book block (spine)
plus width of the book block (back
     side-cover)
plus width of the book block (back
     foredge turn-in)
plus width of the spine (back
     foredge turn-in onto spine).

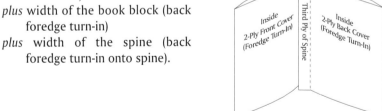

Z-FOLD FLAT BACK with TURNS-IN

The Z-fold at the hinge-folds hides the tapes which are laced into the side-covers behind the Z-fold.

The book block is sewn onto tapes. See *Sewing onto Tapes*, page 187; *In-Tape Sewing*, page 203; or *Blanket Stitch with Slit Tapes*, page 197.

Cover is attached separately. Cut, but do not fold a flat back with foredge turns-in as described above, adding an additional 3" to width of cover.

Measuring Formula

HEIGHT of cover paper equals height of book block.
WIDTH of cover equals width of front foredge turn-in
plus width of book block (front side-cover)
plus ¾"
plus ¾" (Z-fold)
plus depth of book block (spine)
plus ¾"
plus ¾" (Z-fold)
plus width of book block (back side-cover)
plus width of back foredge turn-in

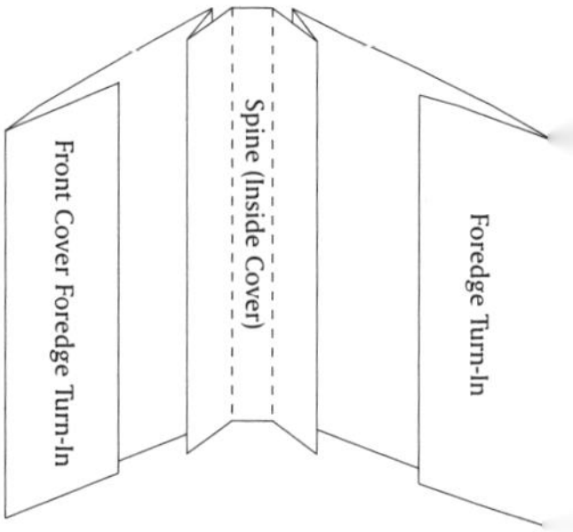

Procedure for the Z-Fold Flat Back with Turns-In

Measure and cut the cover. Fold according to diagram below.

Open cover flat, with the inside of the cover facing up. Mark a dot on each side of the tapes on the hinge-folds. Mark locations of the tapes on the next fold in on the side-covers, which is the mountain peak of the Z-fold. Cut the slits on these folds. Set book block into formed cover. Lace the tapes out the hinge-fold slits and back in the slits on the Z-folds. On the outside of the cover the Z-fold slits are in the valley.

Trim edge of the tapes. Tapes can be attached to inside of the side-covers. I prefer attaching them to the first endsheet.

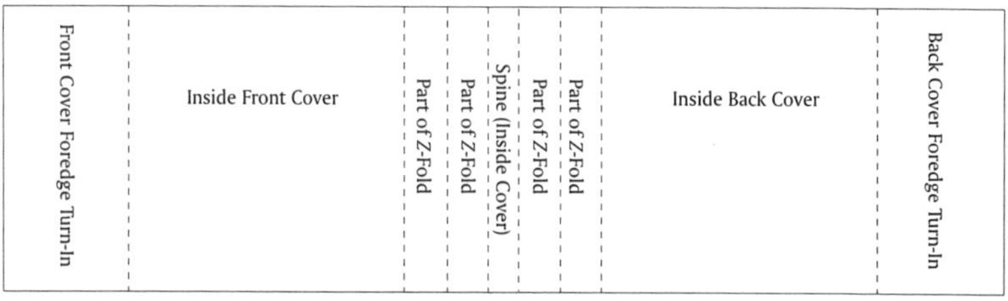

FLAT BACK with BORDERS

the 6-fold cover

The flat back with borders has turns-in at the head, tail and foredges creating an overhang cover. They are folded in that order, tabbed or sewn down. See *Interlocking Tabs,* page 306.

The text block is more securely attached to the cover, since the hinge-folds are reinforced. In addition, the turns-in reinforce all open edges of the cover, which are now two-ply. This allows the possibility of designing an overhang cover.

A one-piece liner can be placed under the turns-in. Or, separate liners can be placed under the turns-in of each side-cover. See *Optional Liner,* page 82.

The turns-in should be at least ¾" on all sides. More than that may be used to obtain a desirable proportion of the bordered turn-in to the remainder of the inside cover. I prefer close to a 2" turn-in, especially on the *Long Stitch/Link Stitch*, page 177. A wider turn-in will catch two of the sewing stations at the head and two at the tail. The remainder of the sewing stations sew through a single thickness of spine-cover.

Measuring Formula for Flush Cover

HEIGHT to cut and fold the cover paper:
the size of the turn-in at the head,
plus the height of the book block,
plus the size of the turn-in at the tail.
WIDTH of the needed cover paper equals:
size of the front foredge turn-in,
plus width of the book block (front side-cover),
plus width of the spine,
plus width of book block (back side-cover),
plus the size of the foredge turn-in.

NOTE: It might seem that if the overhang at the head is ¼" and the overhang at the tail is ¼", that only an additional ½" need be added to the height of the book block. But the overhang must proceed beyond the head ¼" inch on the side-cover, then another ¼" down the turn-in at the head. Thus, ½" is required at the head and another ½" at the tail to yield a ¼" square.

Turn-In at Head

Spine-Edge Turn-In   Spine   Foredge Turn-In

Turn-In at Tail

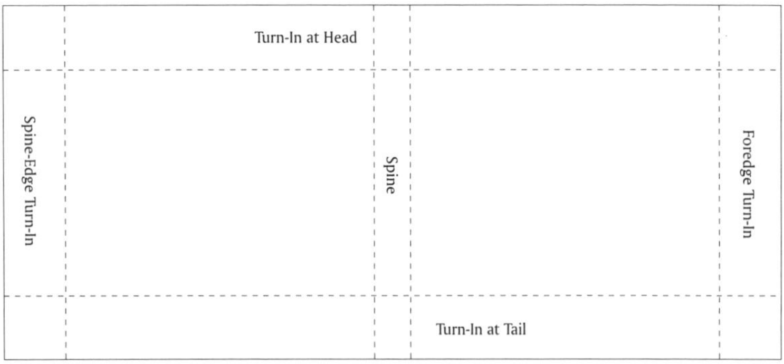

3. Measure and mark the depth of the spine, which will be the same as the depth of the book block. This is the position of the other hinge-fold.
4. Proceeding to the left measure and mark the width of the book block. Add to this ¼" for the foredge overhang. This is where the back cover foredge fold will occur.
5. Add ¼" for the overhang on the other side of the fold. Add to this the width of the turn-in on the back cover. It is probably the same size as the turn-in on the front cover, the head and the tail.
6. Trim off excess paper, tab or sew down the turns-in.

REVIEW, or CONDENSED MEASURING FORMULA

HEIGHT of cover with ¼" overhang equals height of the turn-in at the head and an additional ¼" for overhang on the turn-in,

plus ¼" for the overhang at the head and the height of the book block and ¼" for the overhang at the tail,

plus ¼" for the overhang on the turn-in and height of the turn-in at the tail.

WIDTH of needed cover paper with a ¼" overhang equals:

width of front foredge turn-in and ¼" for overhang of the turn-in,

plus ¼" for overhang of front cover and width of book block,

plus depth of the book block,

plus width of the book block and ¼" for back cover overhang,

plus ¼" for overhang on the turn-in and width of the foredge turn-in.

BORDERED PAPER SIDE-COVERS

Two separate side-covers each having turns-in at the head and tail and at the foredge and the spine-edge. They are folded in that order, tabbed to a spine-pleat or sewn onto tapes See illustrations: *Attaching Separate Side-Covers* page 303 and *Attaching Separate Side-Covers by Sewing on the Tape Supports,* page 305.

Rigidity of separate side covers with borders on all for edges allows for an overhang. Separate liners can be placed under the turns-in of each side-cover. See *Interlocking Tabs*, page 306.

Tapes are sewn or woven through slots on the covers. The attachment of the tapes also fixes optional liners in place. The tapes are the hinges for the cover. See *Stab Covers*, for the example *Hinge-Fold at Spine with Bordered Turns-In*, page 129.

Measuring Formula

This description is for a single side-cover, bordered on four sides, which will have tapes attached. The square of the book will be ¼". This requires an added inch to the height, but only ½" to the width, because there is no overhang at the spine-edge. Construct two of the following:

HEIGHT of needed cover weight paper with a ¼" overhang equals:
height of the turn-in at the head and an additional ¼" for the overhang on the turn-in,
plus ¼"" for the overhang at the head and the height of the book block and ¼" for the overhang at the tail,
plus ¼" for the overhang on the turn-in and height of the turn-in at the tail.
WIDTH of needed cover paper with a ¼" overhang equals:
width of the foredge turn-in and ¼" for the overhang of the turn-in,
plus ¼" for overhang on the foredge of the side-cover and width of the book block,
plus width of foredge turn-in.

FLAT BACK with BOARDS

Most of the bindings in this book are designed for paper covers. However, any of the bindings can be modified to be hard cover and still remain a non-adhesive binding.

Boards as side-covers with a paper spine require three papers to create the wrapper—one horizontal and two vertical sheets. Each board is folded into the horizontal wrapper, then held in place by a vertical wrapper which shows on the inside of the side-covers.

The Pamphlet Bindings, Buttonhole Stitch, Long Stitch and the Long Stitch/Link Stitch binding can each be sewn onto the horizontal wrapper. This is done prior to adding the boards. The spine of each binding is made two-ply to reinforce the spine, but also to add a hinge-fold flap on the inside of the horizontal wrapper. This are needed to attach the vertical wrapper.

PREPARATION
A Wide Hinge

The *wide hinge* is a continuous paper support onto which the book block is sewn. It is not a cover, but used as tabs to attach a cover. The hinge is between the horizontal wrapper and the book block. It is cut to these dimensions:

HEIGHT is the same as the horizontal wrapper, which may be a flush or overhang cover.
WIDTH equals ⅓ width of the book block (front hinge-flap),
plus width of spine,
plus ⅓ width of the book block (back hinge-flap).

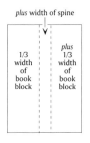

Hinge-Fold Flaps

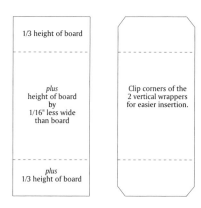

Vertical Wrappers

1/3 width of book block	*plus* width of book block and square, if any (1/4")	*plus* width of book block and square, if any (1/4")	*plus* width of book block and square, if any (1/4")	*plus* width of book block and square, if any (1/4")	*plus* 1/3 width of book block

plus width of spine

Horizontal Wrapper

Horizontal Wrapper

Horizontal wrapper shows on the outside of side-covers and on the spine. Cut, but do not fold the wrapper:
HEIGHT is same as the book block for a flush cover or ½" larger for an
  overhang cover with ¼" square.
WIDTH equals ⅓ width of book block,
plus width of the book block and ¼'''' for square, if any,
plus width of the book block and ¼" for square, if any,
plus width of the spine,
plus width of the book block and ¼" for square, if any,
plus width of the book block and ¼" for square, if any,
plus ⅓ width of book block.

Fold the hinge to fit the spine. Fold the horizontal wrapper at the hinge-folds only. Fold one at a time, fitting the spine of the wrapper around and therefore just slightly wider than the spine of the hinge.

Sewing

Modify the two-ply spine for the particular binding. The Buttonhole Binding will need part of the spine removed. Make the sewing stations on the spine and sew.

Boards

Cut the boards for the side-covers the same dimensions as the book block for a flush cover or ½" taller and ¼" wider for an overhang cover with a ¼" square.

Vertical Wrappers

Cut paper for the inside of each side-cover. HEIGHT of the paper is 1⅔ times as tall as the board. It might be a different color than the horizontal wrapper.
WIDTH will be ¹⁄₁₆" less than the board.

ASSEMBLY
Folding the Horizontal Wrapper

Lay a board on the inside of the horizontal wrapper, next to the book block, on top of the hinge. Grasp the wrapper extending beyond the board and fold it around the foredge of the board. The folded paper will extend slightly onto the book block. Fold the remainder of the wrapper under the spine-edge of the board.

Attaching a Vertical Wrapper

Open the side-cover. Lay the vertical wrapper centered on top of the wrapped board. Run your finger along the head and tail of the board to crease. This will indicate the head and tail folds on the vertical wrapper. Remove and fold the vertical wrapper. Shape the head and tail of the wrapper by clipping angles, much like an envelope flap. This will allow easier insertion.

Insert the flap of the vertical wrapper at the head and tail, between the outside paper of the horizontal wrapper and the hinge. Wrap the remaining board.

Attaching to the Hinge-Fold Flap

For those bindings sewn onto a hinge-fold flap this cover can be constructed after the text block is sewn. The completed cover would be a jacket, fitted over the sewn binding, woven or sewn onto the hinge-flap.

SEPARATELY WRAPPED BOARDS

These separate side-covers are paper-wrapped boards, good for any binding with exposed spine sewing or those bindings with tapes. It is also used for Coptic Binding, but not for the Album Binding. Specific side-covers for the album binding are described along with that binding.

Dimensions

The boards are the same dimensions as the book block for flush covers. For an overhang cover, each board is two squares taller and one square wider than the book block.

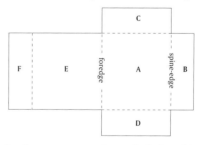

Each board is covered with a single sheet wrapper. Parts *A, B, E and F* are the height of the board. Parts *A, C, D and E* are the width of the board. Parts *C* and *D* are ⅓ the height of the board. Parts *B* and *F* are ⅓ the width of the board. Cut a wrapper for each board.

Procedure

Lay one of the boards on *A*. Close flap *B* over the board, followed by *C* and *D*. Bring *E* over the board and over *B*. Insert flap *F* between *C, D* and *B*. This is the spine-edge of the side-cover. The foredge must be a fold, not a slit edge. For different ways of attaching, see *Attaching Separate Side-Covers*, page 303.

BOARDS with PLEATED SPINE

Wrapping these boards is similar to *Flat Back with Boards*. The difference is this spine is pleated and two separate flaps are attached, one at each hinge-fold. This cover can be used with any binding requiring a spine-pleat and is especially suited to the Unsupported Concertina Binding. The Supported Concertina Binding can utilize its tapes to attach separate side covers as one means of adding board covers, the unsupported cannot.

PREPARATION

Spine and outside of the finished side-cover are the same color. This is the horizontal wrapper. The inside of the side-cover is the separate vertical wrapper of the same or a different color.

Horizontal Wrapper

Fold a pleated spine with side-covers attached. See *Folding a Pleated Spine-Cover,* page 324. Height of the spine-pleat and horizontal wrapper may be the same as the book block for a flush cover. Height of an overhang cover is the thickness of 3 boards in addition to the height of the book block.

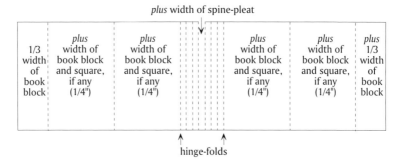

plus width of spine-pleat

| 1/3 width of book block | *plus* width of book block and square, if any (1/4") | *plus* width of book block and square, if any (1/4") | *plus* width of book block and square, if any (1/4") | *plus* width of book block and square, if any (1/4") | *plus* 1/3 width of book block |

hinge-folds

Wrapper for each side-cover must be 2⅓ times as wide as the book block, because they wrap around the boards.

This horizontal wrapper is the pleated spine and shows on the outside of the side-covers. A separate vertical wrapper of the same or a different color will be on the inside of the side-covers, tucked in at the head and tail.

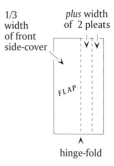

1/3 width of front side-cover

plus width of 2 pleats

FLAP

hinge-fold

Separate Flaps

The hinge-fold flap is pamphlet sewn on inside of the side-cover at the hinge-fold. The wider part of the the flap extends onto the inside of the side-cover.

Separate flaps are made for the front and back side-covers. Hinge-fold of the flap is lined up with hinge-fold of the horizontal wrapper

Each flap extends into a couple of pleats, on the inside of the pleated spine. The sewing of the first and last sections to the pleats will attach the flaps, as well, since they are sewn at the same time.

> 1/3 height of side-cover
>
> *plus* height of side-cover
>
> *plus* 1/3 height of side-cover
>
> Separarte Vertical Wrapper for Each Side-Cover

Vertical Wrapper

Cut paper for the inside of each side-cover. This will be ¹⁄₁₆" less wide than the board. Height of the paper is 1²⁄₃ times as tall as the board. It might be a different color.

BOARDS

Cut the boards for the side-covers the same dimensions as the book block for a flush cover. For an overhang cover, the height of the cover is the thickness of 3 boards in addition to the height of the book block. Width is 1½ times the thickness of the board (approximately ¼") in addition to the width of the book block.

Assembly of the horizontal and vertical wrappers is the same as for *Flat Back with Boards*, page 290.

VARIATION on BOARDS WITH PLEATED SPINE

This variation has a separate horizontal wrapper for each side-cover. The advantage over the horizontal wrapper on the facing page is that this version does not require an extremely wide sheet of paper, since the boards are wrapped individually and the separate spine-pleat is attached to the side-covers. It also permits the outside of the side-covers to be the same or a different color than the spine-pleat.

Each horizontal wrapper is cut to the following dimensions:
HEIGHT is the same as the boards.
WIDTH equals ⅓ the width of the board,
plus width of the board,
plus an additional width of the board,
plus ⅓ width of the board.

Cut, but do not fold horizontal wrapper except for the first fold. Remaining folds are fitted around the board to insure proper fit.

1/3 width of board	first fold goes on spine-edge of the board	*plus* width of board and square, if any (1/4")	second fold, around the foredge	*plus* width of board and square, if any (1/4")	third fold, spine-edge	*plus* 1/3 width of board
		covers the inside of side-cover	covers the outside of side-cover			shows on inside of side-cover at the spine-edge

Separate Horizontal Wrapper for Each Board

Spine-Pleat with Flaps

Fold a spine-pleat leaving extensions on each end as the flaps. The process of folding is the same as for *Folding a Pleated Spine-Cover*, page 324.

Vertical Wrapper and Boards

Dimensions are identical to the vertical wrapper and boards described on the previous page.

Procedure

Fold in one end of a horizontal wrapper ⅓ the width of a board. Place this fold onto the board at the spine-edge. Crease the horizontal wrapper forming the foredge. Bring the remaining edge of the wrapper around the spine-edge to form the third fold. Loose edge of wrapper will be on the inside of the side-cover. Pamphlet sew this fold to hinge-fold of the spine-pleat.

hinge-folds

1/3 width of book block

1/3 width of book block

FLAP   FLAP

Spine-Pleat with Flaps without Horizontal Wrappers

Place the vertical wrapper on the inside of the side-cover, over the flap. Insert edges of the vertical wrapper at the head and tail, between outside paper of the horizontal wrapper and the board.

Attach the other horizontal wrapper to the remaining hinge-fold of the spine-pleat. Wrap the remaining board in the same manner.

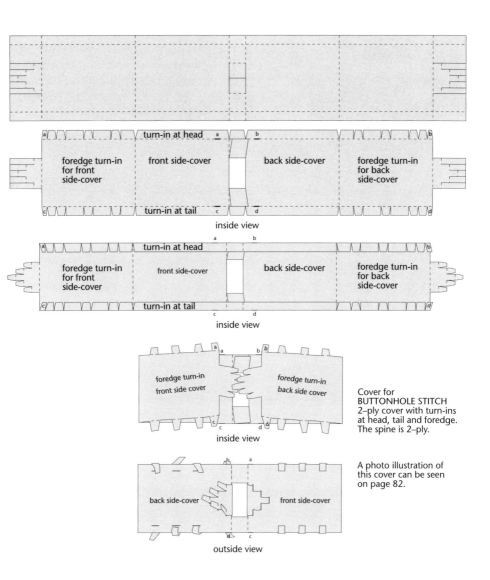

foredge turn-in
front side cover

foredge turn-in
back side cover

inside view

Cover for
BUTTONHOLE STITCH
2–ply cover with turn-ins
at head, tail and foredge.
The spine is 2–ply.

A photo illustration of
this cover can be seen
on page 82.

back side-cover

front side-cover

outside view

This is the most elaborate paper cover I have designed. I think it is worth the effort. Turn-ins at the foredge are with the grain and pose no problems. The turn-ins at the head and tail are against the grain. Choose a paper that will not crack when folded against the grain.

Keith Smith, *Bobby*, Book 100,
in a one-of-a-kind supported Concertina Binding.
Sections are taller than the cover-pleat.
Spine of the book block visible at the head and tail is recessed. 1986.

TAPE SUPPORTS and HINGES

The Coptic Binding, Unsupported Blanket Stitch and Spring Action, are unsupported sewings. Sewing goes from one section into the next, into the next. Structure of unsupported sewing is not as strong as supported sewing, where the stitching goes through or around cord or tape supports or through a continuous support.

Traditionally cord is 6 or 8-cord linen twine. Tapes are ¼" linen, but that is for sewings where the cover hides the tapes. Tape supports can be strips of leather, vellum, 2-ply book cloth or paper. Paper is not recommended, as it will wear and break. If I use paper tapes, I glue book cloth on the back side to reinforce it.

Supports must bend with the side-covers; they are also the hinges. Tape supports can be any width.

Sewing stations for smaller tapes are just above and below the support. Thread wraps the support, holding it to the sections.

Maximum width for a tape would be the height of the book block, in which instance, it would be a continuous support.

Horizontal slits can be cut into tapes for *In-Tape Sewing,* page 203. The slits correspond with the sewing stations pierced into the sections. Slits do not extend beyond the width of the spine. If wrapping is done it would be on, rather than around, the entire support.

CONSTRUCTING a 3-PLY TAPE

Paper can be folded to form a tape support without the use of adhesive. The sewing would keep the layers of the paper tape support together. I strongly advise against paper tapes, as those I made as examples in the first edition of this book have not worn well. If you wish to fold down a tape support, I suggest using book cloth.

Length of tapes depends upon how they are attached to the side-covers. If sewn, they might extend less than an inch onto the side-covers. If woven, they must extend at least ½ the width of a page onto the front and back of the book block. Tapes can be made extra long and trimmed after weaving. This is advisable, as the tips may become crumpled during weaving. Cutting a point onto the end makes the tape easier to weave. Since the tape has considerable thickness, you will generally need to cut slots for weaving onto the side-covers, rather than slits. See *Slots,* which is illustrated on page 82.

For a ¾" wide tape, measure the cover-weight paper a little less than 2¼" in height. From the top edge of the tape, measure down ¾" and mark. Measure down another ¾" and mark. Fold under the top third of the tape at the mark. Fold under the bottom portion of the tape. The turn-in at the bottom will not extend beyond the top of the folded tape, as the folded edge should be hidden on the back of the tape.

CONSTRUCTING A 3-PLY TAPE

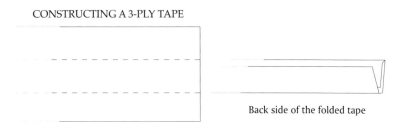

Back side of the folded tape

Attaching to Flat Backs

Several bindings which are sewn onto tapes are the *Concertina Binding*, page 261; *Sewing onto Tapes*, page 187; *Blanket Stitch with Slit Tapes*, page 197; and *In-Tape Sewing*, page 203.

The book block is first sewn onto tapes, with an equal length of tape extending at least 3" onto the first and last pages.

One of the flat back covers can be used. Sewing on the spine is not seen. The tape may be attached to the inside of the side-covers by sewing or by separate, vertically laced tapes.

Tapes sewn to the spine may proceed through slits on the hinge-fold, to outside of the side-covers. They can be sewn down or woven through slots on the side-covers.

A hinge can be used to reinforce the spine. The hinge and the cover are sewn at once. See *Reinforced Spines*, page 83.

HINGES
Weaving a Hinge

A *hinge* is a continuous support connecting the book block to the cover. Sewing of the book block goes through the hinge at various sewing stations all along the spine. Generally narrow, they can be as wide as the book, a liner to be woven or sewn to a separate cover as a decorative element, perhaps using a different color of paper. See illustrations on page 302.

A hinge can as wide as the book can be thought of as the first and last page of a book block. A flat back cover is fitted to the book block and hinge, sewn, laced or woven through the cover. The following is a pamphlet sewn example of a hinge woven to the cover to demonstrate quickly. You can use a multi-section binding also.

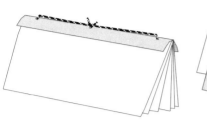

3-Hole Pamphlet Sewing with hinge
to be tabbed to separate side-covers

3-Hole with a wide hinge to be laced into
or sewn to the cover

Preparation and Measurements

Fold one section and cover to fit.

HEIGHT of the hinge of cover weight paper, is at least 3" less than cover. This is so the slits on the cover do not come close to the head or tail, thus weakening the cover.

WIDTH of the hinge equals ½" (to be tucked in)

plus 1" (foredge turn-in onto front cover),

plus width of book block (front side-cover),

plus width of the spine, (if a multi-section binding)

plus width of back cover,

plus 1" (foredge turn-in onto back cover)

plus ½" (to be tucked in).

Even when binding a single section with a pamphlet sewing, the hinge and the cover may accommodate the thickness of the section. There would be two folds placed closely together, on the hinge as well as the cover. The illustration above has only one fold as a hinge-fold since the section is thin, with light weight paper.

Sewing Procedure

Center the hinge on the mountain peak of the section. Mark the sewing stations on the hinge. Pierce stations through hinge and section. Pamphlet sew the hinge and section. Cover is not sewn. It will be attached by weaving.

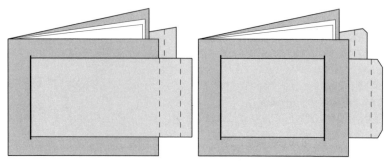

1. Insert flap into slits near the spine on the front and back side-covers.

2. Slip hinge through slits at foredges on front and back.

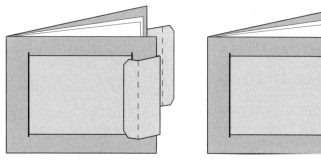

3. Cut angle on edge of hinges for easy insertion. Fold hinge back onto front side-cover.

4. Tuck end of the hinge into the slit.

Weaving the Front Cover onto the Hinge

Open cover flat. On front cover cut a vertical slit 1" in from hinge-fold, the height of the hinge or slightly more to accommodate the hinge. Cut a second vertical slit ⅞" in from foredge. Do the same on the back cover.

Position the cover on and bring front hinge out through the first slit and back inside the cover at the second. Fold the hinge at the foredge onto the top of front cover. Fold the hinge again, this time 1" in from the foredge, with the end of the hinge turned under. Tuck the end of the hinge into the slit. Do the same on the back cover. Variations are up to you. For instance, a smaller tape can be placed near the head and another near the tail of a section. Each is separately pamphlet sewn to the section.

A third tape may be sewn at the center of the spine. The tapes are then attached to a cover.

The same procedure could be accomplished with a long stitch binding. The slits on the cover near the spine can be placed on the hinge-fold or out onto the side-cover as with the pamphlet sewn example. It is important not to have the height of the hinge and slits so large that they weaken the cover.

ATTACHING SEPARATE SIDE-COVERS

Separate side-covers may have turns-in on all four sides with inter-locking tabs. Tapes or hinges can be attached to side-covers by various means. Any turn-in makes the cover stronger and resists being bent.

With a Hinge or Pleated Spine

1. Tapes can be woven through slots on the side-covers.

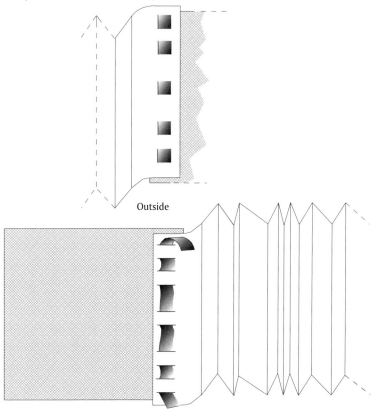

Outside

Inside, prior to tucking the tab

Single sheet side-covers and hinges have corresponding rows of horizontal slits or slots. A vertically laced paper tab weaves them together. See *Tucking the Tab as an Extended Unit*, page 309.

2. A sheet of cover weight paper is cut the height of the book block and twice the width. It is folded in half with fold at the foredge. The hinge is inserted between the two layers of the side-cover at the spine-edge.

Side-cover is attached by sewing or as in example 1, a vertically laced paper tab.

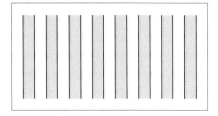

3. Hinges are made extra long. Side-covers are vertically slotted several times at equal or unequal increments. The hinge is then woven through the cover.

4. Hinges are made extra long. Several horizontal slits are made from the hinge-fold out to edge of hinges. Every other portion is removed. The hinge is transformed to several horizontal tabs. Side-cover is slotted and spine-tabs are woven through the cover.

Hinge-folds

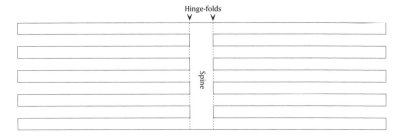

5. Separate side-covers with borders might have turns-in with interlocking tabs on the head, tail and foredge. The turn-in at the spine would not be tabbed, but function as a hinge-fold. The side-cover turn-in at the spine would be sewn or woven to the hinge. See *Hinge-Fold at Spine*, page 128; and *Hinge-Fold at Spine with Bordered Turns-In*, page 129.

With Tapes

6. Single sheet side-covers, with or without foredge turns-in, can be attached by sewing the tapes supports to the board. See the facing page.

7. Tapes can be sandwiched between 2-ply side-covers, then attached by weaving or sewing.

ATTACHING SEPARATE SIDE-COVERS
by SEWING on the TAPE SUPPORTS

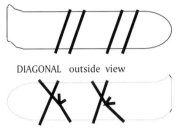

DIAGONAL outside view

inside cover tie-off

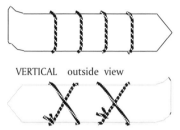

VERTICAL   outside view

inside cover tie-off

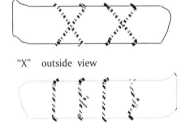

"X"   outside view

inside cover tie-off

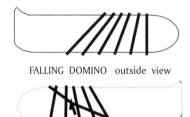

FALLING DOMINO outside view

inside cover tie-off

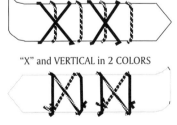

"X" and VERTICAL in 2 COLORS

inside cover tie-off

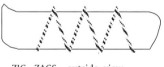

ZIG - ZAGS   outside view

inside cover tie-off

INTERLOCKING TABS

FOREDGE TAB

A foredge turn-in does not need to be tabbed, but can be for reasons of design.

You can invent your own means of tabbing a single turn-in. The following are two examples.

SHAPED FOREDGE TURN-IN as TAB

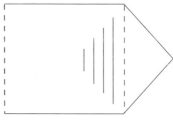

Slit side-cover with
foredge turn-in not folded

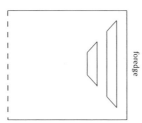

Shaped tab on outside
of side-cover

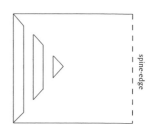

Foredge turn-in tab
woven on the inside

FOREDGE TURN-IN with TABS

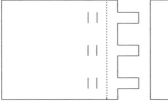

Slit side-cover with
turn-in not folded

Folded and woven
tabs on outside
of side-cover

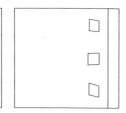

Folded turn-in and
tab endings woven
to inside of side-cover

TABBING BORDERED TURNS-IN

Turns-in at the head, tail and foredge must be sewn down or held in place by interlocking tabs. The following are ways of tabbing at the corners of intersecting turns-in.

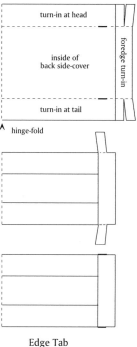

Edge Tab

The foredge turn-in is folded after the turns-in at the head and tail. Therefore, the foredge turn-in is tabbed onto the other turns-in. See *Flat Back with Borders*, page 287. If you are using separate side-covers, the turns-in are illustrated on page 129, *Hinge-Fold at Spine with Bordered Turns-In.*

Unfold the cover so that it lies flat. Notice the creases at each of the four corners create a square. If the head, tail and foredge turn-in are each 1" wide, the squares at each corner are 1" x 1".

1. Slit each square in half vertically to create a tab at each corner The tabs are along the edge of the paper when the cover is opened flat. Each is ½" wide and 1" in height The remainder of the squares at the corner are part of the turns-in.

Edge Tab

2. Fold the turns-in at the head and tail, leaving the tabs unfolded. Next, fold the foredge turns-in. The tabs will now set in ½" from the foredges. With a pencil, lightly mark where the tabs line up on the fold of the head and tail.
3. Open the cover paper flat and cut a slit on the fold to accommodate each tab. Re-fold the cover in the same order and insert the tabs.

   Cover is now ready to be sewn with the book block, after the stations are marked and pierced on the spine.

Mitered Turn-In Tab

1. Fold 2" turns-in at the head, tail and foredge. Unfold the cover so that it lies flat. Notice the creases at each of the four corners create a 2" square.
2. Open the cover flat and remove the 2" square at each corner by cutting.
3. Fold down the turn-in at the head, then fold in the foredge turn-in.

Fold the top of the foredge turn-in back on itself, at a 45° angle from the corner. Measure down ¾" from the corner, along the 45° fold. Place a pencil dot on the head turn-in at the foredge 45° fold. Place another pencil dot beside the other, on the foredge fold.

4. Measure ¾" up from the other end of the foredge 45° fold. Place a pencil dot on the head turn-in at the foredge 45° fold. Place another pencil dot beside it, on the foredge fold.

5. Open the cover flat and cut, connecting the two dots on the head turn-in. This will create approximately a 1¼" slit for the tab.

Cut the foredge turn-in down from the fold between the foredge and the side-cover to the top dot. Cut from the edge of the foredge turn-in up to the lower dot.

This creates the tab which will be inserted into the slit on the head turn-in. The tails of the tab must be folded temporarily to insert the tab into the slit. Once the tab is inserted, unfold the tails as a locking device. When completed, the tab does not show. Follow this procedure with each of the other corners to create the tabs.

Turns-In at the head, tail and foredge may be held in place by interlocking tabs other than at the corners by weaving a tab.

MITERED TAB

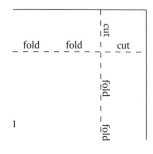

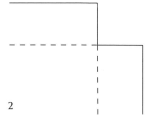

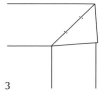

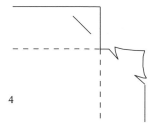

Slit-Locked Tab

This is a single unit tab.

1. Weave the unit. 2. Slit the ends. 3. Lock the tabs.

1. The side-cover and turn-in are slit at once, slightly larger than the width of the tab. A second parallel slit is made. A tab is woven in and out.
2. At the far left, the top edge of the tab is slit vertically down to center of the tab. At the far right, the bottom edge of the tab is slit vertically up to center of the tab.
3. The loose ends of the tabs are interlocked.

     One or more woven and locked tabs can be used on the side-cover. Several may be randomly placed in polka dot fashion or regimented, such as a border. However, if the woven tabs are regimented, as in a straight line, it is easier to weave a single tab the length of the row. This creates a multi-unit tab, as the tab weaves in and out. The ends of the tabs will be finished off by tucking, rather than using the slit-locked tab.

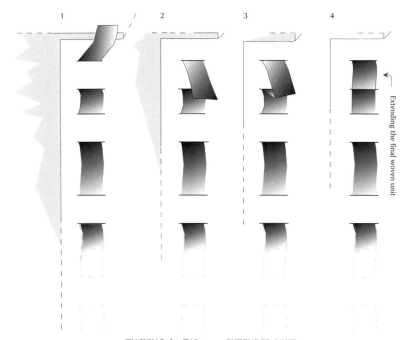

TUCKING the TAB as an EXTENDED UNIT

Woven and Tucked Tab

Each end of the woven tab is folded back. The edge of the tab is then slipped into the previous slit, out of sight between the pleat and side-cover.

In the illustration at the bottom of the previous page is a close-up of tucking the tab, which is described and illustrated on page 303, *Attaching Separate Side-Covers.* When the tab is tucked, the end of the tab extends the final woven unit. It is designed so that the extended units will be the same length as the other woven units.

Rather than extending the previous unit, the woven and tuck tab can create a new and final woven unit.

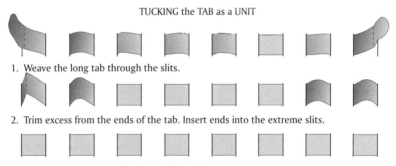

TUCKING the TAB as a UNIT

1. Weave the long tab through the slits.

2. Trim excess from the ends of the tab. Insert ends into the extreme slits.

3. Tuck ends under as the final unit of the design.

This dotted line of tabbing could extend across the length of a head and/or tail turn-in. A dotted line of tab could extend down the foredge of a cover, to tab as well as decorate the turn-in.

A woven tab need not yield a square or rectangular motif. Shape of the repetitive motif is determined by the slits, not the tab.

SHAPING A TAB *Outside View*

These four tab units, *Diagonal, Arrow, S,* and *Square* show a variety in shaping a single long strip as a woven tab.

SHAPING A TAB *Inside View*

The reverse side of the woven strip would look like this.

Dotted Border as Tab

A *Flat Back with Borders*, page 287, may be tabbed down with woven and tucked tabs, which could also hold an optional liner in place. Tabs are woven across each foredge turn-in, creating a dotted, woven border.

With *Bordered Paper Side-Covers*, page 289, the woven and tucked tabs are used along all four turns-in. Each separate side-cover has a dotted border created by the woven tabs. An illustration of this cover is on the following page. For an example of a tabbed and woven cover see *Lexington Nocturne,* Book 93, at the bottom of page 262.

Cut Shapes as Decoration

The motif of the dotted border can be comprised of units of the woven tabs and interspersed with units which are merely cut shapes. The cover or turn-in might be cut away to reveal the color of the liner. The shape would be the same as the woven unit and positioned as if an extension of the woven unit. In the illustrations on the facing page, the middle square of both the head and tail motif are not part of the woven tabs, but are cut shapes in the side-cover and the turns-in. Those two square openings show the color and texture of the paper used for the liner on both the inside and outside of the cover.

DOTTED BORDER TURNS-IN *with liner on the inside*

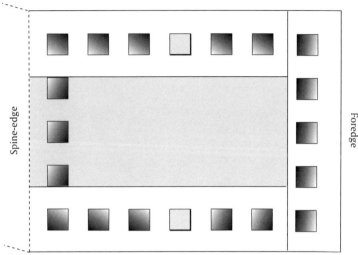

Inside view of back side-cover. Head, tail, and foredge turns-in and liner
are fixed in position by woven tabs.

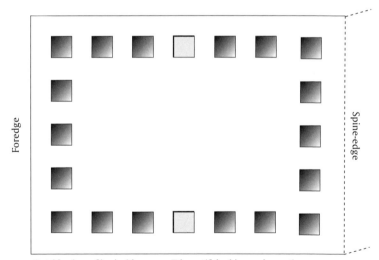

Outside view of back side-cover. Tab motif doubles as decoration

Susan E. King, *I Spent the Summer in Paris,*
1983, above and *Lessons from the South,* 1986 below.
Both books by Paradise Press, the top in conjunction with Visual Studies Workshop Press and
the bottom with Nexus Press. Printed on translucent paper, the unsupported concertinas
spread open to reveal chapters of the books. See illustration in the middle of page 321.

Top: 23 x 32 x 1.5 cm.
Bottom: 27.5 x 17.5 x 1.5 cm.

314

FOLDS-OUT

A fold-out is also called a *throw-out*. The page is "thrown-out" referring to the action of extending a fold-out.

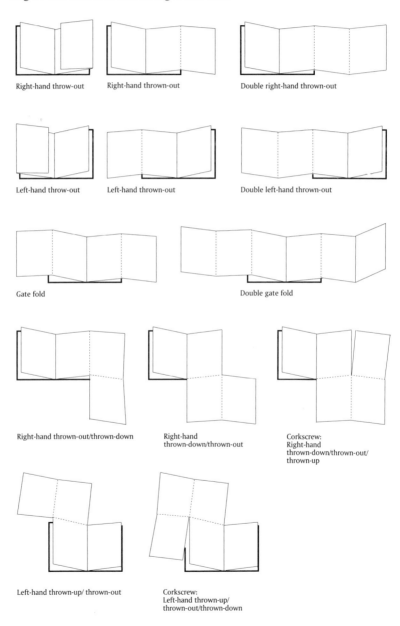

Right-hand throw-out

Right-hand thrown-out

Double right-hand thrown-out

Left-hand throw-out

Left-hand thrown-out

Double left-hand thrown-out

Gate fold

Double gate fold

Right-hand thrown-out/thrown-down

Right-hand thrown-down/thrown-out

Corkscrew: Right-hand thrown-down/thrown-out/ thrown-up

Left-hand thrown-up/ thrown-out

Corkscrew: Left-hand thrown-up/ thrown-out/thrown-down

Cork screw, or compound folds-out, offer the opportunity of investigating a new frontier. A fold book attached to, or within a codex would be a compound fold-out.

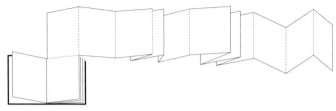

COMPOUND FOLD-OUT:
Page 3 is thrown-up and out to reveal a fold book within the codex.

FOLDS-IN

The fold-out should suggest the concept of a fold-in.

Manipulating a Fold-In

A found codex can be manipulated. One or more folds to some or all of the pages would greatly expand the foredge of the book block.

Conceiving a Fold-In

Imagery and binding of a book might be conceived as a fold-in. Pages would remain flat, not manipulated until after the book is bound. Binding with an expanded spine would compensate for the eventual folds-in. After the reader manipulates the book, the spine-edge and foredge become equal, allowing the covers to be parallel when closed. The imagery would come into registration and alignment after it is folded by the viewer. If the content is text, folding would alter the order, and thus the context of facing words.

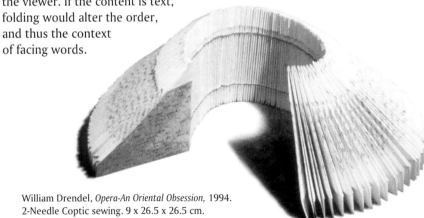

William Drendel, *Opera-An Oriental Obsession,* 1994.
2-Needle Coptic sewing. 9 x 26.5 x 26.5 cm.

BORDER BOOK

A 16-page thrown-out book

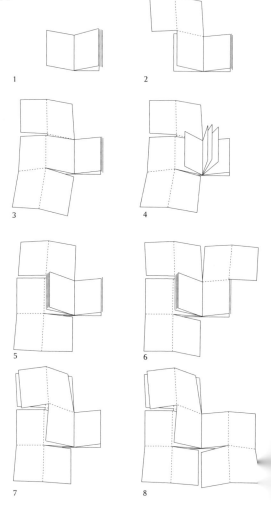

Ideas for content or binding often come from looking at strange features in the history of books. In early-printed books the final word on each page was on a line by itself. As often as not, the final word did not end a sentence. The last word on the page was repeated at the top of the following, as the only word on the first line. Sometimes the carry-over was a partial word, having been hyphenated from the last full line on the page. This carry-over is referred to as the *catchword*.

The concept of a catchword seems ripe to influence a poem of several pages in length. It is similar to a crown of sonnets, which repeats the final line of a sonnet as the first line in the next. Here, it is a lovely transition, whereas the early use of catchwords was for gathering sections in order, not a seemingly awkward lack of faith that the reader could make it from one page to the next without losing the train of thought—which reminds me of the book I am supposed to be describing.

The *Border Book* is a format, not a particular type of binding. This book-as-sketch makes use of the book tradition of the fold-out. In grade school I was excited by books with a map as a fold-out. Since it is at the back of the book it can be extended and constantly in view while the   th

the   book is read. Childhood experiences are a rich source of ideas.
      In the first edition of this manual the Border Book existed only as a
drawn illustration. Julie Chen liked the idea and produced a book using
this format. It is reproduced on the following page. I enjoy seeing my
sketches taken to the next level.
      A throw-out suggests a theme. Reading several pages while one page
remains thrown-out, suggests variation. Concept of the throw-out could
inspire a series of books. The
Border Book is one.

1. The first leaf has a com-
    pound fold-out, which is
    on the verso.
2. When the first page is
    turned, the compound
    fold-out, which is page 2,
    is thrown up and out to
    the left.
3. The second leaf, consist-
    ing of pages 3 and 4, has
    a triple fold-out. When
    page 3 is turned to reveal
    page 4, there is a fold-
    out to the left, then a
    fold-down, then a fold-
    out to the right. This is a
    corkscrew.
4. Pages 5 through 12 do
    not have throws-out.
5. The middle of the book
    is viewed, all the while,
    pages 2 and 4 remain
    thrown-out.

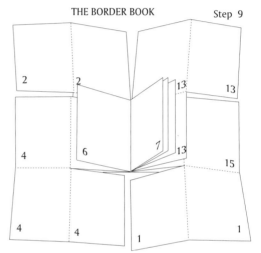

THE BORDER BOOK   Step 9

When this binding book came out in the First
Edition, Julie Chen liked the idea of this book,
which existed only in my head and the drawings
above. Julie took off from this point to make an
edition book with a box. It is reproduced on the
following page. I love the idea of presenting
sketches or devising new bindings. later, I am
rewarded when I see what others do with it.

6. Page 13 has a compound fold. It is thrown up and then out to the
    right.
7. Page 13 is then turned, leaving the folds thrown-out. Page 14 is now
    in view.
8. Page 15 has a triple fold. It is first thrown-out to the right, then
    thrown down, then thrown-out to the left.
9. Page 14 is then turned back onto 15 to reveal page 13 again. Now,
    the border is complete. Pages 5 through 12 can be read again, this
    time in context with the cyclical reading of the ten "pages" which
    orbit the main text block. This is a book-within-a-book, an earth and
    moon book.

Books within Books

The idea of a book within a book has been used by Alan Stone in his book titled *Towers*, published by the Writers Center, 1982. The codex is opened to reveal hollowed out pages containing an oriental fold book which can be pulled out like a tongue. Pages of the codex have not been imaged, only those of the fold-out.

Safety in Numbers, self-published by Scott McCarney in 1986, contains a smaller codex within the cut pages of the larger codex. Both books can be read separately, intermittently, or at the same time.

The influence of the throw-out is exquisitely utilized in The *Book of Doom.*

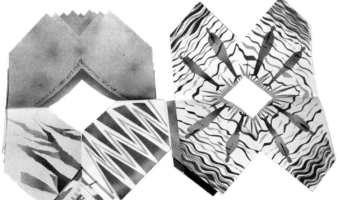

Clifton Meador, *Book of Doom,* Space Heater Editions, 1984. Edition of 25 bound by Philip Zimmermann. Pages fold out and up to four times the size when closed.

Julie Chen, *You Are Here,* Flying Fish Press, 1992. Edition of 100, letterpress printed on Fabriano Roma. Box is 11 x 10.7 x 3.4 cm. Opens to 28.5 x 39.5 cm.

SPINE-PLEATS

A spine-pleat is an Oriental fold book used in a playful manner. Unlike the fold book, the pleat is not a book in itself but a structuring device generally employed as a spine. A pleat could be a throw-out or a pop-up. The spine-pleat can go between the book block and the cover. It is only seen on the inside of the book as endsheets, as the pleats showing between the sections. This is called a *concertina guard*.

If the spine-pleat is heavy paper, it may be used as the cover, itself and called a *cover-pleat*. See illustrations on pages 270 and 280.

Boards can be attached, so only the pleat shows on the outside as the spine. See illustrations on pages 272 and 298.

CONCERTINA GUARD *aka book block pleat*

This pleat goes between the spine-cover and the sections. The pleat is folded with the inside having the same number of valleys as there will be sections. The paper is text weight, usually the same paper as the book block. Pleats are small, about ¾" from valley to peak.

The pleat is folded and, while shut, the sewing stations are marked on the mountain peaks of its spine-edge. When the pleat is opened, the sewing stations will be on the inside valleys. Pleat, sections and spine-cover are all pre-pierced.

The pleat is set into the cover on the spine prior to sewing. The first section is placed into the first valley of the pleat. Section and pleat, as well as cover, are sewn as a unit.

The second section is set into the second valley of the pleat and the two are sewn as a unit.

The concertina guard is used as a spacer to swell the spine, allowing items to be added to the pages without expanding the foredge.

Another benefit of the pleat is to avoid seeing the cracks between sections which show the inside of the spine-cover. Often the cover is a dark color, whereas the book block is generally light. The pleat gives a continuation of the paper stock from section to section, as each mountain peak of the pleat protrudes between sections. In bindings such as the Coptic, when the book is opened between sections the crack is an open gap. If this is not desired, a concertina guard is the remedy.

The concertina guard is folded in the same manner as a fold book page 243. The ends of the concertina guard can be extended the width of the pages of the book, creating endsheets. For procedure of folding leaving the ends unfolded as pages, see *Folding a Pleated Spine-Cover,* page 324.

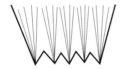 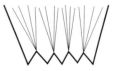

LEFT Sections attached in the valleys: This could be a *concertina guard* with a cover hiding
the pleats on the outside of the book. It could also be the cover, itself, making it a
cover-pleat. It is really only semantics, as long as you see the potential.
RIGHT Sections attached on the peaks: This is a *cover-pleat*. It cannot be a *concertina
guard,* since it does not fit between the sections on the inside of the book. This
attachment offers double hinging action. See *Compound Hinging,* page 261.

COVER-PLEAT

The cover-pleat is the spine, to which sections are attached to the
mountain peaks or valleys. The pleat is constructed of cover weight
paper, as it must support the sections. Sewing stations can be marked on
the spine mountain peaks, as with the concertina guard. On the inside of
the pleat, sections can be sewn in the valleys.

Or, the stations can be in the valleys when viewing the spine-pleat
from the outside. In this instance, the stations are marked from the
inside, on the foredge mountain peaks of the pleat. This is so that all the
folds can be marked at once. A section is sewn to each peak.

In both these examples, the sections are pamphlet sewn to the cover-
pleat. Attaching sections to the pleat creates an unsupported Concertina
binding. If tapes supports are sewn onto the spine to fix the cover-pleat
at a particular width, this creates a (supported) Concertina binding. See
Concertina Binding, page 261.

With sections sewn to the valleys or mountain peaks of the cover-
pleat, separate side-covers can then be attached to the ends of the pleat.
This can be by sewing or by tabbing. See *Attaching Separate Side-Covers*,
page 303.

Sections Attached to the Mountain Peaks

There are more benefits with sewing stations on the mountain
peaks on the inside of the pleat:

1. *Expandable Spine* The spine of the unsupported concertina remains
   expandable, to the total depth of all the pleats.

   This permits an increasingly expandable spine for adding things
   to the pages at any point in time. No matter how many items are
   slipped inside, the closed book allows the covers to remain parallel.

   If the sections are reduced to folios, the ratio of pleats to pages is
   increased, allowing more items to be added to the already bound
   book while permitting the covers to close parallel.

When the front cover is opened and pulled to the left, while pulling the back cover to the right, the sections are positioned across the length of the pleat.

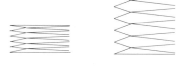

A small pleat will present an oblique stack, a staggered imbrication. The overlap allows part of the first page of each section to be seen at once. Chapter headings or a synopsis of each section can be composed to fit these areas of the first pages. Each section may be treated as a separate volume, several books or short stories under one cover. Area of the first page of each section in view would reveal the title of the different volumes within the single binding. See examples on page 313.

If each pleat is the width of a section, each section will be displayed side by side with no overlapping.

2. *Compound Hinging* Sections attached to the inside peaks is superior, because it creates a double hinge. The peaks and the valleys of the cover-pleat operate in a combined action, allowing the pages to open more freely.

3. *Break between Sections* Movement of the compound hinging is more obvious when turning the last page of a section. The action is dramatic, as the entire section falls to one side. There is a brief interlude of seeing the pleat as a pause before continuing to the next page.

4. *Imaging the Pleat* The interlude could be expanded if the pleat contains text or imagery.

Each portion of the pleat can contain a single picture. The sections are text with intermittent interruptions of the pictures.

Or the reverse, it can be a picture book with text on the pleats.

Each pleat can be treated as part of a picture. The length of the pleat is imaged with one gigantic picture before folding, perhaps a photographic enlargement onto mural paper. Reading the sections is paced by the progressing revelation of the long image on the pleat, portion by portion.

5. *Enlarging the Pleat* The element of the pleat can be developed as an equal to the sections. If the pleats are widened, extending farther from the spine, the turning of the final page of a section is exaggerated as it flops aside to reveal the pleat.

If the width of the pleat is the same as the pages in the section, turning all but the final page of a section yields four facing pages. From left to right, the opened folio gives two pages. Next, one side of a pleat is seen. Connected to that, the first page of the following section is in view.

Enlarging the Pleat

Turning the final page of the section, the four page display is the last page of that section, the pleats as two pages and the first page of the following section. Since the pleat is equal in width, it permits *French Doors* viewing at section breaks. The last page of the left section is grasped with the left hand. The first page of the following section is grasped with the right.

Concertina as *French Doors* format

Both pages are turned at once to the middle of the pleat.

Reducing the number of pages between pleats would exaggerate the *French Doors* effect. Sew folios instead of sections onto pleats. For a variation on this concept, see *French Doors* format, page 257.

6. *Variable size pleats* Another permutation to explore is varying the pleat.

Pleats could gradually increase in width while the section widths remain constant. This would give a foredge display on the closed book.

6a.

Pleats could increase in width, while the section widths decrease inversely. This would maintain the same total width of each pleat/section.

6b.

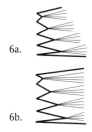

7. *Uniform pleats with reversed exception* Sections of the text block are attached to pleats which are uniform in size. The final pleat is widened to the total width of the book block with pleats. Foredge of this pleat meets the foredge of the book block. This pleat has a section attached on the back side of the pleat. It is a glossary, or blank for note-taking. The final panel of the pleat may even be the back cover.

8. *Uniform pleats with center exception* This spine allows for two volumes of several sections each to be connected by a common back cover. It is a variation on a very old traditional sewn and glued binding called a Dos-à-Dos. An example is described and illustrated on page 253.

9. *Sheets and pleats* Using a small pleat as a hinge allows single sheet boards to be used as pages. A single board can be placed in every other valley. The pleat is closed against the board for attachment. The sandwiched board and pleat can be stab sewn from the outside of the spine and the stitching will not show in the opened

Sheets and Pleats

book. Transparencies and film-positives cannot be folded into sections, as the folded surface would split or crack. Film pages can be bound as sheets and pleats. Metal and glass can form pages of a book. Sewing stations can be drilled through thin metal or glass. These sheets can be sewn to a cloth pleat.

Concentration in creating is like a battlefield surgeon going from one operation to the next. Attitude is that of a child probing with his tongue the tastes of three different flavors of a triple decker ice cream cone. I become giddy playing with permutations.

10. *The next variation would be multiple sheets and pleats* A separate volume can be stabbed to every other pleat. See *Separate Volumes within Concertina,* described and illustrated on pages 126 and 131.

PLEAT as SPINE *attaching separate side-covers*

If the pleats are kept uniform in width, they are the spine to which the sections are attached. The foredges of the two extremes of the pleat are tabs at the front and back of the book block. Separate side-covers must be attached to these pleat tabs, which will serve as hinge-folds for the side-covers. The pleat tabs could be made wider, an inside cover not as wide as the book block. The tabs could fork to become two tape supports. You can invent and elaborate. For examples of attaching separate side-covers, see *Tape Supports,* page 299. Examples are on page 313.

PLEAT as SPINE and COVER *the pleat as spine and side-covers*

If the first and final pleat are extended to page width, the pleat functions as both the spine and the cover.

Either the concertina guard or the cover-pleat can be constructed so that the two extremes are page width. If it is a concertina guard, the two ends can function as endsheets. This is because paper used for a concertina guard is generally text weight, too flimsy to be used as paper side-covers. Separate side covers would be attached over these endsheets.

If it is a cover-pleat, the two ends could be the paper side-covers. Additional width might be included on the sheet to form foredge turns-in. Or, the pleated spine-cover could be used to form heavy endsheets with board covers attached. If boards are to be attached, the endsheet should be made 2½ times as wide as the board, so that it can be wrapped around the board in making a wrapped cover. See *Separately Wrapped Boards,* page 293.

If the endsheet is to be sewn to the board, or a tape woven through the two as attachment, sewing stations or slots will have to be drilled or cut into the boards.

FOLDING a PLEATED SPINE-COVER

A cover-pleat can be extended at each end the width of the pages of the book. These might be used as endsheets with separate board covers attached.

Or, the extension of the cover-pleat, constructed of cover weight stock, can be used as the paper side-covers. Make sure in measuring the side-covers to include width of a pleat. Side-cover equals section width and one pleat. See illustration below.

The same folding procedure is used to construct a book block pleat extended with endsheets. Since the book block pleat is generally text weight paper, the extensions would serve only as endsheets, not side-covers. Separate side-covers would be attached.

The process of folding an Oriental fold book can be modified to fold the pleats and the two side-covers from one sheet. Determine the size and number of pleats needed.

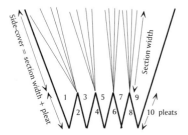

Number of Pleats Needed

To calculate the length of sheet required for the two side-covers with pleats, it helps to draw a diagram. Include the number of mountain peaks on the inside of the spine, which equals the number of sections or folios to be attached:

Write the widths of each portion on the diagram. Add up all the widths for the total width required.

If you are attaching *Sheets as Pleats,* example 9, page 323, you will need twice as many mountain peaks on the inside of the spine as sheets attached. If you are stab binding several volumes into the pleats, you will also need twice as many pleats as volumes. See *Separate Volumes within Concertina,* pages 126 and 131.

Formula for Calculating Measurements

HEIGHT of the sheet required is generally the height of the book block.
WIDTH of the total cover equals:
width of the front foredge turn-in (if any),
plus width of the section and width of a pleat, (equals total width of the front cover),
plus width of a pleat,
plus width of a pleat (equals the total of one mountain peak),
plus width of two pleats for every additional mountain peak,
plus width of the section and width of a pleat, (equals total width of the back cover),
plus width of the back foredge turn-in, if any.

Folding

1. Fold the sheet in half.
2. Measure in from the fold ½ of the total required for the spine (half of the pleats). Mark this on the sheet. Fold at this point, in the opposite direction of the first fold.

Step 1 Fold cover-pleat in half.

3. Flip the folded sheet to the other side. From the initial fold, measure in the same distance. Mark the sheet. Fold the sheet at this point, in the opposite direction of the first fold. This has constructed a W.

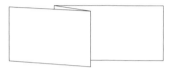

Step 2 Fold back to the left the width of the front side-cover and turn-in, if any.

   The two ends of the sheet are the side-covers with turns-in, if any. If there are to be foredge turns-in, do not fold them until sections are attached to make sure you have the proper width for the side-covers. The folds on either side of the initial fold are the hinge-folds. The center mountain peak is the initial fold.

Step 3 Fold the back side-cover in the same manner, forming a W.

4. Open cover flat and fold at initial fold only. Width from the initial fold to one of the hinge-folds is half of the pleats. Reverse the hinge-fold on top and take it to the initial fold to start the pleating.

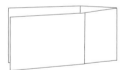

Step 4 Fold in half. Reverse the hinge-fold. Take hinge-fold to center fold to begin forming pleats.

   Continue folding the pleats following directions for *Folding an Oriental Fold Book,* on page 243.

   Sometimes in making the first three folds to form the *W*, I measure the side-covers, instead of the pleats. Then when I fold the pleats, I allow them to be whatever size they turn out. There is less control than the instructions at the top of the page, but it is quicker and at times I am not concerned with measurements but with speed in making up a blank binding.

DECORATING the PLEAT

The pleat has many advantages structurally and logistically. Printing on the pleat uses the pleat as a page. Another area of investigation is the pleat as decoration. It seems appropriate that the decoration is by folding. The following pages illustrate extending the sculptural aspects of the pleat to decorative motifs.

Cuts must not be so drastic as to weaken the structure of the pleat. The primary function of the pleat is to support the attached sections.

A slit can be made and that area folded back while reversing the fold. The hole and the folded area combine as a form.

A semi-circular slit folds down to form a circle. The two-ply fold-down, the space of the hole and the single-ply pleat set up texture as well as pattern, with the possibility of shadows cast through the openings when displayed with a single light source.

Slits can extend over a valley or a peak. The designs to the right are only on the peak. Illustrations 4, 5 and 6 on the following page show the designs alternating on the valleys and the peaks to form a pattern.

By making two horizontal slits extending over a valley or a peak, a portion of the pleat between the cuts can be pushed in the other direction, reversing the fold. If these cuts extend over a peak, the fold on the form is reversed to a valley. The reversed fold presents another opportunity for stations to pamphlet sew a section. See drawing number 3 on the next page.

See drawing number 3 on the next page.

SLIT and FOLDED DOWN
MOTIFS for PLEATS

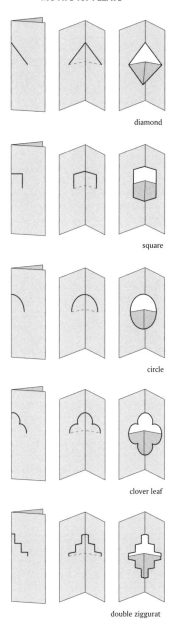

diamond

square

circle

clover leaf

double ziggurat

Close pleat to slit. Open to fold down.

HORIZONTAL CUTS and ALTERNATING FOLDS for COVER PLEATS

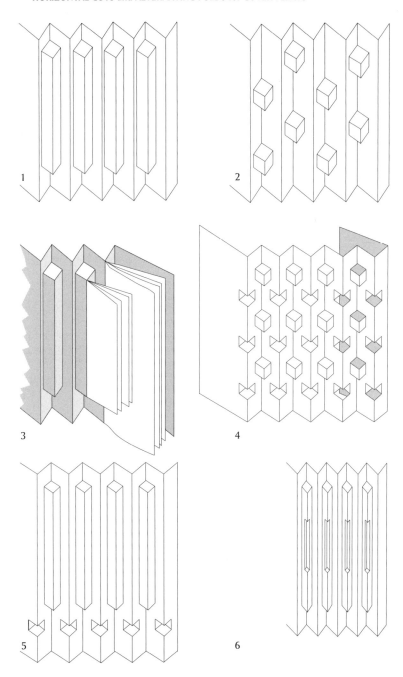

Slit top and bottom of form, perpendicular to the fold. Reverse the fold on the form.

Tape supports, flaps, tabs, fold-outs and spine-pleats are the herbs and spices to give each binding its special flavors, which in time become remembrances. Each time I pick up one of my hand-bound books, I see the text and pictures, of course. But I also smile at the papers, typeface and all the basics of the physical object. I fondly remember how it all came together in that particular piece. Better, I think of where I can go from where I left off.

I lay the finished book down, close it and start anew.

Keith Smith, *Book 151,*
one-of-a-kind, 1989.
Sewn onto (leather) tapes.
Machine-sewn pages of "quilted"
photographic portraits of my
friends. Each page is like a quilt
block. Cover is strips of suede
machine-sewn to a paper cover.
20.5 x 20.5 cm.

CONCLUSION

Binding is not an afterthought. It is one of the inter-related elements: *the page, the picture/text, turning pages and display.*

Structure must facilitate action.

The choice of many possible bindings and even variations of a binding will aid in finding the proper binding for the content of pictures and/or text. Proper approach to binding will allow for the ease of turning pages and for display. Craft is useless without function and accessibility is sterile without content.

There is excitement in binding a blank book. There is more in binding a dozen than the addition of numbers acquired. Self-assurance comes with practice. So does a change in attitude. I am less likely to be uptight about my approach to imaging if I have a number of blank bindings in front of me to play with while I work.

Work is play.

If I image the content prior to binding, I tend to be more willing at risk-taking in my approach to binding. Creativity can only happen if I am willing to fail. If I were not, I would be in the wrong business.

I must take risks if I am to progress. I can afford the luxury of shyness socially, but it is sure death artistically. Matisse said that art is as a crime. I must break the rules, break away from my past solutions to books, break from seeing by habit to find vision. Habit is a form of blindness. "Take courage," I tell myself and indirectly, tell my reader. Like me, enjoy the process of binding and revel in the revelation, "I see!"

KE☉TH

PART 4

REFERENCE

GLOSSARY of TERMS

accordion pleat 1. Several parallel, alternating and closely placed folds. Pleats are usually not pages, but an additional hinging device between the backbone and the aiached folios or sections. Very often the pleat is the backbone, with separate side-covers, rather than a flat back. Pleats also expand the depth of the backbone to accommodate additions to the book block. 2. Also known as the concertina fold.

across aka **all across** 1. Perpendicular to the folds, cover to cover.† 2. Sewing which proceeds from section to section, generally in two or more separate sewings, using paired stations. Examples are *Blanket Stitch with Slit Tapes, 2-Needle Coptic Sewing* and the *Celtic Weave*. Sewing across the spine is always more secure than sewing along the spine. If a thread breaks, only the sewing at those paired stations is affected. If the thread breaks sewing along the spine, the entire binding is compromised.

adhesive Generic for glue and paste. Glues used for binding remain pliable and are used on the backs over the sewing of most bindings. Glue on the backbone may be a heat glue, made from animals. It is archival, in that it may be easily removed, but not in the sense it attracts insects which eat it. Another pliable glue is a poly-vinyl-acetate. Plastic based, it does not attract animals, but is not archival, inasmuch as it is not removable and thwarts attempts at book restoration. Pastes are used to adhere leather to spines, paper to paper and paper to boards. Wheat or rice paste are commonly used.

adhesive binding single leaf binding without sewing using a synthetic adhesive consolidation on the back.* Referred to as *perfect binding.*

against the grain Folding paper at right angles to the grain.

along aka **all along** Parallel to the folds, head to tail.†

angle To move diagonally.†

Asa-No-Ha Toji Japanese name for the stab binding also known as the Hemp-Leaf Binding.

back or backbone 1. The binding edge of a text prior to sewing or adhesive con-solidation.* *Note:* The back differs from the spine, which is part of the cover which overlays this.

back saw Moulding saw or tenon saw used to cut the sewing stations when the book block is held in a finishing press.

backward (reverse) Counter to the direction of the sewing.†

bead 1. Top edge of the book (when viewing the book upright). 2. The little roll formed by the knot of a headband.

beeswax Cake of wax purchased in a small block from a binder's supply. It is used for waxing all unwaxed thread, prior to sewing.

blind A type of book. See *Venetian blind.*

blind embossing Stamping type into leather, without gold or foil.

board or book board A layered stock specifically for side-covers.

bodkin A sewing tool which is a type of awl. Unlike an awl which has a shaft which graduates in thickness, a bodkin has a thin metal shaft which remains constant in diameter except for narrowing at the point. It is similar to a bradawl, which is a carpen-ter's tool. An awl is inferior for piercing sewing stations, as it is difficult to obtain proper size of the opening in the paper. Choose a bradawl or bodkin which will give a hole slightly less than the diameter of the

* GLF refers to definitions by Gary Frost from
A VOCABULARY of TERMS for BOOK CONSERVATION PRACTICE
† *"Glossary of Terms,* based on the work of Pamela Spitzmueller and Gary Frost," a handout in a workshop by Betsy Palmer Eldridge.

needle which will be used in the sewing.

book block or **text block** Total of the collated signatures, sections, folios or sheets, constituting the body of a book.

book block pleat See *concertina guard*.

booklet 1. A one-section binding. 2. A pamphlet. 3. A magazine.

bostrophedon A Germanic term meaning as the ox plows. In a single word, it graphically describes moving across a field, back and forth in a continuing S fashion. It is as if a page of text were read, the first line from left to right, the second from right to left and continued in this alternating manner. This movement and thus the term, describes the Scott McCarney binding. He also calls this the *snake format*.

bone or **bone folder** A flat, polished tool, made of bone or plastic. Paper is folded by hand to a temporary fold. The bone is used to score the fold to a permanent position and to flatten the fold. This is done in a single stroke, as burnishing the paper will scar or make it shiny.

bradawl A straight shafted awl with chisel edge used to make holes for brads or screws. Like the bodkin, a bradawl is ideal for piercing sewing stations in paper in bookbinding. Either tool is superior to an awl for piercing sewing stations.

butterfly sewing An across the spine sewing which utilizes paired stations. Each needle spans, enters the next section, then cross inside to exit the other station. The *Butterfly* is also known as the *Yamato Toji* or *Japanese 4-Needle Sewing*. It is a 12th century binding. The Butterfly is described in *Exposed Spine Sewings*, Volume III of *Non-Adhesive Binding*.

case The two side-covers connected by the spine-cloth or leather.

catch-word In early printed books, the last word on a page was positioned at the foot. The same word was repeated at the top of the next page. Perhaps this served as a bridge in reading from page to page, but its purpose was a guide in collating signatures.

chain stitch *Chain stitch* is an embroidery term. In binding, it is referred to as *link stitch and* they form a chain. Pattern of

interlocking thread in sewing by connecting loops is described and illustrated beginning on page 164.

to change over To continue sewing in the different section.†

clamshell A box for storing a book, hinged to open like covers.

climb To move upward.†

codex (plural: **codices**) A book, bound along one edge. One of the four types of books, the others being the fan, blind and the fold book.

compiled section A signature or section, constructed by assembling two or more folios, rather than folding down a sheet.

compound binding A hybrid book structure of two of the same or differing types of books.

concertina 1. A type of binding, utilizing the concertina fold. 2. The concertina fold is also called an *accordion pleat*.

concertina guard A form of construction securing sections to folded stubs with a pamphlet stitch and, in turn, sewing the stubs together to form a text block.*

content Statement within the book of text and/or pictures. In a no-picture book, it is the cast shadows, cut shapes, holes, et cetera. *Note:* To avoid confusion in this text, content is never used to mean satisfied.

continuous support sewing Use of a single support, as opposed to sewing onto cords or tapes. The paperback sewings in Volume II of *Non-Adhesive Binding, 1- 2- & 3- Section Sewings*, are examples. It is important to reinforce the spine on the cover. Folding or pasting a second ply of paper in this area strengthens the sewing.

to continue on To continue sewing in the same section.†

core A support. It might be a cord or rolled material to form a cylindrical support, generally out of leather. The endband is formed on a core.

cover stock or **cover weight** Heavy paper used for covers as opposed to text weight used for book blocks. Commercial printing papers generally come in both cover weight and text weight.

covering Forwarding is followed by Covering and Finishing. If the outside of the boards are not full leather or cloth, the area of the board that is not covered with cloth or leather is covered with decorative paper. The paste-down is made on the inside of the boards.

crease A fold induced by pressure marking or die debossing, not cutting.* Other binders refer to this procedure as a score.

creep The successive protrusion from the outermost folio to the innermost within a section or signature.

crossbar The wooden dowel held above and parallel to the base of the sewing frame by threaded posts. The crossbar is often slotted to accept threaded hooks.

curl The distortion of a sheet due to differences in structure, coatings or moisture from one side to the other.

deckle In papermaking, the width of the wet sheet as it comes off the wire of a paper machine.

deckled-edge The untrimmed feathery edges of paper formed where the pulp flows against the deckle.

digital scan Half-tone photographic images created on a computer scanner. I do not use the term *photograph,* reserving that dear term for silver prints.

display Presentation of the object, generally through turning pages. Books with one-sided display, the fan, blind and fold book might be displayed fully extended on a table or wall displayed. Books with unusual formatting may be presented in the round as sculpture, the pages not meant to be turned. *Note:* To avoid confusion in this text, display is never used as a verb.

drop To move downward.†

dos-à-dos A specific traditional format of two connected codices which have a back cover in common.

duodecimo aka **12mo** A sheet folded down to create a section of 12 sheets or 24 pages. See *folio, quarto, sexto, octavo and Z-fold.*

endband Wrapping and beading decorative thread, usually of colored silk or cot-

ton, at the head and tail of codices. Thread is wrapped around a core and periodically stitched into the book block. "Imitation" machine-made headbands are sold by the yard and pasted onto the backbone of commercial hard cover books.

Note: The term *headband* is often erroneously used, if the band described includes or is specifically at the tail. Therefore, it is better to use the term endband, rather than headband, as it includes the bands sewn at both the head and tail.

end paper In tradition binding, the sheet which is glued down on the inside of the cover board, extending across the gutter as the first page.

endsheets The first and last folio or section of a book may be blank and perhaps a nice laid paper in a particular color different from the bulk of the book block. Endsheets function as a mat surrounding a drawing. It is blank space to clear the mind before the introduction of the content of the opus.

enter To pass from the spine side to the fold side.†

exit To pass from the fold side to the spine side.†

F&Gs *Folded and Gathered* The F&Gs are the assembled signatures ready for sewing.

false kettle The (true) kettle stitch is the proper sewing procedure for ending one section, changing direction of movement in adding the next. The true kettle drops and links, slips and climbs. A false kettle would fail in one of these steps, usually failing to slip under in order to lock. True and false kettle stitches and link stitches in general are described in *Exposed Spine Sewings,* Volume III of *Non-Adhesive Binding* and in *Bookbinding for Book Artists.*

fan A book, bound at one point. One of the four types of books, the others being the *blind, codex and* the *fold book.* Fans and blinds are used by South Sea Island cultures.

finishing Finishing is decoration of the book after forwarding and covering.

first section In the sewing procedures, the term first does not necessarily mean the beginning of the book. On the bench, you may very well start sewing from the back, towards the front of the book. In that instance, the "first" section to be sewn is the final section of the book. See *Face Up and Face Down*, in *Bookbinding for Book Artists*.

flap A continuous support sewn to the back and extending on each side of the hinge-fold. Covers are attach to the flap.

flat back Sewing without rounding the spine.

flat back cover Paper cover with two folds which delineate the spine from the side-covers. These folds create the hinging action of the cover and are called hinge-folds.

flush cover 1. A cover whose front and back panels are the same dimensions as the pages. 2. In commercial binding, a cover that has been trimmed with the text block, so that cover and text block are the same size. See *overhang cover*.

fold, see *accordion, hinge-fold, fold out, gate fold and thrown out.*

fold book A book, whose binding is mechanical; the sheet is folded back and forth upon itself to create pages. One of the four types of books, the others being the fan, blind and the codex.

fold-out See *throw-out*.

folio aka **fo** A sheet folded in half to yield a section or signature of 4 pages and two leaves. See *quarto, sexto, octavo, duodecimo and Z-fold.*

foredge 1. The front edge of a book. 2. The edge of the side-cover and book block opposite the spine.

format The size, style, type page, margins, page set-up, etc.

gate fold Two facing fold outs in a codex. Each fold out is hinged on the foredges of an opened folio. When the gate fold is opened or thrown-out, there are four facing pages, the two at each extreme extend beyond the book block.

forward In the direction on the sewing.†

forwarding After the book is sewn, forwarding is gluing the back, plowing, rounding and backing, sewing the endbands and attaching the boards. Forwarding is fol-

lowed by covering and finishing.

gate fold Two facing fold-outs in a codex. Each fold-out is hinged on the foredges of an opened folio. When the gate fold is opened or thrown-out, there are four facing pages, the two at each extreme extend beyond the book block.

gathering Assembling the folded signatures into the proper order for binding. See *F&Gs.*

grain The direction in which most fibers lie which corresponds with the direction the paper is made in commercial production machinery. *Note:* To avoid confusion, this is the only definition of *grain* used in this text.

gutter 1. The blank space or inner margin, from printing area to binding. *Note:* To avoid confusion, this is the only definition of *gutter* used in this text.

half hitch A type of knot for Tying-off, when there is only one loose end of thread. The needle slips under a stitch and is pulled until there is a small loop. The needle proceeds through the loop, before the thread is pulled tight. Half hitch is diagrammed with the knots in this book.

head and **tail** The top and bottom of a book when stood upright. They are at right angles to the backbone and foredge. *Note:* Only definition of head or tail used in this text.

headband Wrapping and beading decorative thread, usually of colored silk or cotton, at the head and tail of codices. Thread is wrapped around a core and periodically stitched into the book block. "Imitation" machine-made headbands are sold by the yard and pasted onto the backbone of commercial hard cover books. *Headbands* is generally misused to mean both the headband and the tailband. The proper term is *endband.*

Hemp-Leaf Binding The stab binding also known as *Asa-No-Ha Toji.* There are four traditional Japanese stab bindings. The others are the *Yotsume Toji* or *Japanese 4—Hole Binding;* the *Kikko Toji* or *Tortoise-Shell;* and the *Koki Toji* or *Noble* binding, which is also referred to as the *Kangxi* binding, after its reputed originator.

hinge-fold The folds on either side of the spine, delineating the side-covers from the spine-cover. See *Flat Back* cover.

horizontal wrapper See *wrapper*.

implied compound binding A inventive folding of pages or itinerary through a book that suggests a hybrid book structure of two of the same or differing types of books.

imposition The laying out of pages on a sheet, so that they will be in numerical order after the sheet is folded down as a folio or section or signature.

to the inside Toward the head or tail.†

jaconette A thin coated fabric used to reinforce a spine or joint in a book box.

jog To knock up and level to an edge, preferably at the head to keep text in registration.

Kangxi Binding Japanese name for the stab binding known as the *Noble*. This binding is also referred to as *Koki*.

kerf cuts made with a back saw across the section folds of an unsewn text. * See *sewing stations*.

kettle stitch sewing procedure of ending one section, changing direction of movement in adding the next. The sewing drops backwards and links, slips and climbs. See pages 213 and 215.

Kikko Japanese name for the stab binding also known as the *Tortoise-Shell* binding.

Koki Japanese name for the stab binding known as the *Noble* binding. This binding is also referred to as *Kangxi* binding, after its reputed originator.

lap To pass over a support or sewing thread.†

leaf 1. A sheet. 2. Two pages, back to back; a recto/verso.

link To pass under another thread.†

loop To circle around a support or sewing thread.†

moulding saw Backsaw or tenon saw used to cut the sewing stations when the book block is held in a finishing press.

octavo aka **8vo** A sheet folded in half three times, to yield a section or signature of 16 pages, with 8 leaves. A sextodecimo or 16mo, has 32 pages with 16 leaves. See *folio, sexto, octavo, duodecimo* and *Z-fold*.

one-of-a-kind A book conceived and executed as a single copy. I do not use the word unique, meaning "special" to define a single copy item, as the term applies to production work as well. *Note:* Some librarians define a book as an item which must have more than one copy. Consequently, they do not recognize or purchase one-of-a-kinds.

1-on Sewing 1-on applies to sewing multi-section sewings along the spine: In addition to using the kettle stations at the head and tail, every sewing station is used. The middle stations lap or loop the supports.

open ended Open ended stations refer to the use of the head and the tail as sewing stations. The support is not pierced. It is a passive station, that is, the thread wraps around the head or tail, marking the change-over.

opened folio The two facing pages at any point to which the codex is opened.

Oriental fold book See *fold book.*

overhand knot Half a square knot. For instructions how to tie, see *Knots*, page 72.

outside The position on the mountain peak of a section, as opposed to the valley, which is called the inside.

to the outside Away from the head or tail.†

overhand knot Half a square knot.

overhang cover A cover larger in size than the pages it encloses. (The amount of the side-cover that extends beyond the book block, bordering the head, foredge and tail is called the square.) See *flush cover*.

pack To loop several times around.†

packing Tapes and raised cords can be packed. The sewing thread may be packed loosely or solid, so that the support is not seen as a reinforcement. See Tacket Binding on page 148, as well as many examples of packed cords in *Non-Adhesive Binding* Volume III: *Exposed Spine Sewings.*

page 1. One side of an unfolded sheet. 2. That portion of a folio or section or signature bordered by folds and/or the edge of the sheet.

pamphlet 1. A one-section text. 2. A booklet. 3. Type of stitch, the *B* stitch, used to sew a booklet.

pamphlet sewing A type of sewing used to bind a pamphlet.

pamphlet stitch This is a *B* stitch, as opposed to a *figure 8*. Pamphlet "stitching" is relegated to single sheets which are stabbed. Pamphlet "sewing", also a *B* stitch, is used to bind a booklet, sewing in the gutter. See pages 89 through 106.

paste See *adhesive*.

perfect bound 1. Adhesive binding. 2. Binding of a book which has no sewing and no folds on the backbone. The book therefore has no sections, signatures or folios, only a stack of sheets. The back is glued. Commercial paperbacks are generally (imperfectly) perfect bound. Thus, unfortunately there is a general low esteem for any book with paper covers. In the past, the main difference between trade books which were paperback and hard cover, was the latter was sewn. Now, many publishers are reducing the quality of their hard covers and are using perfect binding, rather than sewing them.

pleat An Oriental fold used to attach sections, rather than as a complete book in itself. Also known as a concertina, concertina guard or accordion fold. See *accordion pleat*.

ply In this text, the term is used as one piece of paper, rather than the process of making paper in layers. Two-ply is only used in this text to mean a sheet folded back upon itself for reinforcement. This fold could optionally be sewn down. The term is never used to mean duplex, a type of commercially made paper with a different color on each side of the sheet.

production books A book made in an edition, whether by hand or published (printed).

punch Metal cylindrical tool with sharpened hollow shaped end for cutting and solid head for striking with a hammer to cut through paper. Shapes are usually various diameters of circles and, rarely, squares, diamonds, oblongs.

quarto aka **4to** A sheet folded in half twice, first against the grain, then with the grain, to yield a section or signature of 4

leaves or 8 pages. See *folio, sexto, octavo, duodecimo and Z-fold*.

ream Five hundred sheets of paper.

recto/verso Two pages, back to back; a leaf. Recto is a right hand page. Verso is the back of that leaf, not the page facing the recto in the opened folio. *Note:* Recto does not mean front; verso does not mean back. A recto or a verso is a front side when it is viewed. Each becomes a back when the page is turned and it is not in view. Recto/verso is convenient terminology for folding and collating signatures.

saddle wire or **saddle stitch** In commercial binding, to fasten a booklet by wiring it through the fold or the side of the single section. The machine is adjusted to the thickness of the opened section and uses a spool of wire. It is looped through the section, cut and crimped, similar to stapling.

score 1. To indent with a bone folder. 2. A light surface cut made to facilitate folding or flexing in card or board.* See *crease*.

section 1. A sheet folded down to yield eight or more pages, such as an octavo, sexto or duodecimo. 2. Two or more loose folios compiled. *Note 1:* To avoid confusion, section is never used to mean a *portion*. *Note 2:* If the sheet has been printed, then folded down, it is referred to in printers' terminology as a *signature*. Any signature can be called a section, but only a section which has been printed is technically a signature. See *signature*.

self cover A cover of the same paper as the text block.

sewing path The journey of the needle and thread, in and out of the sewing stations, in constructing a sewing.

sewing stations or **stations** 1. The mark or the pierce along the spine-fold of the cover and the backbone of the section or folio showing the positions of the sewing. 2. Path of the needle through paper to create the stitches on the spine. If made with a saw, they are called *kerf stations*.

sewn vs **stitched** Sewing refers to the thread path along the valley and mountain peak, as opposed to set in from the fold. That is stabbing. Stabbing is stitching, not sewing. Path of the needle limited to the gutter is not "stitching," but sewing. Sewing is done with stitches. Therefore, "stitches" is appropriate when referring to sewing in the fold, but stitching equals stabbing.

sexto aka **6to** A sheet folded down to create a section of 6 leaves or 12 pages. The sheet is first folded against the grain with a Z-fold, dividing the sheet into thirds. That is then folded in half with the grain. See *folio, quarto, octavo, duodecimo* and *Z-fold*.

sheet 1. An unfolded piece of paper. 2. A leaf. 3. The full size of the paper before being folded down into a folio or section. 4. In single sheet bindings, a sheet is two pages back to back; a recto/verso.

side-cover Front and back cover, as opposed to the spine.

signature A specific type of a section, differing from the general term of section, in that a signature is a sheet that first has been printed. Signature is a printer's term for binder's word *section*.

simple/compound Terms used only to differentiate basic bindings from hybrids constructed by combining two or more basic types of books.

slip (v.) To pass under itself.†

slit A slit is a severing with a knife. It has length, but no width. See *slot*.

slot A slot is an opening, constructed by two slits, parallel and no more than about ⅛" apart. Slots, rather than slits, are needed to accommodate the thickness of the inserted photographs or weaving a tape or flap, to help prevent buckling of the sheet.

Smythe-sewn Commercial method of machine-stitching a book.

span To climb and change over to another section.†

spine or **spine-cover** 1. The depth of a bound book, connecting the two side-covers. The spine covers the back or backbone. 2. That part of the book that is visible when it is on the shelf. It is sometimes referred to as the backstrip.

spine-tab A strip woven onto the spine.

square or **square of the book** 1. The projection of the side-cover beyond the book block. 2. Only the part of the cover that extends beyond the book block and borders the head, foredge and tail. (The total surface of the cover is referred to as an overhang cover.)

square knot Reef knot. For instructions how to tie, see *Knots,* page 72.

stations See *sewing stations.*

supported sewings Sections sewn together around common tapes or cords which go across the back, perpendicular to it. The supports are generally attached to side-covers.

swelling Thickness added to the backbone by the accumulation of sewing threads or any guards.* See *swelling the back,* page 68 and *expanding the spine pleat,* page 272.

tab A narrow strip woven as means of attachment.

tail 1. The bottom edge of a book when standing upright. 2. The edge opposite the head and perpendicular to spine and foredge.

tailband See *endband* and *headband.*

tapes Woven fabric supports, usually linen, onto which the sewing occurs. They are usually ¼" wide and always are non-adhesive.

tenon saw Moulding saw or backsaw used to cut the sewing stations when the book block is held in a finishing press.

tension Regulation of tautness. Uniform shape and tautness is desired. Betsy Palmer Eldridge says that the tension varies with each sewer. It varies even if one person stops for a break. It is best to start and sew the entire book at once. The operative word is snug. Tension should not be loose, but neither should it be tight. I find that men tend to sew too tightly. Link stitches lose their teardrop shape when pulled tightly.

text block See *book block.*

tie-off Joining two threads with generally a square knot at the beginning or end of a sewing. If the tie-off has only a single thread, a half hitch is used.

ties-down The threads which extend from the endband, in on the spine to the next station to anchor the endband. The tie-off may enter a station on the section or link under a support at that station.

throw-out A fold-out. The action of unfolding of a fold-out or throw-out is referred to as thrown-out. A throw-out might be a single fold, gate fold or any other page which is larger than the book block and folded down for storage. Traditionally refers to a fold-out at the end of a book containing a map. The map is thrown-out, so that it remains visible while any other page in the book can be read and turned.

turn-in A folded over edge of paper for reinforcement by making the edge 2-ply.

types of books There are four basic types of books, determined by how they are bound: 1. at one point is called a *fan*. 2. at two points is the *Venetian blind*. The fan and blind are used by South Sea Island cultures. 3. across one edge, is the *western codex*. 4. alternate folds back and forth upon itself is the *Oriental fold book*. The other three types of books are sewn. The fold book's binding is mechanical.

unsupported sewings Sections sewn directly together, without tape or cord supports.

Venetian blind or **blind** A book, bound at two points. One of the four types of books, the others being the *fan, codex* and the *fold book*. Fans and blinds are used by South Sea Island cultures.

verso See *recto/verso*.

vertical wrapper See *wrapper*.

wheat paste An adhesive, like rice paste, used to adhere leather to the spine and decorative papers to the board. For formulas of making wheat paste, see *Wheat Paste* in *Bookbinding for Book Artists*.

with the grain Folding paper parallel to the grain of the paper.

wrapped stations Head and tail of the sections used as sewing stations. Passive, as opposed to a pierced or slit stations.

wrapper Paper covering board covers without the use of adhesives. See *Flat Back with Boards*, page 290 and *Separately Wrapped Boards*, page 293.

Yamato Toji Japanese name for the 4-needle sewing, across the spine. It is also referred to as the *Japanese 4-Needle Sewing*, as well as the *Butterfly* sewing. It is sewn across the spine, utilizing paired stations. Each needle spans, enters the next section, crosses inside to exit the other station. Yamato Toji is described in *Exposed Spine Sewings*, Volume III, *Non-Adhesive Binding*.

Yamato Toji or Japanese 4-Needle Sewing is not to be confused with the the Japanese 4-Hole Stab Binding, which is described in Volume I of *Non-Adhesive Binding, Books without Paste or Glue*.

Yotsume Toji Japanese name for the 4-hole stab binding.

Z-fold Procedure to create a 6 and a 12 page section. The sheet is first folded in thirds, against the grain (the Z-fold). Folding the Z-fold in half once, with the grain, gives a sexto. Folding the sexto in half with the grain gives 12 leaves or 24 pages, called a duodecimo. See *folio, quarto,sexto, octavo and duodecimo*.

NOTES

1. page 30   Gary Frost, email: gary-frost@uiowa.edu.

2. page 50   All the traditional single sheet bindings described on page 50 are stabbed; the books have to be pried open. I have devised single sheets sewings which are sewn to open flat to any page. See description of Non-Adhesive Binding Volume IV: *Smith's Sewing Single Sheets* on page 351 in this manual.

3. page 66   My thanks to Anne Castrodale.

4. page 66   Sawing sewing stations is not described in this book. It is generally limited to book blocks with at least eight sections. Using a saw is described in *Exposed Spine Sewings*, Volume III, *Non-Adhesive Binding* as well as in *Bookbinding for Book Artists*.

5. page 80   Keith Smith, *Non-Adhesive Binding* Volume III, *Exposed Spine Sewings*, ISBN 0-9637682-4-7.

6. page 106   Pamphlet stitching is not the same as pamphlet sewing although they both use the same sewing pattern. As Betsy Palmer Eldridge admonished me, it is not just a subtle use of terminology, but understanding the difference between sewing and stitching.

   Sewing takes place on the fold of the section. This permits the fold to function as a hinge permitting the pages to open flat.

   Stitching takes place in on the sheet close to the spine-edge. The pages cannot open flat. Examples are the Album Binding and the Japanese 4-Hole Binding. These are stab bindings. Stitching is stabbing, not sewing.

   Pamphlet sewing requires sections. Pamphlet stitching is limited to binding single sheets which are stitched to a pleat.

7. page 107   Each picture must be subordinate to the total. The photograph is not the "picture", unless it is bled to the edges. Everything in view on the open folio is the picture. That includes text and borders, if any. When photographs are centered, with the larger page taking up slack, the photographs are composed, but the page, the opened folio and the book are not.

8. page 123   Kojiro Ikegami, *Japanese Bookbinding*, Instructions from a Master Craftsman, Weatherhill, First Edition 1986.ISBN 0-8348-0196-5.

9. page 171   Penland School, Penland NC 28765-0037. Workshops in various crafts, including papermaking, marbling and bookbinding. Catalogue available. Telephone 704 765 2359.

10. page 188   Various true and false kettle stitches as well as Sewing onto Tapes and Raised Cord sewing is covered in *Exposed Spine Sewings*, Volume III of *Non-Adhesive Binding*. ISBN 0-9637682-4-7. The kettle stitches and many more approaches to Sewing onto Tapes as well as Recessed Cord sewing is elaborately described in *Bookbinding for Book Artists*, by Keith Smith and Fred A. Jordan. ISBN 0-9637682-5-5.

11. page 223   Anne-Catherine Fallen, *The Lively Dance*, The Writer's Center, 1983.

12. page 272   Other illustrations of the crown spine of Book 96 are shown in *Structure of the Visual Book*.

Acknowledgments

Indebtedness to my beloved Scott. Thank you for understanding.

Grateful appreciation to those who have taught me how to do bindings: Kathy Amt, Linda Crabill, Betsy Palmer Eldridge, Joan Flasch, Gary Frost, Hedi Kyle, Fred Jordan, Julie Leonard, Barbara Mauriello, Valerie Mayse, Scott McCarney, Todd Pattison, K. Noël Phillips, Pamela Spitzmueller and Philip Zimmermann.

I wish to thank Betsy Palmer Eldridge who studiously combed through every line of text, every drawn illustration of the First Edition, noting the mistakes. She then invited me to her home and took the time to go over these with me. Those corrections were made in the second printing in 1991.

My thanks to all those who permitted me to reproduce illustrations of their bindings, especially Bert Weijermars, who, after buying the first edition, bound a sample of each of the sewings. After photographing the bindings, he bound the photographs in a lovely Long Stitch with Chain binding with gold stamping. He sent the book to me as a gift. I have received many gifts, some of words, some as objects. It makes my efforts worthwhile.

Photo Credits

Almost all the photo-digital reproductions were made from my slides. Slides or prints were scanned into my computer. I then took the liberty to alter the photographers' work by removing the background around the objects via PhotoShop.

Wish You Were Here by Emily Martin, was photographed by Meryl Marek; *Gaudy Nights* by Barbara Mauriello, photographed by Christopher Erb. Book by Roberta Lavador photographed by Walters Photographers; book by Mary Maynor photographed by Charlotte Randolph. Books by Rosemary Bell, Nancy Brandt, Jane Cameron, William Drendel, Christine Forsythe, Gary Frost, Claudia Lee, Mary Ellen Long, Peter Madden, Scott McCarney, Adéle Outteridge, Kitty, Spangler, Bert Weijermars and Philip Zimmermann were photographed by the book makers.

INDEX of TERMS

accordion pleat aka concertina fold 261
action 23, 24 30, 31
album 50, 132 album covers 134
Asa-No-Ha Toji 119
awl 43, 63
back (backbone) 17, 65,
backbone, swelling the 52
bead 174, 175, 271
beeswax 43
bench, sewing on the 79
blind 249
board or book board 40, 290-296
board with slot 67
bodkin 43, 63
book block or text block 38, 65
bone or bone folder 39, 42, 47
book block pleat 319
bordered turns-in 129, 287
bradawl 39, 43, 63
catch-word 316
chain (link stitch) 164-170, 177-186, 207-218
codex see types of books 24
Collapsible Star 237
compiled sections 51, 52
compound binding 31, 249-282
Concertina Binding 261
concertina guard 319
content 23, 24, 28-32
cords see supports
covers, paper 283-298
covers, layered 84
covers, reinforced 84
cover over a continuous support 83
cover-pleat 131, 320
cradle 67
crown spine 272
crow's feet 52
deckled-edge 48

display 20, 28, 30, 37
dividers 39, 42
dos-à-dos 249-251
drill, paper 42, 133, 138
duodecimo aka 12MO 57
elements of the book 20, 35, 37
end papers 61
endsheets 61
English method of sewing 79, see German method
fan 21, 24, 50, 223, 243, 249, 250
flap 299, 300
flat back 283-298
flush cover 207
fold book 50, see types of books 243-247, 249
fold-out see throw-out
folio aka fo 50, 51, 52, 54, 55, 56, 57, 58
foredge 38, 52, 65
foredge, fold on the 107
foredge turns-in 284, 285
foredge with border 107
format, multiple-page 19
French Doors 25, 256-260
gate fold 314
German method of sewing 79, see English method
gouge 39, 43
grain 45, 46, 54, 55, 56
guard see concertina guard
gutter 17
half hitch 73
head 38, 65
Hemp Leaf 119
hinge-fold 17, 285-296
hinge-fold flaps 291, 295
hinges 23, 24, 27, 41
hinging, compound 261
itineraries through a book 27, 28, 31, 249
imposition 57, 58, 59, 60
Japanese 4-Hole Binding 50, 110
jig 67
jog 64

Kangxi Binding 123
kettle stitch 191
Kikko 114
Koki 123
laced tab 303. 304
leaf 23, 24
liner see optional liner
long stitch bindings 141-170
mountain peaks see peaks
needle, ballpoint 68
needle, threading the 70
Noble 123
octavo aka 8VO 51, 52, 53, 54, 55, 56
one-of-a-kind 48
opened folio 18
optional liner 82
Oriental fold book 50, see types of books 243-247, 249
overhand knot 72
overhang cover 85
packing 148
pamphlet sewing 89-105
pamphlet stitching 106
paper cutter 49
paper drill see drill
papers 36, 81
peaks and valleys 17, 19
perfect bound 12
photo attachment 140
pleat 261-282, 294
pleat, decorating the 280
post and nut 42, 133
punches 42, 83, 133
quarto aka 4TO 50, 51, 53, 54, 55, 56, 57, 58
raised cords 193-195
Rapidograph™ 48
recto/verso 17
reef knot see square knot
reinforcing paper covers 81, 83, 84, 284-296
Also see optional liners; bordered turns-in, foredge and spine-edge turns-in
section 50, 57

REFERENCE of PHOTOGRAPHIC ILLUSTRATIONS

BOOKS on BOOKS

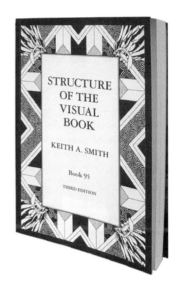

Concept
Structure of the Visual Book, keith a smith *BOOKS*, Expanded Fourth Edition 2003, discusses concepts of ordering a book of pictures by means of a group, series, or sequence. Pacing is stressed by composing the pages as well as the individual pictures. Utilizing the space between pictures is part of the awareness of time in books. 432 pages with 453 photographic illustrations by 145 book artists.
$35
ISBN 0-9740764-0-6

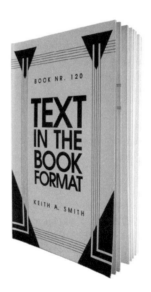

Concept
Text in the Book Format, keith a smith *BOOKS*, Expanded Third Edition, 2004, is a concern for conceiving text as a book experience. This differs from writing a running manuscript or the single sheet format. A book experience cannot be fully revealed in a recitation but demands holding the physical object and turning pages conceived as *part* of the content. The format is not treated as a vessel, but allows writing to emanate from the inherent properties of the book—the opposite of sticking words into the object. 240 pages with 48 pages in color.
$25.00
ISBN 0-9740764-1-4

All the books are printed on archival paper. Available either as Smythe sewn paperback, or, in sheets, folded and gathered sections, if you wish to hand bind your own copy. Individuals or stores can order directly from keith a smith *BOOKS*.
Besides store discounts, there are group discounts available for individuals ordering 6 or more assorted titles. Email for information, or check the web site.

How To Bind
Non–Adhesive Binding, Volume II:
1– 2– & 3–Section Sewings, keith a
smith *BOOKS*, First Edition, 1995. Written and drawn illustrations for 122
sewings which yield four, to perhaps a
hundred pages imposed as one, two or
three sections. Almost all of these
sewings on continuous limp paper supports were devised by Smith, as the
book was written. Photos of bindings
by 28 contemporary binders and
artists. 320 pages.
$30
ISBN 0-9637682-2-0

How To Bind
Non–Adhesive Binding, Volume III:
Exposed Spine Sewings, keith a smith
BOOKS, First Edition, 1995. Variations
on raised support sewings with packed
cords or endbands as change–over
rather than using kettle stitches.
Descriptions of sewings across the
spine include 2–Needle Coptic, Greek
Binding, Celtic Weave and Caterpillar.
Most of the sewings were devised by
Smith as the book was written. Nine
various Coptic sewings are described.
Photographic illustrations by contem-
porary binders are shown. 320 pages.
$30
ISBN 0-9637682-4-7

To order, or for a free brochure on all titles, contact:
Keith Smith, 22 Cayuga Street, Rochester, NY 14620-2153
Telephone or FAX: 716 473 6776
or Email: ksbooks@netacc.net
Web Site: http://net2.netacc.net/~ksbooks

How To Bind
Non–Adhesive Binding, Volume IV:
Smith's Sewing Single Sheets, keith smith
BOOKS, First Edition, 2001. These sewings
can be used to bind sections, and/or single
sheets of paper, board, plexiglass and even
metal. The bindings open flat to any page,
unlike traditional post-bindings and stab
bindings commonly used to bind single
sheets. This attribute makes handsome and
functional albums for photographs. Smith
devised these sewings to make one-of-a-
kind books from large inkjet prints. There
are five Coptic sewings, two sewing raised
cord and one sewing onto tapes—all with
single sheets.
paperback or in sheets: $30
ISBN 0–9637682–8–X

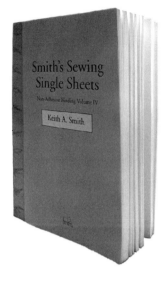

How To Bind
Non–Adhesive Binding, Volume V:
Quick Leather Bindings, keith smith
BOOKS, First Edition, 2003. Hard cover
quarter leather bindings are constructed
without paste or glue using archival pres-
sure-sensitive sheet adhesive. No binding
equipment is used, just needle, thread,
scissors, metal straightedge, X-Acto knife
and a self-seal cutting surface. Sections are
sewn through the spine as continuous support sewings.
    Smith devised 17 new sewings for this
book. You can also sew any of the 122
bindings from Volume II as hard cover,
quarter leather. This approach makes
leather binding simple and—quick.
paperback or in sheets: $30
ISBN 0–9637682–9–8

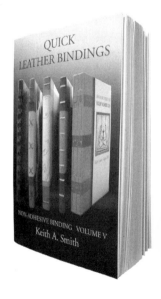

To order, contact: Keith Smith, 1115 East Main Street, Suite 219, Box 8, Rochester, NY 14609-6152
Telephone or FAX: 585 482 2496
or Email: keith@keithsmithbooks.com
ORDER ONLINE: www.keithsmithbooks.com

How To Bind
Bookbinding for Book Artists, First Edition,
1998, keith smith *BOOKS.*

Bookbinding for Book Artists presents a
simple approach to binding in cloth or un-
pared leather. Household tools are substi-
tuted for traditional binding equipment.

Three bindings are described:
Pamphlet Binding with Boards gives a hard
cover book with only 4 to 32 pages.

Flat Back is shown as sewn onto tapes as
a book of 24 to 100 pages.

Tight Back and the *Hollow Back* are presented as leather bound books, rounded
and backed.

Over 400 detailed drawn illustrations
augment the text with 60 photo reproductions of books by 19 contemporary binders
and book artists. 432 pages.

paperback or in sheets: $35
ISBN 0–9637682–5–5

Autobiography
200 Books, An Annotated Bibliography,
First Edition, July 2000, keith smith BOOKS.

200 Books is a memoir as told through
all the books made by the author.

Text and pictures describe the 199 previous books by Smith with over 550 photo
reproductions. The text gives background
of the author and describes why each book
was made with references to other artists.
Sometimes there are detailed descriptions
of how the imagery was technically
achieved. 336 pages.

hard cover or in sheets: $35
ISBN: 0–9637682–7–1

ORDER ONLINE:
www.keithsmithbooks.com

COLOPHON

Book 128
was originally written in the spring and summer of 1990.

The Revised & Expanded Edition
was modified on a MAC Super 266 G3 MINITOWER from September to
December 1998.
Text was formatted as it was imported and re-written using Quark
XPress. Drawn illustrations were imported from Macromedia FreeHand
and Adobe PhotoShop and then refined.

Books without Paste or Glue
was periodically proofed on a Macintosh G5 with a Hewlett Packard
LaserJet 2300. The book was sent to the printer on CD, postscript, for
direct platemaking at 1200 dots per inch for the type and 150 line
screen for the drawings.

Typeface is Amerigo BT.

Photographs of the books are by the author except for photo credits listed on page 344. Drawn and photo-digital illustrations are by the author.

Cover design is by Scott McCarney.

This fourth printing of the Revised & Expanded Edition is offset in 2000
copies on Finch Vellum 80 lb. text and cover with film lamination. The
book is Smythe-sewn, paperback.
Additional copies are available unbound, folded and gathered, for any-
one who might wish to hand bind their own copy of this book.

Keith A. Smith
August 2005

KE◉TH